The Secret Life of
Fighter Command

The Secret Life of Fighter Command

*The men and women who
beat the Luftwaffe*

By Sinclair McKay

Aurum
Press

First published in Great Britain
2015 by Aurum Press Ltd
74–77 White Lion Street
Islington
London N1 9PF
www.aurumpress.co.uk

A catalogue record for this book is available from the British Library.

HB ISBN 978 1 78131 295 7
PB ISBN 978 1 78131 531 6
eBook ISBN 978 1 78131 478 4

2015 2017 2019 2018 2016

1 3 5 7 9 10 8 6 4 2

Typeset in ITC New Baskerville by Saxon Graphics Ltd, Derby
Printed and bound by CPI Group (UK) Ltd, Croydon, CR0 4YY

Contents

Chapter 1   The Celestial Ballet   1

Chapter 2   The Vision of Wings   16

Chapter 3   The Seduction of Flight   35

Chapter 4   The Lines in the Heavens   53

Chapter 5   The Secret Under the Hill   69

Chapter 6   We Are At War   87

Chapter 7   Dress Rehearsals   103

Chapter 8   'Interesting Work of a Confidential Nature'   118

Chapter 9   Blood Runs Hotly   131

Chapter 10   Alert   142

Chapter 11   The Sky was Black with Planes   151

Chapter 12   Nerve Endings   169

Chapter 13   Big Wing   180

Chapter 14   'We Will All Be Here Soon'   192

Chapter 15   'Resist Until the Very End'   216

Chapter 16   'This Was War and We Were Fighting'   228

Chapter 17   A Dog Called Heinkel   245

Chapter 18   Rhubarbs   263

Chapter 19   Knitting, Smoking and Great Literature   280

Chapter 20   Death Will Send No Warning   292

Chapter 21   Grounded   302

Chapter 22   Afterlife   320

Endnotes   329

Further Reading   335

Index   337

Acknowledgements   345

Chapter One

The Celestial Ballet

'Be calm,' Hitler had told the Berlin crowds. 'He is coming. He is coming.'

Late on the afternoon of 7 September 1940, the warmth of summer lingered in the hazy air over England; and the graceful whorls and curls of white in the blue sky above the South Downs might either have been innocent clouds or the last traces of a distant aerial fight. On the chalk ridges and green slopes below, and in the bustling lanes of south coast towns from Portsmouth to Dover, civilians were making the most of the temporary lull and were tensed for the next attack. For the past few weeks, huge numbers of people had watched with guileless fascination as, high above, planes had swooped and swerved, describing wide circles as they chased one another. From that distance, even an exploding fuel tank hit by gunfire – a split second of glittering gold and orange, followed by the plane simply falling out of the sky – was hypnotic rather than frightening.

It was almost a different war. Across the grey waters of the Channel, on the continent and deep in the darkness of Europe, the conflict had been lumbering, ugly, brutally functional. Vast tanks that jerked and manoeuvred in unnatural lines, vast guns roaring beyond human reason; and everywhere the mortal wreckage of red, glistening viscera. But here, high above in the blue, no one could look away from the Spitfires and the Messerschmitts. Every fleet movement, from climbs to dives, had an innate elegance, a geometrical beauty – even as the pilots were flying for their lives.

British pilots had been fighting continuously in these skies for days and weeks; physically and mentally, they had been taken to the edge. The fear that kept them focused during sorties left them exhausted in the aftermath, with the result that many of these men were working by pure instinct. That summer, their squadrons had faced an enemy that seemed not only relentless but also apparently limitless in number. No matter how many German planes they shot out of the sky, the next day brought fresh formations. Perhaps a few RAF pilots sensed just how heavily the odds were stacked against them. Yet, paradoxically, even if they had not been required to risk their lives on an hourly basis, these men would still have been desperate to fly. (By contrast, think of the soldiers who drove tanks; imagine if they yearned to drive a tank for the love of it.) The nature of this war in the air was technologically new, yet as old as Arthurian legend. The RAF pilots were not just warriors. Flying, for them, was a metaphysical pleasure.

But that Saturday, this 'celestial ballet', as one mesmerised onlooker had described it, took on a different character. There were specially trained plane-spotters at Dover, at Folkestone, at Lympne, and dotted around the north Kent coast. The job of these volunteers – many of whom, proud men, had served in the First World War – was to report, instantly, the type and the numbers of enemy bombers flying in overhead. On that Saturday, the Observer Corps heard the storm before they saw it; at first a pervasive note, a deep unearthly hum, like some distant male choir. In their small dugouts – often not much more than rudimentary wooden huts – the bells of their telephones had started ringing a little while beforehand. 'He' was coming; Hitler, characterising the German air force and its massed bombers as the physical projection of his will, had announced his intentions in a speech to hundreds in Berlin.

A few days before this, the British had launched a bomber assault on Germany; on the night of 25 August 1940, the pilots had flown their planes to the very limit that fuel would allow. Their targets were Berlin's airport and other strategic sites. As with all bombing raids, there were imprecise hits, collateral damage.

Compared with what was to follow years later, the destruction was not great. But the response to that August raid was incandescent; the Führer's aim was changed. Forget the RAF airfields and the convoys and the neat tactical targets. Instead: pour hellfire down upon the civilians of London.

The intelligence gathered from Y Service operatives (the 'Y' short for 'wireless'), who were listening in to Luftwaffe messages had confirmed that 'he was coming.' The operatives of the coastal radar stations had looked into the cathode ray tubes and seen the assembling force represented as an electronic echo. The number of blips was unprecedented. That afternoon, stations in Dover and Rye picked up the same readings.

The low unearthly hum deepened, acquiring a new timbre or vibration. The Observer Corps volunteers would have been among the first to see them, at 4.15 p.m., through their binoculars. Rows of black dots that grew larger, resolved, drawing closer to the White Cliffs, perfectly unstoppable. These men were not there merely to report on the appalling spectacle. From their small posts on hills high above the sea, on the edges of fields, with instruments like astrolabes set out on tables before them, they started telephoning their observations to the local Observer Corps headquarters in

Maidstone, Kent. They reported the numbers of enemy bombers that were flying towards and over them, along with the height at which they were flying (calculated by means of that specially designed instrument). The Observer Corps – like the coastal radar operatives – were among the first to feel the horrified thrill of atavistic awe; rather than the usual enemy formations, these disciplined rows of aeroplanes, black in the sunlight, seemed to be coming line after line. First, about 100 were seen; then 200. Then yet more were reported, coming from different angles, different aerodromes, but heading for one target. An estimated 1,100 German aeroplanes flew in over the south coast that Saturday afternoon. On previous occasions, large formations had fragmented, broken off in varying directions, feinted, lured British pilots into redundant battles while others snaked towards their bombing targets. At tea-time that warm day, these hundreds of German planes were making their way high across the orchards of Kent towards the brown industrial air of the nation's capital. Waiting until the last possible moment, in order to conserve fuel, RAF pilots, based at aerodromes ringing the capital and dotted throughout the swards of Kent and Sussex, awaited their orders to intercept.

Before any orders went out, the aerodromes needed – very quickly – an idea of where pilots were to fly to, and how many would be needed. They needed to be able to comprehend the scale and purpose of this gargantuan raid. Such intelligence was secretly gathered beneath a property on the northwestern edge of London, in the heart of what poet John Betjeman called 'Metroland'. In the gardens of Bentley Priory – a grand eighteenth-century house that had once hosted poets and princes – was a large chamber buried some thirty feet beneath the earth. It was to this room that the calculations of the Observer Corps volunteers, together with the readings from the new radar stations, were phoned through, to be instantly received and analysed by volunteers from the Women's Auxiliary Air Force (WAAF) in what was called the Filter Room; their calculations – translated into vectors and co-ordinates – were then passed to the Operations Room.

There, on a large map, coloured counters were deployed to represent the forces that were flying in. From here, the intelligence radiated outwards again on telephone lines, to aerodromes up and down the land. The secret bunker and the grand house formed the headquarters of Fighter Command. Bentley Priory was, throughout that summer, the crucible in which the course of the war was shaped.

This cat's cradle network of intelligence – the bluff old Observer Corps men, the dedicated and intelligent women, and the eager young civilian scientists looking after the brand-new radar technology – had been painstakingly devised by a commander who was misunderstood and treated with cold contempt by his superiors. Air Chief Marshal Sir Hugh Dowding was an austere figure who had throughout his life in the RAF seen the science of flying turn from a rare miracle of daring and aeronautic skill to a new, modern branch of warfare. His Fighter Command system was designed with tremendous skill and care, the armourer's science and guile supporting the knights of the air.

Despite the availability of some intelligence, none of the women or men who worked in this futuristic control room – with its dials, its headsets, its different coloured lights and colour-coded clocks marked out in red, blue and yellow – would have known earlier on that Saturday precisely when or where the enemy would decide to strike, and with what sort of force. That lunchtime, some of the women, in their uniforms, had taken advantage of the good weather during their breaks; they had lain outside on the grass behind the grand house, smoking cigarettes, listening to the thoughtful hum of bees investigating local wildflowers. Underground, the women on duty were doing what they normally did on quiet days: knitting, writing; though they always had their specially designed telephone headgear at the ready for an alert. Young Gladys Eva, then nineteen, was playing bridge with some of the more senior men; her knack for the game was one of the attributes that had smoothed her recruitment to this top secret establishment.

By 4.30 p.m., the day had been so pleasant that there was a slight haze rising even above the streets of central London. To the east and the north of the capital, the air had a thicker, almost orange quality; though this was not the season of domestic coal burning, the great industries of the East End and the vast docklands kept going with their larger concerns. Fighter Command was about 24 kilometres (fifteen miles) west of here, sitting on the ridge of green hills that enclose the city like a bowl. It would have a grandstand view.

This was the day which would end with many in London convinced that their world was being torn apart. And yet, paradoxically, this was also the day – 7 September 1940 – which would prove that Fighter Command had triumphed.

That afternoon, the young WAAFs who were about to start their watch hurried around the side of the handsome Italianate house (complete with an imposing bell tower that had, for the purposes of the conflict, been painted a dull green and black by means of camouflage). On the west of the house was the concrete entrance to what was called The Hole.

Down hard concrete steps, the young women would descend some thirty-five feet into a world of artificial light, an hermetic chamber of maps and markers, sharp-eyed observations and focused tension. The Operations Room was bursting with techniques so new that the enemy had not fathomed the extent of them. *Reichsmarschall* Hermann Goering had, before the war, happily boasted to the likes of

American ambassador Joseph Kennedy that his air force, the Luftwaffe, was unquestionably the best in the world. The lethal skill of Goering's pilots was, by the summer of 1940, perfectly obvious; yet the urgent question of how one successfully could fight off such skill – so central to Dowding's system – came to dominate the conflict.

Equally, this was an enemy fighting a kind of war so novel that Dowding's forces were still learning on their feet. And on this day, the Nazi strategy changed dramatically. Before, it had striven to disable Fighter Command. Now, thwarted, it appeared to be set on mindless, murderous vengeance.

At around 4.35 p.m., anyone living near the banks of the Thames on the estuary – the people of Essex and north Kent – would have heard the low yet piercing drone louder than ever before; and they would have seen the first wave of some 350 German aircraft, an almost Wagnerian spectacle. No matter how fast the defending pilots could be alerted and sent into the sky to try and intercept them, this vast force – the mightiest enemy to have made such an incursion into British territory for almost a thousand years – were within minutes of their targets.

Back in the Filter Room, the young women and their commanders, receiving the information from so many observation and radar stations, understood the sickeningly relentless progress of the aggressors. This was the city in which their families still lived. For WAAF officers like Patricia Clark, there were fresh memories of having watched recent air battles with her parents on the fringes of London. The women triangulated the areas over which the Luftwaffe was heading, the lives under the deadliest threat. Very shortly, the working-class populations of East Ham, Poplar, Plaistow and Beckton – and on the south side of the river, Woolwich – felt the ground beneath them undulating, the unsure foundations of their homes shifting, as the first bombs fell.

From the Filter and Operations Rooms, the women had been able to furnish the squadrons at Uxbridge to the west, and North Weald to the east, and Biggin Hill and Kenley to the south, with vectors and altitudes. Young pilots, with not a great deal of training but a huge amount of courage, were thousands of feet up in the air, swooping down to engage against this outrage. As the German bombers got the great East End docks in their sights, the hugely outnumbered Spitfires and Hurricanes did astonishingly well in the circumstances; seventy-four enemy aircraft were annihilated. A further seventy-odd were reckoned damaged. In other words, a disproportionate percentage of the attacking forces sustained lethal or serious injury. And yet the outrage continued.

The daytime raid had merely been the first act. At 8.10 p.m., with the last traces of hazy crimson gone from the sky, another lethal black wave of bombers materialised from the thickening darkness of the east. The Thames beneath the Germans was now a dully luminous serpent, twisting, rippling, betraying the city. The targets, many already burning fiercely, were hit more intensively. At Purfleet, the Anglo-American Oil Works went up in a lurid blaze.

Upriver, Woolwich Arsenal – that great historic citadel of gunpowder, explosives and fissile material – bellowed black and molten yellow as stores detonated. There were fires at the Siemens Bros works. Damage was done to the southern outfall sewer that stretched out to Crossness. The vast gasworks by the claggy, thickly flowing Thames at Gallions Reach nearby were also hit, and orange and blue flames rose high into the indigo sky. The percussive waves of noise that could be felt as well as heard were described by one East End resident as being like the mighty footsteps of an enraged giant.

That giant seemed to be stamping everywhere; every bomb that did not hit an industrial objective would instead find a domestic target. South and east London were very densely populated, with houses bunched in terraces around a vast expanse of factories, docks and processing plants. As the blue twilight settled into the total darkness of London blackout, the German bombers mocked the cover of night before turning back by illuminating the city in blazing oranges and scarlets. Houses were sliced in two in a fraction of a second, their occupants instantly dismembered; roads and railway lines were bisected. Midnight came and yet more waves of bombers flew over. Against daytime raids there was some semblance of a chance of engaging the enemy properly. At night, in 1940, pilots were still largely flying blind and into a disorientating pandemonium. 'Has a Blitz begun?' wrote pilot George Barclay of 249 Squadron of that night. 'The Wing Commander's coolness is amazing and he does a lot to keep up our morale – very necessary tonight.'[1]

Meanwhile, the personnel emerging from the Bentley Priory 'Hole' at midnight, at the end of an eight-hour shift, saw the unnatural sunset of flame in the east. For WAAF officer Gladys Eva, taking a quick break from the relentless underground duties, the horror was immediate. 'God, I cannot tell you,' she says now. 'We'd been working downstairs, so we knew what they were doing to London, once they started to bomb. You would go out of the Hole and the whole of the sky would be lit. You could see London easily from Stanmore. And we had been plotting them all the while, so we knew they were over in vast numbers.'

There were other elements to the armoury of Fighter Command: the plump silvery barrage balloons floating on ropes in the air, a spectacle that Londoners had taken a while to get used to; the huge wheeling guns and the piercingly bright lights of Anti-Aircraft Command. But with a determined enemy thrusting through, they could offer only limited protection that night.

Yet this is assuredly not a story of failure. Completely the reverse. The Blitz, terrifying and deadly though it was, was Hitler's tacit admission of failure to gain mastery in the Battle of Britain. This is the story of how an institution – part military, part civilian – carefully built up and yet very often improvised, found a completely new way of waging a war, projecting it into the skies throughout the hard years to come.

The headquarters of Fighter Command had seen many pivotal days and nights already, and would see many more before the war was finally played out. The later years would bring V-1 and V-2 missiles, as well as the extraordinary tension of D-Day in 1944. Bentley Priory saw many huge successes, as well as harrowing disasters, right the way through to the end.

The story of the Second World War's fighter pilots, men such as Alan Deere, Richard Hillary, Roger Bushell and Douglas Bader, is clearly one that cannot be celebrated enough; indeed, their story seemed to have been imprinted in the national consciousness even before the Battle of Britain began. The images are so familiar as to seem like clichés from innumerable John Mills films: the absurd cheerfulness of the pilots in the face of death or mutilating injury; the aerodromes with their concrete hangars; the young fighters running for their fighter planes, taking to the skies in small metal constructions that now look as if they could barely survive collision with a flock of geese.

Then there are those battles in the skies above, now pressed into national folk memory as seen from the ground – skies swirling with curling contrails, moments of mad exhilaration when German pilots swoop in so low that they can be seen in their cockpits; and then the moments when these young men are shot out of the sky, planes spiralling down, distant explosions in far-off fields.

Added to this is the folk-memory of the individualistic nature of the courageous RAF squadrons; the lightning-fast decisions taken at stations like Hornchurch and Debden and Northolt and Duxford; then, after the fighting, the accounting of the dead, and the swift, deliberate insouciance of the surviving fighting men. As such, the images convey a sense of cohesion and assurance; it is startling to think now that so much of this was extemporised.

And even the flashing lights of the Fighter Command Operations Room – the special clocks with the differently coloured sectors, the futuristic looking, brightly illuminated panels, the WAAFs spending hours leaning across the table map like croupiers, moving the tiny markers that signified the different sorts of enemy waves and their positions – was a system that had to be adapted constantly to new emergencies.

It doesn't take much now to imagine the asphyxiating weight of anxiety on Hugh Dowding, the architect of a system for which he was to receive next to no thanks. He was remembered by all who knew him as a reserved man; and during these days of national crisis, this grave figure would be found in his office in Bentley Priory, the windows facing out west towards Harrow, his desk sparse, save for the in-trays of seemingly illimitable paperwork that had to be done even in emergencies. Even at the height of the Battle of Britain, Dowding faced poisonous office politics; superiors who wanted to get rid of him at any cost.

In May and June 1940, the people of Britain had been galvanised by the unnerving rout of the British Expeditionary Force in France that had led to the evacuation of Dunkirk. The brave voyages of the Little Ships were instantly mythologised by press and public alike. The returning soldiers – half-starved, almost hallucinating with tiredness – were greeted at railway stations as though they were film stars. But after a long Phoney War (or 'Bore War') in which public and military alike had seemed perfectly confident of Britain's ability to hold back the Nazis, the next few weeks were to be marked with a mass cognitive dissonance. Hitler's invasion was widely anticipated, yet the public and the returned soldiers contrived somehow to press on with a kind of black good humour.

In Parliament, Winston Churchill – who had been Prime Minister for barely a month – made reference to the pilots of the RAF. 'The battle of France is over,' he proclaimed on 4 June 1940. 'The Battle of Britain is about to begin.' And so the coming conflict had been named before it had even started. Churchill too referred to RAF pilots in Arthurian terms; the new chivalrous knights, brave men of the airy realms, who would now be doing battle to protect the honour of the nation. His words might have been a response to the fury among so many ordinary British soldiers about the RAF's perceived lack of help during the Dunkirk crisis. The soldiers were wrong; the pilots had been fighting, all right. And behind the scenes Dowding too had been bitterly fighting to preserve the forces that he needed for the confrontations to come.

But the story and the life of Bentley Priory extends much further out and further back. It begins in another age, another reign, as dreams of flying took on corporeal life. And it also encompasses that point at the outbreak of war when a nation was jolted into modernity; not just in technological terms, but also in terms of meritocracy, the dissolution of old class structures, and in the ability of a younger generation of women to find a voice in this new world.

It is a story that extends across Britain too; not just to take in all the pilots in all the squadrons in those strategic positions, but also the personnel keeping up with events on the ground. From the ever vigilant Observer Corps, dotted around the country in their little exposed huts; to the anti-aircraft gunners, posted on hills and in parks, doing what they could in the hours of darkness to beat back an enemy that was all but invisible; to the dedicated young women from Bath to Suffolk, in underground control rooms, who were overseeing the very earliest days of radar. At these far-flung bases, young women recruits found a strong taste of independence that they might not otherwise have had; the responsibility and the skilled work brought commissions for some, like Eileen Younghusband, and the eye-opening experience of entering formerly male strongholds.

But what they all found was a life of needle-sharp intensity. Not merely in terms of duty, but also in off-duty hours: the romances, the dances and even the unauthorised pet dogs on base. Looking back now, we tend not only to imagine the war in black and white, but also to assume that it was conducted very much on one note. The veterans, by contrast, recall the vivid range and depths of emotion that the period inspired. It is worth repeating that in an age before computing, Fighter Command's accuracy in the plotting and interception of enemy planes was genuinely astonishing. Above all it is a story about a group of young men and women thrown together in extreme circumstances and immediately growing both in maturity and experience.

There is a sharp difference between the lives of the fighter pilots and those of the bomber crews, who belonged to a separate RAF branch of command. The work of the bombers, the cruel precariousness of their existence and the crushing weight of their function, was by its nature unrelentingly haunting, especially in the later stages of the conflict. By contrast, even though the sacrifices made by the fighter pilots were vast, there was something perhaps less philosophically burdensome about their war; right from the start, there was even a sort of purity about these duels in the sky. Which is why, despite the mortality rates, despite the hideous injuries and disfigurements, such battles still now tend to be associated with the cleanness of blue skies and white clouds.

The story is also in some ways a portrait of a younger generation in microcosm; or at least of everything that the younger generation wanted itself to be. Long before American GIs came over with their irresistible music and attitude, the pilots and the women of RAF Fighter Command embodied a certain style and cool. They were sharp, sophisticated, amusing, attractive. Like their opposite numbers in the Luftwaffe, it is true that many were, at least initially, drawn from the more rarefied levels of society. But where the Prussian princes and minor noblemen of Germany were noted both for exquisite social manners and high seriousness, the RAF fighter pilot was – at least for the consumption of an eager public – an indomitably cheery, even slightly raffish young man. At the time of the Battle of Britain, the average age of a fighter pilot was twenty. They were not even old enough to vote (the age of majority then was twenty-one); yet anyone halfway sensible would have understood the depths beneath that studied insouciance. The memories one hears now – either from those long gone or those wonderfully still with us – are tinged with an unusual amount of humour, as well as of poignancy; surprisingly, some of their stories are very funny. There is also an unusual lyricism, and a lingering sense of spirituality too. It makes their achievements all the more breathtaking.

Bentley Priory was at the heart of the sort of war which will never be fought again. Those pilots achieved a victory that it will be given to no one else to win. All the control rooms, all the aerodromes, all the exquisitely designed aircraft, all the airmen with poetry in their souls, came together in one unique national moment: an island fighting to ensure that its soul remained intact.

Chapter Two

The Vision of Wings

From the beginning, there had been a curious mix of pure addictive adventure, the exhilaration of climbing beyond the clouds, and the extraordinary, concrete power that these flights could bring. Even before aeroplanes, in the middle years of Victoria's reign in the nineteenth century, young men were looking up at the sky and daydreaming that Britain's empire might be further strengthened from high above. In 1863, in the secret woods of Hampshire around Aldershot that had been closed off for military training, Lieutenant George Grover and Captain Beaumont were enthusiastically preparing to rise high above the green canopy, having been given hesitant permission by their superiors.

Their means of doing so was by balloon. The two men were very excited about the possibilities that it represented, chiefly for watching over the enemy's activities from a safe distance above. Such contrivances had already been used to a limited extent over the battlefields of the American Civil War; the French were also exploring the possibilities. It would take a dedicated amateur balloonist, Captain James Lethbridge Templer, to make a more persuasive case, as he did when, fifteen years later in 1878, he proudly presented his own balloon, made to his own designs, to the military engineers and scientists at London's Woolwich Arsenal. The first British military use of aviation came in South Africa in 1884, and in Sudan the year afterwards. From above, it was possible for observers to make out not merely enemy movements, but also artillery that might otherwise have been hidden. This new omniscience was hated and feared by those on the ground; even from the start, war in the air engendered a permanent sense of insecurity.

However, when air technology took a vast leap forward in 1903 with the work of the Wright Brothers, senior British military figures were resistant to the innovations that immediately suggested themselves. Others weren't. The Germans, inspired by Count von Zeppelin, who had made a maiden flight in the dirigible that bore his name in 1900, had developed a strong fixation with the potential of airships. The deadly possibilities of such craft were not lost on the popular fiction writers of the day. Indeed, in 1909, an early cinema film called *The Airship Destroyer* concerned an invasion of such ships (depicted via some basic animation techniques) throwing down bombs and missiles on a helpless populace.

But there was the soaring romance of flight too. In 1909, the *Daily Mail* began offering cash prizes for astonishing feats of aviation. Not only did men love risking their lives to fly into the clouds; millions of readers thrilled to their exploits too. In that year, Louis Blériot successfully – and stunningly – made a flight across the English Channel. In the midst of aero-hysteria, Chief of the General Staff Sir William Nicholson observed to his colleagues: 'It is of importance that we push on with the practical study of the military use of aircraft in the field … Even with the present type of dirigibles and aeroplanes, other nations have already made considerable progress in this training and in view of the fact that aircraft will undoubtedly be used in the next war, whenever it may come, we cannot afford to delay the matter.'[1]

The military and senior politicians in Whitehall naturally did delay the matter. The following year, Colonel J.E.B. Seeley announced that 'the Government does not consider that aeroplanes are of any possible use for war purposes.' Yet that war was coming; it was foreshadowed in popular fiction which was filled with hysterical paranoia about the hostile intentions of continental enemies. The novelist Herbert Strang eagerly seized upon all the adventurous possibilities that aeroplanes presented and used them in story after story. Notable was the stirring 1910 effort *King of the Air*, in which bandits kidnap a diplomat – and two daring young men in a flying machine subdue the kidnappers by flying around their stronghold and dropping explosives upon them.

Cinema added a fresh dimension to the flying craze. Daredevil pilot Claude Graham-White took his plane up with a film camera in 1911; beguiled audiences were shown breathtaking – and hitherto impossible – views of London taken from hundreds of feet in the air. The moving images induced disorientation in many. And those who had read their science fiction might also have felt a pang of unease; from street level, all cities look indestructible. This was the first time that everyone could see how – from above – even a grand capital of stone and marble suddenly started to seem a little more vulnerable.

By 1911, there were just six military aeroplanes in the whole of Britain; by contrast, at this stage, France had a total of 208. At last, the authorities understood the need to catch up. And soon, there was a Royal Aircraft Factory at Farnborough, Hampshire, the presiding genius of which was a talented engineer called Geoffrey de Havilland. It often took the enthusiasm of civilians to help the military hierarchy see fresh possibilities. In 1912, the Royal Flying Corps was formed, overseen with keen interest by Lieutenant General David Henderson.

There were several branches to the Corps: the Military Wing, the Naval Wing and the Central Flying School. To ensure a minimum of tension between army officers (the War Office ran the school), it was decided that it should be run by a naval officer: Captain G. Paine was selected. There was one initial setback: he had yet to learn to fly. Paine was taught in the space of ten days. The Central Flying School was established on high ground outside a small village called Upavon in Wiltshire, a location noted immediately for its bitter wind, cold, and rugged terrain that should, as one observer pointed out sardonically, have produced the hardiest imaginable aviators.

Real air-power innovation was coming from the Italians; in 1911, when declaring hostilities against the Ottoman Empire, they deployed a handful of aeroplanes (with a grand total of thirty-one qualified pilots) to carry out operations in north Africa. In November of that year came the first ever instance of aerial bombing. Pilot Lieutenant Gavotti dropped grenades from his cockpit upon the settlements of Taigura and Ain Zura. It was not too long before the explosives were being refined elsewhere; and it was the Bulgarians, also in an extended skirmish with the Ottomans, who bombed the town of Adrianople. The editor of *The Aeroplane* magazine was the first to declare in a headline: 'Destroyed By Fire Bombing'.

Despite all this, back in Britain, Colonel J.E. Edmonds pooh-poohed aerial warfare as a 'German bogey' and claimed that in Africa, Italian bombs had fallen so slowly that 'Arabs' and 'Turks' had ample time simply to step out of their way. But the Italians – the more cosmopolitan of whom were at that time in the grip of the Futurist Movement, with its emphasis on the thrilling nihilism of the new technology – saw it differently. As Michael Paris wrote: 'The success of the air detachment resulted in a wave of patriotic air-mindedness and the north African pilots became national heroes, creating an image of the dashing aviator and the mystique of the air service which was not dispelled until the poor performance of the Italian Air Force in the Second World War.'[2]

In 1912, Major Frederick Sykes was out in Italy, closely observing and reporting back on the evolution of flying tactics. Sykes was to become a key figure in the months and years to follow. He also helped design the emblem that has lasted to this day: the brevet, or pilot's wings, which is awarded to fully trained pilots. The original badge involved a representation of the wings of a swift, picked out in white silk, a crown on the top. It was given royal approval in February 1913. You still occasionally hear the expression 'earned his wings'.

In 1912, one man who signed up for flying lessons at Brooklands in Hampshire was the young Winston Churchill. He was fearless about it; but that is not the same thing as having a talent for it. Churchill grew so addicted to the adrenaline thrust that came with leaving the ground at speed that at one point, he was going up ten times a day. In 1913, his instructor, Captain Gilbert Wildman Lushington, was killed in a separate plane accident; this and the disappearance of yet another pilot over the Channel so unnerved Mrs Churchill – Clementine – that her husband was persuaded to drop the lessons, at least temporarily.

At around the same time, an experienced, rather stolid military man also signed up for lessons at Brooklands. Hugh Dowding's desire to fly was nothing to do with ambition or passion; it was, according to his biographer Basil Collier, a 'desire to gain knowledge likely to be useful to him as a soldier'.[3] Dowding longed to return to India, where he had been a lieutenant with the Mountain Artillery in Rawalpindi, relishing the exercises and adventures that he had found in remote jungles and on mountains. But the gaining of his wings was to change the course of his life permanently.

The outbreak of the First World War brought a wider variety of unanticipated mortal danger for freshly trained aviators, from the precision of anti-aircraft guns to the phenomenon of planes 'icing up' high in the winter skies. Moreover, in the early stages of the conflict, aerial combat regularly lacked a specific focus or aim, while pilots were required to fly in highly unsuitable wet, misty or rainy conditions. In all the noise made by enthusiastic newspapers, the proximity of death was consistently glossed over. There was a point in the First World War when the average life expectancy of a newly qualified pilot was barely weeks once the man had earned his wings. This was an era before flyers were equipped with parachutes. If a propeller stuck, or if the enemy's bullets had hit home and the plane went into a stomach-quivering drop, the only hope was that a steep dive would produce enough wind resistance on the propeller to start it revolving again. If not, then either the body was crushed beyond recognition, or was sometimes bisected by impact, or the pilot endured the horror of being burnt alive. Yet there was still a romanticism about flying that was completely absent from the despair in the trenches below.

Some of the work – especially that involving attacks – had an element of the experimental about it but was nonetheless vital: for instance, pre-emptive bombing strikes on Zeppelin sheds in northern Germany, which were cheered on by Churchill.

The man appointed in 1915 to take command of the Royal Flying Corps – Hugh Trenchard – shared Churchill's passionate belief that an air force should go on the attack with bombing raids. Trenchard had little faith in the idea that aircraft could be used protectively. 'The aeroplane,' he said, 'is not a defence against the aeroplane.' A glowering and often spectacularly maladroit figure socially, who came from a bankrupt and impoverished family at a time when one needed money to rise to the higher levels of military life, Trenchard nonetheless quickly won loyalty among his associates. In fact, he had had the most unquantifiable military career. As a young man in serving in South Africa, he acquired a nickname: the Camel. This was because, like a camel, he did not drink and neither did he ever seem to speak. Such social graces seemed beyond him.

But Trenchard was very good at sports such as polo – notably besting Winston Churchill on one occasion – and this won him a retinue of admirers. He was also, according to his biographer, 'impatient of all orders but his own' (something of a recurring leitmotif in many airmen). Several years later, he was in charge. But he and his pilots were feeling their way in the dark.

A huge test for the Royal Flying Corps – and a foreshadowing of the crucial defensive actions of the Battle of Britain – came in 1915 when the Germans started launching their dirigibles across the North Sea to bomb the British mainland; when the attacks began, it initially seemed as if there was no way to stop them. On 19 January 1915, there was a raid on the blameless seaside town of Great Yarmouth, and bombs were dropped near Sandringham (the royal family had reportedly been moved to London) and the town of Sheringham. Obviously the deaths and injuries that resulted were inflicted upon civilians. The outrage stoked by this and similar raids was vast.

Count Zeppelin himself, interviewed by an American newspaper in February 1915, was the image of insouciance. 'War in the air is bound to become a vital factor in the strife between nations,' he said. When asked about the killing of civilians, he responded: 'No one regrets that more than I do.' Those Zeppelin crews subsequently returned to kill many more women and children, regretfully or not.

But eventually a defensive system was established combining very powerful new searchlights, set to cross beams and hold the Zeppelin in their light 'like scissors'; anti-aircraft guns; and, most importantly, fighter pilots sent up to counter the Zeppelins in the air. They faced a range of difficulties. The first was altitude: in mechanical terms, their aircraft could easily reach 10,000 feet – but in a plane with an open cockpit, on an autumn or winter evening, the temperature would be bitingly low. Although the fur-lined leather jacket was already in place, as were the gloves, the standard clothing of the pilot that we associate with Fighter Command and the Second World War was still evolving in 1915. Goggles were widely disliked at first because they restricted the all-important field of vision. But all pilots eventually acceded to them – with no windscreen to speak of, to fly at speeds of 128 to 160 kilometres per hour (80 to 100 miles per hour) without them was tricky.

The silk scarves that later became such an important leitmotif were introduced as the best means – and material – for wiping dirt and oil from the goggles in mid-flight. Meanwhile, oxygen equipment was primitive or non-existent. For many of us, the idea of being 15,000 feet above the ground – that is, over ten times the height of The Shard tower in London – in an apparently fragile and open construction of wood and metal would be intolerable. The men's courage was certainly understood and celebrated, though; a twenty-year-old pilot called James McCudden became nationally famous, his missions over the battlefields of France celebrated especially in the pages of the *Daily Mail.* This ace also flew defensive missions over London (and bitterly, his death in 1918 was caused not by his return to the Front or enemy fire, but by an engine fault).

And the prototype Fighter Command, fighting a prototype London Blitz, did have some startling success. Late one night in the autumn of 1916, Lieutenant William Leefe Robinson, stationed at Hornchurch, was ordered to go in pursuit of an airship that was menacing northeast London. Fighting enemy bullets, black fog and the danger of immolation, he brought the monster down in a blinding ball of orange.

His superiors knew that it would make for excellent newspaper copy. Here is how the normally grave *Manchester Guardian* described the young hero: 'A glimpse of him revealed the sharp firm cut features of a very intrepid young man. He did not carry a superfluous ounce of flesh, and his features seemed hewn from granite.' Moreover, when Robinson showed his face in public in the following days, he was mobbed by ecstatic crowds, and the police had to hurry him away in cars. The cult of Fighter Command's pilots had its antecedent here.

Indeed, the wider exploits of the Royal Flying Corps – taking on the likes of the diabolically skilled Baron von Richthofen, also known as the Red Baron – were eagerly taken up by the popular press. This is where the stories in boys' papers and real life became quite deliberately entangled. It has been suggested that in an era when war had become hideously industrialised, reducing whole countries to poisoned wildernesses, the idea of fighting above, in the free air, pilot to pilot, had an irresistible purity. It almost seemed organic; a natural form of conflict, as opposed to the mechanical horrors taking place on earth. These early air battles were somehow not faceless; they could instead be dramatised in newspapers and boys' journals with real passion, and indeed a sliver of compassion, on both sides.

The element of kinetic poetry in this new world of flight was captured by a young German pilot a few years later, when he became one of the country's leading film directors. F.W. Murnau, who had first served in the trenches, joined the *Luftstreitkrafte*, the German First World War air force, later in the war and the experience was clearly echoed in his later productions, both in the swooping fluidity of his camerawork and in specific set-pieces. In 1926's *Faust*, there is a famous scene in which Mephistopheles takes the eponymous alchemist for a ride in the sky: they glide through foggy air, over vast mountain peaks, over dark forests, over twinkling waterfalls and rivers. During that first global conflict, the new young pilots must occasionally have forgotten that they were involved in war at all.

Another striking film features stark monochrome documentary footage of young *Luftstreitkrafte* pilots. We see one young man coming in to land, removing goggles, then face-wrappings, then earplugs. He turns to the silent camera and smiles quizzically. This young German was a fighter ace responsible for at least twenty-two downed planes. In the footage, he is seen to be wearing a distinctive cross: the honour known as 'The Blue Max'. The shrewd-looking young man was Hermann Goering. He had originally joined the army but had been persuaded by a friend to take up flying. The man who was to become Hitler's deputy in the 1930s was quite at home within this pioneering new flying force; among the *Luftsreitkrafte*'s recruits were many German aristocrats, such as Walter von Bulow-Bothkamp. Goering himself, though nothing so exalted, was nonetheless the son of a career diplomat and acutely aware of the smarter circles. It is fascinating now to look into the eyes of this First World War hero, this fighter ace, and to imagine how he transformed over the ensuing years.

Among the notable pilots on the British side, William Sholto Douglas – who was later to head Fighter Command – had himself flown in two-seater Sopwiths in France; it was here he gained experience of ground-strafing, shooting from the air at targets on the ground. Meanwhile, Hugh Dowding initially found himself posted to France with No. 6 Squadron. According to Collier, in the opening stages of the war, encounters between enemy pilots – even when firing upon each other with Mauser pistols – were random and even exploratory. On one occasion, Dowding wrote a letter to his sister that made him sound rather younger than thirty-two years of age: 'I have had plenty of excitement since I have been out. 2 smashes without getting hurt. Peppered by "Archibald" [an anti-aircraft gun] without getting hit, 2 bullets through the plane one day and today a scrap with a German biplane … Nobody seems to get hurt; the nearest was one fellow who got a bullet flattened against his bullet-proof seat.'[4]

In 1917, as the war below crushed so many hundreds of thousands of corpses into the mud, early cinemas showed *With the Royal Flying Corps,* a carefully timed propaganda epic; again, as with the pilots of Fighter Command in the Second World War, the dashing images helped cement the idea of a certain cheerful insouciance in the face of constant danger. There were the aces, whose exploits were to be pored over by schoolboys across the land: James McCudden, Mick Mannock, Albert Ball, and their elegant arch-nemesis, von Richthofen. At this time, the names of aircraft manufacturers began to take on a patina of the same glamour: de Havilland, Sopwith, Fairey, Short Brothers.

Meanwhile, one particular German advance became a byword in its own right: the Fokker. This new breed of plane had the lethal innovation of a machine gun that was precisely synchronised with the craft's propeller, enabling a huge increase in both firepower and accuracy. The British answer was the DH2 – a plane which featured a forward-firing Lewis gun.

The Royal Flying Corps did not only operate in the damp skies of northern Europe; squadrons were shipped out to Egypt too. From there, missions were carried out in Syria, Palestine and Mesopotamia. The aeroplane was changing the geography of Empire, and of the Earth. Royal Flying Corps pilots were making sorties over the fringes of Russia and taking their planes up above the northwest frontier of India. It was becoming obvious to many that control over a nation's skies would be the key to any future conflict.

In 1917 a hugely influential report from General J.C. Smuts gave the following assessment of how aeroplanes might change the world:

> As far as can at present be foreseen, there is absolutely no limit to the scale of its future independent war use. And the day may not be far off when aerial operations with their devastation of enemy lands and destruction of industrial and populous centres on a vast scale may become the principal operations of war, to which the older forms of military and naval operations may become secondary and subordinate.[5]

Smuts recommended that there should be a dedicated Air Ministry. Not too long afterwards, such a ministry was established, with Flying Corps enthusiast Lord Rothermere as its first Secretary of State. In April 1918, the separate wings of the Royal Flying Corps, naval and military, were gently detached. It became its own independent creature: the Royal Air Force.

Many of the flying names that would go on to find illustrious resonance in the decades to come had gathered for the First World War; in December 1916, New Zealander Keith Park, having fought at the Somme, was transferred to the Royal Flying Corps. Much of the knowledge and skill he acquired in matters such as formation flying was picked up on the hoof; the encounters with enemy aircraft were equally improvised affairs, a very long way from the meticulous planning that Park would later put in at Bentley Priory.

The philosophy of what was to become Fighter Command was formed towards the end of the First World War, as the defensive strategy coalesced. By 1918, this was an air force that understood both about bombing and about parrying bombs. The capital's protective system had been pulled together into a body called the London Air Defence Area. According to John Ferris, even in those early days of flight, there was remarkable sophistication:

> Within one minute, the headquarters at LADA could receive and process reports from thousands of observers, place them before commanders and despatch orders to the aircraft standing ready on the runway. These aircraft were in the air within two and a half to five minutes. By the end of the war, this system was on the technical verge of conducting ground-directed interception of enemy bombers at 20,000 feet [6,100 metres].[6]

In 1914, the Royal Flying Corps had gone into a conflict for the conduct of which it had very little to guide it. By the end of that war, it had grown into an institution with its own fresh-minted traditions and also – thanks to a large injection of money from Lord Cowdray – its own grand gentleman's club, the RAF Club, in London. There were 188 combat squadrons, 22,647 aircraft and 291,170 officers and men. All these pilots and engineers might have thought that there was some stability in this mighty new fighting force. The inter-war years were to prove quite different.

After the war, empires dissolved like dreams; the Ottoman caliphate, the Habsburg dynasty. Lines on maps lost all meaning, new lines seeded fresh hatreds. And for those nations that retained their colonies, the air was increasingly the means by which control was exercised as convulsive shocks coursed through Europe and out into the Middle East and north Africa. In Britain, Winston Churchill, now combined War and Air Minister, understood the opportunity and the danger; and he invited Hugh Trenchard to head the new service.

But there was no guarantee that the RAF would be permitted to retain its independence. The conclusion of the war had brought with it the assumption – amid the slaughter of so many young fighting men – that there would be no further war like it for at least ten years. And on all sides, no one had any money left. The services had to contract. In March 1919, the RAF, barely formed, was slashed. Its 22,000 aircraft and 240,000 personnel were reduced to around 200 planes and 30,000 personnel.

The core philosophical question of the period – and the unresolved dilemma that was to be faced in 1940 by Hugh Dowding, and by his vociferous, furious opponents – was this: what was the RAF for? If the realm was to be defended from the air, how best was this to be achieved? Giulio Douhet, a pioneering French pilot whose writings came to be studied eagerly within the RAF, had this to say: 'The command of the air will be achieved when the enemy's planes are reduced to a number incapable of developing any aerial action of real importance to the war as a whole.'[7]

In other words: strike first and take the fight to them. Attack not only the airfields and aerodromes, but also the plane-making factories, and their fuel suppliers, and the roads and the rails used by the suppliers. Yet an alternative in emphasis had been outlined by Frederick Sykes in 1918: 'Strategic interception has not been frequent in history, owing to the great skill demanded of the leader, combined with the great mobility and efficiency of the troops under his command. It is the ideal strategy for the new Arm – the Air Force.'[8]

Another theory arose: that of the 'knock-out blow'. If only the elusive blow could be landed, hostilities could be ended almost immediately. From the air, such a blow could come in the form of massive bombardment, as foreseen in all those Edwardian science-fiction dystopias. As J.M. Spaight wrote: 'The nations may fear to unleash the monsters they have bred. That would be the greatest, the most welcome contribution that an air-power could make to the next war – that the next war never in fact comes.'[9]

Hugh Trenchard might not have been the most academic of men, but the subject of bombing – and the concomitant ethical issues – was frequently in his thoughts throughout the early 1920s; for as the technology of flying evolved, so too did its destructive potential. 'There can be no question that a bombing squadron is a more powerful offensive weapon than the fighting squadrons,' he said in 1924. 'It strikes either at the nation or at the air forces on the ground whereas the fighter can only strike at the air force. Therefore, it may be stated as principle that the bombing squadrons should be as numerous as possible and the fighters as few as popular opinion and the necessity of defending vital objectives will permit.'[10]

What about the prospective bombardment of civilian populations, though? What was the RAF doctrine on this subject? There was never any suggestion that innocent civilians – women, children, the elderly – would be targeted. Likewise, hospitals and schools were to be avoided at every possible cost. But Trenchard had been looking with some interest at the changing industrial landscape and the potential it offered. He was vehemently fascinated by the rise of workers' movements; the growing strength of the unions in the mines and in the steel foundries.

'[He] singled out several industries as being particularly important: iron and coal mines ... chemical production facilities, explosives factories, armament industries, aero-engine manufacturers, submarine and ship-building works, gun foundries and engine repair shops,' wrote Philip Meilinger.[11] But it wasn't just physical damage Trenchard was interested in; it was psychological sabotage. By making targets of such establishments, he could undermine the morale of the workers; if the destruction became sufficiently intense, then they could be made to rise up against their employers, and against the state, by simply refusing to carry on. In the war to come, both the Germans and the British would seek to probe these nerves to the limit.

Despite the screw being turned on the new Air Force's budgets, it was also quickly understood within the Air Ministry and Whitehall that there is always a war somewhere. And the British empire needed policing and patrolling – or to put it another way, controlling. Hugh Trenchard was very quick to see that the RAF could become indispensable in such a role.

'Trenchard ... suggested to Churchill that the RAF be given the opportunity to subdue a festering uprising in Somali-land,' wrote Philip Meilinger. 'Churchill agreed.' And thus a new empire of the air was assembled; valuable experience for those who would find themselves in positions of responsibility come 1939. Throughout the 1920s, steadily increasing numbers of RAF planes were deployed to India, Afghanistan and Iraq, and even more sent to Egypt, Transjordan and Palestine. As a last resort, rebels would be bombed 'to compel compliance'.[12]

Back in Britain, the gentleman amateur approach to training was made much more formal and professional. A dedicated RAF college was established at Cranwell in Lincolnshire; in essence, it was the pilot's equivalent of

Sandhurst (indeed, a few years later, in 1933, it gained its own grand purpose-built headquarters, designed by architect James West and inspired by the Royal Hospital in Chelsea).

As the 1920s wore on, Trenchard himself was fast becoming not so much a leader as an unlikely idol to many existing and aspiring pilots. His nickname was 'Boom' – a reference to his loud and intimidating voice when angered. The most prominent of his admirers – who joined the RAF under the assumed name of 'Shaw' after his First World War exploits in Arabia – was T.E. Lawrence. Lawrence later wrote: 'The word Trenchard spells out confidence in the RAF … We think of him as immense.'[13]

Thanks to enthusiastic collusion between Air Minister Winston Churchill and Hugh Trenchard, the policing of the Middle East from the air was expanded. And it was at this point, in the early 1920s, when the philosophy of the RAF bifurcated most visibly. Out in the Middle East, the bomber held dominion. T.E. Lawrence, who had lived and fought among the Bedouins in the First World War, aiding their attacks on the Ottoman forces, somehow found a way of conflating his Arab romanticism with his adoration for the work of the RAF. It was a semi-mystical business: when a village was targeted for 'recalcitrance' and then bombed to pieces and burned to ashes, any Iraqi who witnessed such horrors, Lawrence reasoned, would not see it as Western eyes saw it. The bombing would be understood in terms of destiny. 'It is not punishment, but a misfortune striking from heaven.'[14]

Less metaphysical was the view of Hugh Trenchard, expressed to Parliament. 'The natives of a lot of these tribes love fighting for fighting's sake,' he said. 'They have no objection to being killed.'

He shared his private thoughts on these knotty matters with a colleague whom he had not previously warmed to:

Hugh Dowding, who in the late 1920s was sent out to Palestine. It was a serious gesture of confidence. After the war, Dowding was head of 1 Group at Kenley. He rose to the rank of air commodore, moved to Inland Area headquarters at Uxbridge (just a few miles away from the Fighter Command HQ-to-be at Bentley). Then in 1924, he was sent out to Baghdad, in a period during which the RAF were seeking to quell uncountable numbers of different sects and tribes in a landscape that was often far from hospitable to their advanced technology; a land of rough mountains and vast marshes, as well as sand plains. Dowding acquitted himself well and in May 1926 came back to Britain to join the Air Ministry as Director of Training.

In 1929, he was given possibly the trickiest job of them all; a posting to Palestine requiring nimble, fleet judgements. Any mistakes could well result in a conflagration that might sweep across an already fissile Middle East. The country, at that stage, was a British protectorate; the Balfour Declaration of 1917 had promised a home for the Jewish people – and although the fulfilment of that promise was some way off, tensions in the region were high, especially in the vortex that followed the collapse of the Ottoman Empire. For Dowding, this was quite a cauldron to be thrown into; instructive and educational, an invaluable experience.

Dowding seemed bemused by this new world. 'The Arab legion is a curious force run entirely on Oriental lines,' he wrote to Trenchard. 'It is cheap, and has a great deal of rough effectiveness; but I imagine if certain of its methods appeared in "The Spectator", there would be something of a sensation.' Dowding's nickname among colleagues, quite early on, was 'Stuffy'; yet he did have a bone-dry sense of humour.[15]

The peace of those interwar years grew yet more uneasy. In the early 1930s, the Great Depression and its aftershocks rippled across every continent; and as economic hardships began to grate ever more painfully on the ordinary people, fissures were opened in the body politic in many countries. It was understood at Cabinet level as the decade dawned that Britain would have to construct an ever more advanced air fleet; yet there were also those who saw this new air age as the harbinger of Armageddon. Both sides were to be proved right.

Chapter Three

The Seduction of Flight

In 1932, when German voters made the Nazi party the largest political force in the Reichstag, practically every British schoolboy – and a great many pilots to be – were reading the first adventures of a new hero created by Captain W.E. Johns (not a captain at all in reality – but he was a very experienced former pilot). That year saw publication of *The Camels Are Coming*, a collection of short stories featuring the young James Bigglesworth, known more familiarly as 'Biggles'. In his first – surprisingly dark – adventures, Biggles was a Great War ace in the Royal Flying Corps, somewhere between 1917 and 1918.

Biggles's world (friends Algy and Ginger soon popped up) was one of continual hazard and 'red mists', of love betrayed and dead friends avenged, as he went flying off in search of treacherous Germans. At the beginning, there was more consumption of whisky and cigarettes than one would expect (these refreshments were swiftly replaced in later stories with milk). There was also a sense of mortality; in the early books, Biggles felt fear keenly. This did not stop him killing many enemy pilots. He also lied about his age in order to get into the Corps. Biggles was seventeen as his exploits began.

Johns was writing with terrific authority; he had flown with the RFC during the First World War and appeared to have had nine lives. Propellers had flown off his aircraft, while he had got lost in mists, and had been forced to ditch into the sea – all this while over home territory. He also got caught up in terrifying dogfights in 1918, one of which brought him down in enemy territory and resulted in him being made a prisoner of war. But the Biggles adventures – as they went on, Johns brought them up to the present day and indeed had his hero take on the Nazis – were infused with the lyricism of flight itself. Above all, James Bigglesworth loved to fly.

Nor was Biggles the only literary pilot competing for attention. The astoundingly prolific children's author Percy F. Westerman – who had spent a little time in the Royal Flying Corps in 1918 as a navigation expert – soon added to his wide range of adventure stories with entries such as *Winning His Wings* (1919), *Unconquered Wings* (1924), *The Riddle of the Air* (1926) and *Standish of the Air Police* (1935). These were aimed at boys who would never have the opportunity to travel abroad unless they were seeking their fortune in a far corner of the empire. But boys were allowed to daydream, and authors such as these were able to tell them that flying was every bit as extraordinary and marvellous as they could imagine.

Daydreams were not solely the province of the young. These daring literary heroics were matched in real life by spectacular RAF displays in the 1930s, vast pageants at Hendon in north London, several of which were organised by Wing Commander Keith Park. These events were frequently attended by royalty, as well as thousands of eager members of the public. Here were elaborate acrobatics, close formation flying, gimmicks such as giant catapults and floodlit displays of night flying: 'The Sky Is Their Stage'; 'The Thrill of the Year'. The spirit of such events goes on now at the annual Farnborough Air Shows. Back in the interwar years, long before technology smoothed the flight paths of all pilots, here were real daredevils, diving and swooping, making impossible turns. There were pyrotechnics; fighters would 'attack' other planes which would come down amid simulated flames. There would be simulated bomber raids (it is difficult to imagine modern audiences finding this an acceptable means of escapism); even, a little later, action involving barrage balloons. It is possible, in the febrile 1930s, that these mad air shows provided some subliminal reassurance.

Among the early air show daredevils was a young pilot, inducted into the air force in 1929, called Douglas Bader. Though he was later made hugely famous in biography and film, over-familiarity takes nothing away from the story of Bader's genuinely breathtaking achievements – a man who had agonisingly lost both legs in a plane crash in 1931, who painfully learned to walk again on primitive artificial limbs, was then retired from the RAF, but came back and went on to fight brilliantly in the Battle of Britain.

Even away from the thrills of the 1920s and 1930s air show spectaculars, the young pilots – who themselves worshipped at the altar of the First World War 'aces' – perfected terrifying new tricks: one pilot impressed by 'climbing out of his rear cockpit in mid air and crawling forward to tie a handkerchief about the joystick in the empty front cockpit, then getting back into the rear cockpit ... Bader did it too, finding it diverting to be straddled across the fuselage like a bareback rider, holding on with the heels while the hands were tying the handkerchief.' Then, at the Hendon Pageants, Bader and his team would make the crowds (and the journalist from *The Times*) swoon with 'the cleanest trick flying' performed before 'hundreds of thousands crowding hillsides'.[1]

The annual Hendon shows were no empty spectacle; they were tableaux of potential, presented not only for domestic audiences but for continental eyes too, and for observers yet further afield. They featured an element of sabre-waving that would not suit modern tastes. In the earlier shows, in the 1920s, highly specific set-pieces depicted 'Arabs' (RAF men sporting Bedouin costumes) attempting theatrical uprisings, only to see the pride of the RAF swoop down on their 'native villages' (props which were destroyed amid convincing flames and fireworks). Britain's might, in the form of her Empire, now extended to the heavens; and rival powers out in the East, for instance, such as Japan, would be implicitly invited to take note of the courage, the ingenuity and the mechanical know-how.

Among those looking on, fascinated, in the early days was Germany's Erhard Milch, later to become a senior Luftwaffe commander. Before he joined the Reich Aviation Ministry in 1933, Milch had pursued a successful career in civil aviation. The Hendon visit beguiled him and he later wrote warmly of his conversation with someone from the Bristol Aeroplane Company. They discussed fuel injections: 'My English then was very bad,' wrote Milch, 'but he explained everything so kindly that I understood. We had nothing of the kind in Germany at that time.'[2] That was not quite true.

But the very nature of the new warfare caused anguish outside of the RAF, and particularly in some Cabinet circles: it was felt that the destructive possibilities of bombing would grow so enormous that it would paradoxically become a weapon that could never be used. Some politicians worried: what if this horrific weapon was unleashed upon Britain by its enemies? In the industrial areas of the Midlands and north, there was mass unemployment, with squalor and poverty on a scale that seemed closer to the nineteenth century than the neon glow of the 1930s. Nor had the preceding years been much easier for working men and their families; an economy shrunk to the bone, the apparent indifference and hostility of many politicians and the ruling class, and other factors – the acute sense of ingratitude for all the terrible sacrifices of the First World War – helped the trade union movement enormously. Those same politicians in the 1930s looked at the seething resentment of the workers and calculated how much enemy bombing it would take before they rose up and overthrew the established state.

Elsewhere, the newspapers were in the time-honoured business of stoking anxiety. Then, as now, fear sells. A report from the *Evening News* in January 1935 ran:

> If war came tomorrow, London would be an inferno of exploding bombs, of gases drifting in poisonous clouds through the streets, of flames leaping from building to building. Squadron upon squadron of enemy aeroplanes – hundred after hundred filling the sky – would rain down death upon the city. There would be no escape from the destroying horror – except flight from the doomed capital of Empire.

The urgency was not misplaced. Under its commander-in-chief Hermann Goering, appointed by Hitler in 1934, the Luftwaffe, as the German air force was now known, flew out from behind black clouds of secrecy. Though expressly forbidden by the terms of the Versailles Treaty, research and rearmament had been proceeding in the clearings of distant, obscure forests: pilots trained, planes perfected, weaponry honed. Goering – who had brought the concept of the concentration camp to Germany after it had been pioneered by his own father in southern Africa some thirty years beforehand – was a swaggering showman. In the interwar years, having joined the Nazi party, Goering had become a bloated morphine addict, the dependency starting after he was injured at a Nazi rally. The pale blue uniform that he was later to devise for himself, added to his undisguised lust for the vulgar trappings of high society, speak of a serious imbalance at the core of the man. But Hitler's trust in him meant that his growing Luftwaffe was taken very seriously.

In Whitehall, meanwhile, fevered calculations were being made. Officials tried in the early 1930s to project what Germany might soon be capable of. It was reckoned that they could drop anything from 300 to 900 tons of explosives every day. London was the presumed target; many believed that the Germans would soon have the capability to turn the capital into an inferno miles wide. Even the more optimistic voices held an undercurrent of dread. A Home Office report declared:

> Even if unlimited money and resources were available, it would be impossible to prevent heavy casualties and great destruction of property. All that can be done is to take whatever steps financial and other considerations allow on the one hand to inflict as much damage as possible on the attackers, on the other hand to minimise the effects of air attack upon the morale of the people and the working of essential services.

The presumption was that the very first day of such an attack would result in tens of thousands of deaths.

Air Chief Marshal Sir Edward Ellington studied the maps and drew his own chilling conclusions in 1934. He hypothesised the Germans marching into the Low Countries and setting up a range of aerodromes. Such bases would make London almost absurdly easy to attack; a short distance across the water, a dreadful head start on the defenders before they could know that the attack had been launched, and the Germans would not spend long in their enemy's airspace – just drop the bombs, turn, and back to base. Ellington's proposed solution? For Britain to occupy and defend the Low Countries before they could be overrun.

Prime Minister Stanley Baldwin had been thinking of those enemy bombers. Famously he believed that nothing could ever stop them getting through: 'I think it is as well for the man in the street to realise that no power on earth can protect him from being bombed.' More than that, 'Who does not know that if another great war comes, our civilisation will fall with as great a crash as that of Rome?' he asked in 1933.

Yet there was another side to this neurosis; the knowledge that whatever the enemy did to us, we could do back to them. There were those in Whitehall who tried – vainly – to make such calculations too. In the event of British and German populations being struck repeatedly and unstoppably, in the event of entire cities going up in flickering plumes of searing heat, which side would lose its morale first? Which population would be the first to turn on its leaders to beg for the horror to stop?

This had been a major preoccupation in Germany long before Goering and the Nazis came to power. At the 1920s height of the Weimar government, many civic leaders had been reading authors such as H.G. Wells (in *The Outline of History*, Wells had painted a vision of the results of total war from the air; elsewhere, other authors had gone so far as to suggest that chemical bombardment could induce mutations). In 1927 (a year after Germany was allowed by the League of Nations to have defensive military and naval arrangements), the German Air Defence League was formed. It asked experts from many fields to prophesy what would happen if German cities came under heavy bombardment. Chemists were drawn in with the hope that they might be able to suggest ways of neutralising the poisons that could be rained down. Architects were consulted about ways that buildings, streets and neighbourhoods might be somehow made more bomb-proof; could apartment blocks and road layouts be reconfigured so as to minimise the effect of blasts? The country was clearly experiencing a jangling paranoia in the wake of the First World War, a belief that the vengeful Allies might yet seek to crush Germany further.

As soon as Hitler came to power, the Nazis sought to intensify that national neurosis. Just months into 1933, 'the Nazis rehearsed air attacks to simulate the vulnerability of the Reich,' wrote Peter Fritzsche. 'The most spectacular was an air raid over Berlin … "unknown foreign" aeroplanes bombarded Berlin.'[3] The objects dropped on this occasion were leaflets, outlining the ever-present horror that might fly overhead at any time. One newspaper helpfully underlined the point by declaring that next time it could be chemical weapons or incendiary bombs. The shadow of the enemy bomber came to loom large in propaganda; one magazine cover of 1934 depicted a map of Germany and, menacing it from all sides, various types of bombers. Every arena of municipal life was touched; in schools and factories, everyone was urged to learn how to use gas masks, and how to get to gas shelters in an orderly fashion.

There was also a sickly emphasis on the terrifying detachment of bombers; the height at which they flew and the preternatural power which that gave them. It was pointed out that unlike soldiers on the ground, fighting clearly defined lines, defending sacred territory, the pilot of a bomber high above could not even see the physical demarcations of national borders. Why show respect to something that – from such a distance – seemed so insignificant? As the decade wore on and the Nazis' grip on power tightened, some canny lateral thinking took place about making the civilian population more aviation-minded. The new sport of gliding had – like many outdoor pursuits in

Germany – been enjoying a vogue but when the Nazis came to power, they made it all the more popular. Gliding clubs popped up all over the country, heavily subsidised by the Nazis. The German gliders were launched from high hills, hauled to the top by eager teams waiting for their turn to soar. The idea was to quietly train as many people as possible in the principles and science of aerodynamics. As many as 60,000 German people held gliding licences in the 1930s.

The propaganda had a double edge. By terrorising its own population with the prospect of total war, the Nazis were clearing the way towards making their own version of it completely acceptable.

Back in Britain and within the RAF, not dissimilar arguments – in philosophical terms – were taking place. But there was also a much more serious focus upon building up Britain's defensive capabilities. This led to furious in-fighting within the Air Ministry; by concentrating solely on self-protection, some argued, Britain was effectively ceding potential control over the whole of Europe to the Nazis. As the arguments raged, recruitment raced on. Unlike the army, which even by the late 1930s was run very much as though it were still in the late Victorian era – officers most often educated at public school, and a great proportion with private incomes – the RAF was attempting to trawl more varied waters for new candidates. The levels of skill that the new generation of pilots would need meant that the Air Ministry could not afford to overlook genuinely promising candidates. The inception of the Royal Air Force Volunteer Reserve in 1936, as Martin Francis noted, 'opened up the service to lower middle class grammar school boys looking for an alternative to dreary clerking jobs in the city ... All recruits to the RAFVR shared the same initial instruction, and commissions were only awarded later, on the basis of performance in training.'[4]

There were also a number of highly experienced instructors in the air force who had risen up through apprenticeships; a long way from the amused, confident aristocrats who went at it as a hobby. In Geoffrey Wellum's haunting account of his own time as a pilot in Fighter Command, he dwells on the flight lieutenants who patiently tutored him when he was barely eighteen years old: though they were older and wiser, and their aviation experience was obviously far greater, they wouldn't allow him to call them 'sir'; he was in training to be an officer and they were thus his juniors in terms of rank. Therefore they would call Wellum 'sir' and he would refer to them as 'Flight'.

Wellum himself was not grand, hailing from the comfortable middle-class fringes of Epping Forest in London. But in the mid-1930s, the RAF was becoming publicly known for its dashing, suave, better socially connected recruits. A man who would shortly make a name for himself was Peter Townsend, (later, in the 1950s, he made an even bigger name for himself as the lover of the Queen's sister, Princess Margaret). The son of Lieutenant Colonel Edward Townsend, a Burma district commissioner, the fourteen-year-old Peter was enraptured by the sight of three Armstrong Whitworth biplane fighters making a landing in the fields of his English public school, Haileybury.

Five years later, at the age of nineteen, he went to Cranwell to enrol at the Royal Air Force College. Townsend was in some ways the very archetype of the young RAF pilot; darkly handsome, socially assured, not boorish but instead languidly confident, at least outwardly. It can never be reiterated enough that flying – even simply for training purposes – could in fact be intensely frightening. The masks that these young pilots wore must have been easy for barmaids, publicans and batmen alike to see through. But in the 1930s, it was still a service that was struggling to find respect from either the Army or Navy. Townsend later wrote:

> The RAF's impudent claim that priority should be given to air defence rocked the sea-dogs and the Colonel Blimps. It was unbearable that the old country should have to look for protection to pilots of the RAF, whom the old guard tended to despise as the rag-tag and bob-tail of the nation's youth, beyond the fringe of respectable society, with their pub-crawling and noisy sports cars.[5]

Nor did the Colonel Blimps really understand either the grave souls of these outwardly flippant youngsters or their poetic need for the sky. Even as a small boy, Townsend had felt it: 'Unlike the sea, [the sky] was changing and ethereal,' he wrote. 'Unlike the gloomy, invisible depths of the sea, the air was full of enchantment.' He also understood very well as an adult that the euphoria he experienced when flying opened up other philosophical possibilities: 'I was never a fatalist, but the more I flew, the more certain I became of some will beyond our own.' This was a sense that a great many pilots shared.

Elsewhere, Patricia Clark, the daughter of that era's bestselling romantic novelist Denise Robins, was to join Fighter Command as a WAAF to play crucial roles in the Operations and Filter Rooms – and she had been partly inspired in that direction by the fact that her brother and cousins were, in the 1930s, drawn in to become pilots. As a very young woman indeed, one of her very first 'dates' – although the term would probably horrify her – was with a young man who already had his own aeroplane: 'When I was a teenager – I think I was the only person who dared do this actually – I went with him when he wanted to fly. He would take me down to Lancing on the south coast. And we would beetle up Brighton front in his little Moth – where he would go down as low as he could over the piers, skate over the top of them and scare everybody. He was absolutely mad.

'Being as young as I was,' she continues, 'he was the brother that I had never had, but had always wanted. He took me out in London in the winter and the roads were all frozen. He had this beautiful car and he was practising skids. And after we had done this for about an hour, he said: "Well, now we'll practise kissing." And I had never kissed a boy before so I thought, well, that's not a bad idea as I don't know how to do it. So he said, "Right." And he bent down and pressed his mouth on mine – and it went on and on and on and on. I was breathless, he was breathless. Eventually, he took his mouth away and said, "That's a record. I counted to one hundred that time."'

Incongruous innocence and impetuosity seemed oddly defining leitmotifs of many young pilots. But the Colonel Blimps had a point; from Cranwell to Duxford, Hornchurch to North Weald, the RAF men really were roaring around in newly bought motor cars and drinking heavily in country pubs. Writing of that period, novelist Jane Oliver declared that 'to the average citizen … these noisy young men were just a nuisance, with their tendency to pick fights on the least provocation, to drive almost continuously to the danger of the public, to break all the comfortable conventions.'[6] There were moments of tension in smart restaurants when more reserved army officers were faced with the prospect, at another table, of these boys in their blue uniforms with their 'long hair' and – to military eyes – slovenly standards of dress. Meanwhile, certain public bars near aerodromes could be monopolised. One exception to the drinking (though not to the fast cars) was young Douglas Bader, who claimed that he had never liked the taste of beer, or any other alcoholic refreshment, and so avoided it. But he was happy to be in the company of those who didn't.

Yet this was far from being yobbishness. There was a great deal of stress involved in fighter training: not merely the tough instructors and exams, or the anxieties of navigating before the days of radio technology, using only compasses, maps and even Bradshaw's railway timetables to work out where exactly the plane was, as the fuel gauges dropped lower. These very young men had entered a world in which death was frequent and common, yet always came as a stomach-punch of shock. Trainee pilots who had barely started shaving would make friends, form close bonds with their fellows, shake off the tension of spins and rolls and engine seizures with beer; and then watch, with horror, as a comrade in the air experienced engine trouble, or stalled, and couldn't pull the plane out the death-spin. Such intimate acquaintanceship with mortality at so young an age had a tremendous psychological impact.

In that febrile atmosphere, the British welcomed a visit in 1937 from a diplomatic German Air Mission. At that stage, new Prime Minister Neville Chamberlain did not regard war as inevitable. He was pursuing appeasement; although it is difficult to find anyone now who does not view his aims with contempt, it is important to point out that for those who had lived through the First World War, there was a certain honour in trying to avoid sending Britain's working men into a fresh hell; honour, too, in at least attempting to make a lunatic dictator back down from a mania for conquest that might result in the destruction of the Continent.

The senior Luftwaffe commander who led the 1937 mission to Britain, Erhard Milch (the man who had so carefully watched and enjoyed the RAF's earlier Hendon pageants) was carefully steered away from classified technological developments; but he was allowed to meet crews and inspect planes. He and various other figures from the Reich Air Ministry were taken on quite a grand tour: from the aerodrome at Hornchurch to RAF Odiham in Lincolnshire to Mildenhall in Suffolk.

A couple of pilots remembered awkward moments, as Milch inspected cockpits and enquired about reflector gun-sights, which the men had been warned not to talk about in any detail. But Milch was not there to undertake espionage. He in turn talked relatively freely with his British counterparts about Luftwaffe developments. There was said to be an atmosphere of 'intimacy'. Yet away from the eagerness of obsessional men, there was a carefully unspoken darkness. Milch was keeping a larger secret of his own. By 1937, the Luftwaffe as a force was some distance ahead of the RAF in terms of numbers and squadrons. On Milch's return to Germany, he was interviewed at great length by Hitler and reportedly praised very highly all that he had seen. Only a man supremely confident about the superiority of his own forces would have dared to do that.

Yet Milch's visit was mirrored – more informally – by a particularly remarkable encounter just a few months before. It came about when two British pilots – Squadron Leader Herbert Rowley and Flight Lieutenant Richard Atcherley – took it into their heads, independently of their superiors, to fly over to Germany to see what the country's air force was like. The story, long kept classified, was unearthed by Vincent Orange several years ago.[7] As well as providing astonishing, illuminating detail on the sluggishness of British intelligence in that period – detail which, knowingly or otherwise, Rowley passed on to the then politically marginalised Winston Churchill – there is also a curious tone of rambunctious comedy: two RAF boys, with a heightened appetite for drink, in the middle of Hitler's Germany in 1937.

They flew out early one morning in a Percival Gull monoplane and, having stopped off in Kent and then Amsterdam, made straight for Berlin, landing at one of the city's main airfields. Their arrival seemed to cause no consternation whatsoever. As Orange noted, 'they were charged a nominal sum to house their aeroplane.' There was still so much about aviation that was new.

Britain had an air attaché in Berlin; Rowley and Atcherley called on him. From the start, senior Luftwaffe figures were also keen to meet them; at the grand British Aero Club, the pilots were introduced to Colonel Friedrich Hanesse of Germany's Air Intelligence Service and told him – with winning frankness – that they were simply 'out to see as much as they could'. What followed was the sort of VIP visit more normally accorded to senior Air Ministry dignitaries. Rowley and Atcherley found every door open, and a chauffeur-driven Mercedes waiting to convey them wherever they wished.

Meetings and appointments were set up at air bases and air production factories. Obviously this was not one-way traffic; their German hosts were clearly anxious to hear as much about the RAF as they could. But underneath was something that – for those few brief days – pushed to one side notions of nationalism. The English and German pilots – experts at what they did – already knew one another. Atcherley, for instance, knew the Luftwaffe head of research and development, Ernst Udet, from a very different life; both men had performed acrobatic stunts at well-paid American air shows. In just a few years, Udet had progressed from stunt flying to a position of serious power within the Luftwaffe; and he told the two British pilots about his new project, the Junkers Ju 87, otherwise known as the Stuka, a plane with an extraordinary capacity for near-vertical dives, giving the pilot lethal firing accuracy.

When they returned home Rowley wrote a long and considered memo not to his direct superior but to Wing Commander Charles Anderson, who ensured that his friend Winston Churchill was privy to what Anderson regarded as shortcomings and deficiencies in the organisation of the RAF.

If there was a general idea that RAF pilots were largely recruited from the more well-to-do strata of society, there was a parallel notion, in the late 1930s, about their Luftwaffe counterparts, remembers Patricia Clark. Before the war, she and her sister had been sent to Switzerland – and then Germany – for their education. This was not unusual; many girls from rarefied backgrounds completed their educations over there. There were formal dances – and smart young women were sought out as partners.

'Just nearby Munich, there was a training establishment for air force cadets – Luftwaffe – and they were being taught how to behave as gentlemen in the mess,' says Mrs Clark. 'An appeal went out to foreign visitors who would be willing to go – at invitation – to partner these cadets while they were learning to dance. My friend and I both put our names down and sure enough we were carted off to this party.'

The prelude might not have been terrifically elegant – but what followed was. 'There, we sat around in a ballroom and the Luftwaffe cadets all wore white gloves, very old fashioned. Music would start. They would come across the room, click their heels, bow. "May I have your permission to dance?" And then you would get up, dance round the floor. Then they would bow, click their heels, hold your hand and thank you. Very formal. Quite fun, really a giggle, because we were very young. Once or twice we made friends with some of the Luftwaffe pilots and they were just like any ordinary English students.' Nor did they ever discuss politics. 'They weren't Nazis or anything – though whether they belonged to the

Nazi party – well, they probably did, because they had to. But there was no sign of anything like that.'

She remembers vividly how strange the atmosphere was, in 1938, to a young girl who paid very little attention to politics. 'In my Swiss school, there were girls from all over the world. I had a German friend at the school called Hannah – she was Jewish, not that that meant anything to me in those days because the school was completely non-religious – and she wanted me to go to spend Easter holidays with her in Frankfurt. I was allowed to go, which was very interesting because Hannah's parents, one or other of them, was with us at all times. If we went to play tennis, if we went to the cinema, we always had an adult with us. It was only much, much later on, after the war had broken out and I started to learn about what really went on there, that I realised that there was a ruling, if you like, that as long as there was a foreign person with the Jew, they wouldn't be touched. It was a safeguard for them. So they needed to make sure that Hannah was never on her own without me there.

'Of course I didn't know that,' adds Mrs Clark. 'Anyway, I decided that it would be nice to learn German. I persuaded my mother to let me leave the Swiss school and go to Germany as a paying guest and I was billeted with a professor who was supposed to teach me German for a year. I had a wonderful time in Munich! Now that was the year before the war. And all that time I was there, I must have been blindfolded.'

Indeed, the truth of what was happening beneath the placid middle-class surface of life chills Mrs Clark as she thinks back on it; certainly, when she joined Fighter Command later, she was able to piece together exactly what a nightmare regime the British were fighting.

In the middle of 1938, the uneasy period of Anschluss and secession, of the appropriation of Austria and the

Sudetenland by Germany, Britain's Minister for the Co-ordination of Defence, Sir Thomas Inskip (a figure not held in universally high regard in the services) outlined the strategy for the days to come. The priority was that the mother country should be protected above all else. 'It would seem in accordance with strategic principle,' he said, 'that the decisive place and the decisive time for the concentration of our air forces would be somewhere over our own territory at the outset of a war.' Fighter planes were the thing; fighter pilots would be at the forefront of the coming conflict.

But were there enough aeroplanes for the job? In 1930s peacetime, air production in Britain was a fraught and uneven business (unlike in the sleek and modern early days of Nazi Germany, where the government was able simply to commandeer the successful aviation company Lufthansa). In Britain, with so many mixed and confusing signals about military intentions being beamed out from Whitehall, it was a matter of some anxiety for the RAF hierarchy that there would be any suitable planes with which to beat off the enemy.

Chapter Four

The Lines in the Heavens

It seems surprising that it was as late as the mid-1930s that the wooden aeroplane finally evolved into something approaching its modern form. Visionary engineers at Vickers Supermarine and Rolls-Royce were combining new metal structures that used lighter alloys with new engines. One particular aircraft designer, who had spent many years specialising in flying boats, had been giving particular thought to the future of fighters. His creation is now immortal, and symbolises the triumph of Fighter Command.

Reg Mitchell – known as RJ – born in Stoke on Trent in 1895, had been mesmerised by aeroplanes since news of the first Wright Brothers flights took wing around the world. As a young boy, he would make functioning toy aeroplanes with any bits of wood, bamboo and fabric he could find; his childhood home was filled with his imaginary and futuristic designs, and the prototypes were flown in the family's garden. Mitchell's precocious flair for engineering, plus his increasing passion for aeronautics, took him after his apprenticeship in the Potteries to the Supermarine plane factory just outside Southampton, in Hampshire. He joined at the tail end of the First World War, devoting the interwar years to innovative new civilian passenger planes that would win prizes.

Just as the community of pilots was genuinely international, the same went for aeronautical designers; as a result, intelligence was unusually keen. By the early 1930s, designers in Britain had a shrewd idea of what was happening among their German counterparts. This was certainly the case with R.J. Mitchell.

And their disquiet spread upwards; Sir Hugh Dowding (who at the time held the title of Air Member for Research and Development) and Supermarine's Sir Robert MacLean were anxious that Britain should have a new type of day and night fighter. It must have a 'low landing speed and short landing run', a speed of 402 kilometres per hour (250 miles per hour), a steep rate of climb, sharp manoeuvrability and a proper all-round view.

Mitchell, a fair-haired man with pale blue eyes and a seemingly permanent expression of anvil-like determination, went to his drawing board in 1932; the technical demands and complexities of the new beast were all-absorbing and it was only in 1934 that a prototype was ready to be tested. The new plane, streamlined and modern, still had an open cockpit, wooden propeller and fixed undercarriage. The tests were extremely disappointing. It attained only 370 kilometres per hour (230 miles per hour) and there were problems with cooling the powerful Rolls-Royce engine. Mitchell himself was extremely dissatisfied; nonetheless, the plane was given a name, and the name stuck. It has been suggested that 'Spitfire' was the inspiration of Sir Robert MacLean; possibly it was a reference to the way that the plane's machine guns spat flames. But the term was also, at that time, a slang term for a particularly hot-willed woman. Scarlett O'Hara, heroine of Margaret Mitchell's *Gone with the Wind*, would have been described as a spitfire.

In 1936, a prototype Spitfire took to the skies for the very first time, piloted from Eastleigh airfield in Hampshire. It was obviously a closely guarded secret, yet the local press could not help noticing the marvel scorching through the heavens above and no one was particularly minded to muzzle journalists. 'Keen observers in and around Southampton have recently been interested in the high-speed performances of a remarkable plane which has made occasional flights from Eastleigh Airport …' disclosed the *Southampton Echo*, 'here is a plane out of the ordinary.'

The first Spitfire, on its test flight, was still unpainted and as Mitchell's son reports, the cowling had a kind of yellow-green factory finish colour to it. The first test pilot was Captain J. Summers, known as 'Mutt'. He was thrilled with the plane, commenting on its 'remarkably good' handling, the 'powerful and light to operate' ailerons. The cockpit, he concluded, was 'very comfortable and all controls accessible and very well laid out'.[1] There were some critical notes; he had difficulties with the clear canopy over the cockpit, finding it almost impossible to open at high speed (which would make an emergency bail-out especially fraught); there were also concerns about giving the brakes a new air reservoir.

But this test was not quite a seal of official approval; there was another RAF test to come, at Martlesham in Suffolk. The plane was taken up and put through all sorts of different manoeuvres, gaining the instant thumbs-up. The pilot this time was Humphrey Edwardes-Jones – later an air marshal and a KCB. Later he recalled: 'I flew the aircraft for about twenty minutes and found it delightful to handle with no problems in normal flight. I was very much aware of the unusual audience the flight had attracted and was therefore determined to make no mistakes in my approach and landing.'[2] However, he was aware on approach of the plane's nose coming up slightly; moreover, he quite forgot to lower the undercarriage – remembering just in time, climbing, and then going in for another landing. On the basis of this short flight, the ultimate decision lay with Edwardes-Jones. The Air Ministry asked him if the Spitfire would be suitable for a new generation of novice pilots. He took a deep breath and said yes – with the proviso that they were given very strict instructions about the undercarriage.

With a speed quite remarkable for the normally sclerotic Whitehall, an initial order was placed with Supermarine for 310 Spitfires.

Four years quite literally on a drawing board; and now Mitchell's vision was being realised. All this came at a time when – unbeknown to many of his colleagues – Mitchell was suffering terribly with rectal cancer. He very rarely said a word to colleagues about his illness; nor could you now guess from photographs what he was going through. Mitchell's obsession with aviation was one of the things that sustained him; he worked intensively, but also with love.

'There was in fact no mystique about Mitchell's design,' wrote C.F. Andrews. 'It was a straightforward merger of all the technical knowledge of the time into one composite piece of machinery … Everything came right at the psychological moment – a rare event in aircraft and engine design.'[3]

In fact, Mitchell's intensely driven nature was a key element; his wife gave a beautiful description of how enraptured he was with his work. 'He'd be talking to you one moment and the next minute, he'd be miles away, and you knew he had thought up something new,' she said. 'He loved snooker but even in the middle of a game, he would suddenly put down his cue and out would come an old envelope or a scrap of paper and as he began to draw, he would give me a rapid explanation of the diagrams he was making.'[4]

Mitchell never lived to see his creation carrying out the work that would make it immortal. When he died in June 1937, tributes flowed from all corners of the aviation industry, as well as from the Air Ministry and from pilots too.

And his work went on. With a great deal more draughtsmanship and testing, the refined Spitfire formally entered RAF service in 1938. What made the Spitfire stand out at first was its speed; designed as a means of intercepting enemy bombers, the aircraft had to be supple in its manoeuvres. Mitchell had specially designed a thinner elliptical wing for this purpose.

It is a single-seater aircraft; and when you look at one at close quarters (surviving Spitfires are exhibited in museums across the world), it strikes you just how tight and small that seating space is, and how petite and bijou the entire craft is. So much so that while you can imagine soaring through the firmament at speed, you also understand how thin is the skin – a shell or 'monocoque' of sheet aluminium – that protects you from bullets, or from the explosion that could rip you and the aircraft apart. The Spitfire is undeniably beautiful, an ageless work of aesthetic skill. But you gaze on it and think that there is also something toy-like about it; something brave yet frail and vulnerable. The interior of the cockpit is so thin and cramped that you wonder how it was possible to get the thing airborne, let alone loose volleys of machine-gun fire from it.

The Spitfire could reach speeds of 560 kilometres per hour (350 miles per hour); and it could climb to 4,572 metres (15,000 feet) in six minutes (the eyeball-pressing G-force was terrific). Still so little was understood about the potential and indeed the hazards of aviation. One minister in the 1930s, for instance, was convinced that it would never be possible for any pilot to dive-bomb; the effects of gravity on the body would be so severe that he would black out or even die before he even got close to his target.

Yet it is difficult to find any instances of a fighter pilot who did not immediately fall in swooning love with the Supermarine Spitfire. For Adolph 'Sailor' Malan, a notoriously tough South African Royal Flying Corps veteran, the Spitfire was only superficially an efficient killing machine; much more, he said, it was 'a perfect lady with trim sweet lines'. Pilot M.A. Liskutin said more straightforwardly that it was 'love at first sight'. At North Weald, Hurricane pilot Peter Townsend observed his Spitfire colleague Bob Tuck fall head over heels: this was a very serious romance. 'So enchanted was he with the Spitfire,' wrote Townsend, 'that he believed in time it affected his character, maturing him and giving him an inner balance.'[5] Elsewhere, young pilot Geoffrey Wellum – who likened his maiden voyage to dealing with a racehorse or a kangaroo – gave the game away with the more Freudian images he used. He was almost put into a trance by the plane; not just by the beautiful curve of its wings, but also by the way, on his first flight, the plane seemed to be leading him, guiding him through the clouds and the skies; a young man being seduced:

> Elation! We sweep effortlessly about the sky, upwards between two towering masses of cumulus cloud and through a hole like the mouth of a cave, beyond which lies a valley leading into clear sky. We climb up to the very tops of the clouds which stretch away … the very shape of the Spitfire wing is a thing of grace and form … Curved leading and trailing edges, not a straight line anywhere. It's beautiful.[6]

The French pilot Pierre Clostermann went a little further with his appreciation of the craft. 'How beautiful the machine seemed to me, and how alive! A masterpiece of harmony of power, even as I saw her now, motionless. Softly, as one might caress a woman's cheeks, I ran my hand over the aluminium of her wings, cold and smooth like a mirror, the wings which had borne me.'[7]

The most amusing para-erotic reaction, however, came from Lord Balfour of Inchyre, who was wartime Under-Secretary of State for Air. 'I know I fell in love with her the moment I was introduced that summer day in 1938,' he wrote. 'I was captivated by her sheer beauty; she was slimly built with a beautifully proportioned body and graceful curves just where they should be … Mind you,' he added with a jocular flourish, 'some of her admirers warned me that she was what my mother called a fast girl, and advised that no liberties should be taken with her until you got better acquainted.'[8]

In the years to come, the mesmerism would spread beyond pilots and Air Ministry officials. The Spitfire was soon to acquire a devoted following among the general public. Even if, as many argue, it was ultimately the Hurricane – a less fleet but more robust plane which had come into service in 1937 – that was to prove the more effective machine, the morale-boosting properties of the Spitfire were simply beyond measure; a machine that inspired so much confidence in pilots and public alike was a completely new phenomenon.

The Spitfire was also to prove remarkably versatile – a plane that was just as good for photo-reconnaissance missions as it was for intercepting and firing upon enemy planes. But what about its firepower? In the earliest days, Air Chief Marshal Dowding wanted more. He also wanted bulletproof glass, an initial suggestion that drew sniggers from politicians. But, as he later remarked acidly, if such glass was deemed good enough for Chicago gangsters, then it was certainly good enough for his pilots.

One of the more startling aspects of the Spitfire to today's hermetically sealed, pressurised flying public is the fact that at 15,000 feet, the pilots could still roll back the canopy of the cockpit (and indeed, had to do so in order to bail out); Geoffrey Wellum mentioned opening the canopy on a couple of occasions when, either during dogfights or in the terrifying moments when he was lost in clouds, low on fuel and trying to find his way home, he desperately needed to free himself of his oxygen apparatus and breathe freely.

By the start of the war, fighter pilots were still wearing Sidcots, the flying suits that had been devised towards the end of the First World War. These were so named after their inventor, Sidney Cotton, a maverick and often random figure. He had noticed back in 1916 that he suffered less from the biting cold in the air if he was wearing his oiled overalls; the Sidcot suit went through many incarnations but was most familiar as a green cotton garment with air-proof silk, to be worn over the blue RAF uniform, with a range of optional extra inner fleece or fur linings and a detachable fleece or fur collar. There was a large zip, buttons and large patch pockets. Cotton's original prototype featured large amounts of expensive fur. By the outbreak of war, this extravagance had been tempered a little. The suit was light, not bulky; nothing could be allowed to hinder the pilot's range of movement. The leather flying boots were also lined with fleece or fur; at the altitudes that the new Spitfire was capable of, the cold would otherwise have been agonising for the fighter pilots.

The Spitfire was, of course, not the only fighting aircraft available to the RAF. As well as the ineffective Fairey Battle, a little earlier in development was the Hawker Hurricane which – as many have pointed out – came to be unfairly overlooked when the story of the Battle of Britain was retold and invoked. Like the Spitfire, the Hurricane was a response to the need to evolve beyond the old biplanes. Like the Spitfire, it could hit hitherto unimagined speeds of around 482 kilometres per hour (300 miles per hour). Like the Spitfire, this was a craft that pilots could not wait to master. It was delivered to the RAF late in 1937; Squadron Leader John Gillan tried the beast out in some style, flying from Edinburgh down to Northolt in West London, and recording a steady ground speed of 656 kilometres per hour (408 miles per hour).

Rates of aircraft production in the increasingly dark days of the 1930s provoked complaints that the men who worked in the factories were simply not up to the job. What is more, the emergence of the economy from depression – in the south and the Midlands, there was increasing affluence, and not just among the property-owning middle classes – meant that recruitment was more difficult; so many rival jobs and rival wages were competing for workers' attention. For instance, the motor industry was beginning to move into a new gear of mass production; a great many young workers were needed for those assembly lines.

But there was no temptation to nationalise the aviation industry; instead the government and the Air Ministry somehow wanted to rationalise the expertise of all these established family firms. Equally, the firms wanted a little more coherence from the Air Ministry. In 1938, the Society of British Aircraft Constructors got in touch with the Ministry to ask that it should pretend that the country was in a state of war. The implication was that that way, everyone could do their jobs a little more effectively.

In fact, amid a seemingly haphazard development programme, and a faith that British industry would deliver in the end, the Air Ministry had made one solid organisational change several years back which was to prove very important. In 1936, the Royal Air Force had bifurcated into two main wings. Bomber Command would oversee all bombing groups, the planes that were to fly over and attack enemy territory. And Fighter Command, as well as overseeing the defensive fighter squadrons, would look after anti-aircraft defences and the work of the Observer Corps, the unsung men who were, in essence, to act as human radar. Fighter Command soon moved into its new premises amid the green north London hills. It was from his office in Bentley Priory that, in the immediate run-up to war, Air Marshal Sir Hugh Dowding would design an innovative – and misunderstood – system of defence that was to prove more than vital in the days that lay ahead.

This brilliant defensive wheeze had been initially inspired in some aspects by pulp fiction. There was quite a craze for the idea of death-rays in the early years of the twentieth century. They were the imaginative and innovative stuff of lurid popular fiction: in William Le Queux's novel *The Mystery of the Green Ray*, 'violet and orange rays passed through tourmaline and quartz' turned green, blinding their targets on the spot. It recurred in popular culture, making appearances in 'Sapper's' Bulldog Drummond stories and in the 1932 Hollywood adaptation of Sax Rohmer's Fu Manchu series. At around that time, certain scientists, members of Parliamentary committees and senior military figures were hoping such a weapon might be developed by the British.

Suggestions poured into the Air Ministry. Could such a ray be aimed at a plane and cause it to burn and explode? Or could it somehow, magnetically, draw a plane off course and out of the sky? There were rumours that a group of German scientists were close to perfecting such a nightmare weapon. A group of scientists at the Radio Research Station in Slough, Buckinghamshire, were obliged by the Air Ministry to look into claims that a death-ray mixture of X-rays, ultraviolet and radio waves, when properly directed, had the power to make birds fall from the sky.

The Superintendent of the Radio Research Station, R.A. Watson Watt, set to work with his colleague Arnold

Wilkins to try and work out how – and in what quantity – radio waves could be made to interfere with the workings of planes or to make their crews insensible. This naturally is a story of serendipity. For those dead-end researches led directly to a more fruitful line of work that would prove invaluable both in 1940 and in the years to come. Arnold Wilkins found that if radio waves were directed at an approaching plane, it was possible to pick up their reflection. In other words, it would be possible to mark where the plane was in the sky. So it was in 1935 that the first proper glimmerings of Britain's radar defence system were seen.

There had been attempts before. Even now, on the wider, emptier stretches of Kent's coastline, there are monuments to such efforts: grey, curved sculptures – 'sound mirrors' they were called as far back as the First World War – which were intended to detect the noise of incoming aircraft. These constructions look as though they form part of a prehistoric landscape; yet the future was an invisible world of pulses and waves.

The science of radio was, then, immensely attractive to scientists and amateurs alike; the very language of ionospheres, dipoles and cathode rays had its own poetry. Watson-Watt had, as a younger man, worked with the Royal Aircraft Establishment at Farnborough, Hampshire; his job was to detect thunderstorms with a very primitive radio direction-finder. This wasn't a matter of domestic weather forecasts; the early Royal Flying Corps craft were very fragile. Even flying through certain forms of cloud – let alone thunderstorms – was considered hazardous.

The Radio Research Station was staffed by a team of mainly young men, highly dedicated yet also comically slapdash about other areas of life. They were made piercingly aware of the seriousness of the work. When he joined as a Junior Scientific Officer in 1935, E.G. Bowen was made to sign the Official Secrets Act. He was also told that if he broke it in any way, he would be hanged by the neck 'until life was extinct'.[9]

Bowen had gravitated towards this field thanks to a youthful obsession with radio; it was less a job and more a glorious chance to pursue an abiding love. In his memoirs, Bowen wrote of the affection inspired by Watson-Watt and the all-important patronage of Dowding. When it came to the theory of radar – which would require expensive research – Dowding himself needed more than what he termed Watson-Watt's calculations. He needed some form of evidence that such a system could be made to work. With very primitive equipment, a transmitter in Daventry and a volunteer aircraft, Watson-Watt barely succeeded in demonstrating that he could register the 'reflection' of the aircraft.

The funding was granted, a larger team was assembled and more hush-hush headquarters were established on the Suffolk coast, on a spit of land near the remote village of Orford. The bleakness of the land had a poetry of its own; in this watery world of shale and seaweed, frets, haars, the murmur of waves and the lonely cries of wheeling marshland birds, the young boffins set up base at Orford Ness, shifting heavy machinery, great masses of Bakelite, metal and diodes into rudimentary buildings with concrete floors. On dark nights, as the sea whispered, the villagers in Orford could hear a pervasive unearthly hum: the music of silica valves, filament voltage, electricity and dull ruby heat.

Similar experiments in the principles of radar were being conducted in Europe, and in America too. But in Suffolk, they were coming at it with the intensity of men who knew that the very location where they were working – the Suffolk coast – would be intensely vulnerable if the Germans ever launched an invasion.

Early breakthroughs were the cause of intense excitement; the sky was full of echoes. Before they could start detecting planes, the scientists at Orford Ness found that the radio waves bouncing off the ionosphere, ninety-six kilometres (sixty miles) above the earth, were the sounds of mainland Europe; obviously too disparate to be pinpointed, but allowing a possibility of range, a radar that could go over the horizon. In June 1935, the boffins managed to capture their first proper echo, the trace of a flying boat which was travelling up and down the coast. This done, the advances were swift; their range soon expanded to radar coverage of sixty-four kilometres (forty miles), then 128 kilometres (eighty miles), then 160 kilometres (one hundred miles).

The dream was to establish stations around the Thames Estuary that would be able to detect incoming German bombers. It was very quickly understood that for such a system to work, there would need to be proper co-operation between the stations; the sharing of co-ordinates and positions that would allow for triangulation. The villagers in Orford – an absurdly quiet place, with little more than a pub, a greengrocer and a vicar – had to wonder as these dishevelled young men took themselves off through the shale and gorse for all-night work sessions, armed only with cake and bottles of beer.

But by 1936, with the vaulting leaps in know-how – an increasing number of test flights, detected with ever greater success – a move to more accessible premises was needed. The radar pioneers, driving around the coast of Suffolk, eventually came across a country house that would suit them perfectly. This was a redbrick late Victorian extravaganza – all towers and Tudor-style chimney pots – overlooking the mouth of the river Deben and the sea. The property, belonging to Sir Cuthbert Quilter, was for sale. And so it was that Bawdsey Manor, and its surrounding lands, was bought for £23,000.

The men of the radar team instantly loved their new home: the work might have been extraordinarily intense, but it was punctuated with cricket on the front lawn and sailing in the sea below. It was in this youthful atmosphere that the world's first fully functioning radar station was established. Vast metal masts were erected on the hill behind the house. Workshops and laboratories were established in the house's towers. So high up (relative to the surrounding landscape) was Watson-Watt's office, overlooking the river, that larky fighter pilots would dare each other to fly past his window as close as they possibly could. In this exhilarating environment, what became known as the Chain Home system evolved and grew. In those years before the war, atop high cliffs on the coast around Britain, small stations started to appear.

Robert Watson-Watt later wrote: 'Radar is at once a science and an art ... what it achieves depends only in part on physics. It depends very greatly on people.' He reiterated what he had written in a 1935 memo to the Air Ministry: 'You need not hope for any help from the enemy in your attempts to locate him by the light, heat, sound or ordinary radio which he sends out. You must put up a short-wave radio frontier which he must penetrate.' And Watson-Watt's tone was always one of indefatigable optimism. In 1954, looking back, he wrote that 'we can extract all the information we require from a radar echo which contains only one hundredth of a billionth of a billionth of the energy which we send out to produce the echo.'[10]

To begin with, five stations were set up, dotted around the Thames Estuary. The information on aircraft positions they provided would be collated and filtered – the start of what would become known as the Filter Room. The Chain Home stations began to multiply; the Dover station was set up in 1937, and perhaps the most conspicuous and (as it was later to transpire) most vulnerable station, on the Isle of Wight, was soon to follow. The nature of the work being done at Ventnor was kept from the islanders, who could only marvel and speculate about the four huge masts, each 106 metres (350 feet) in height, that were built on top of St Boniface Down. In 1938, it was the 'Chain Home Low' stations – those not directly on the coast – that picked up the signal from Prime Minister Neville Chamberlain's plane as he flew out to meet with Hitler at Munich. It then also tracked his return.

Air Chief Marshal Dowding was watching these developments with grave interest, absorbing the potential of what could be done and worrying about what yet could not. Young men such as E.G. Bowen were by now exploring the possibilities of installing radar equipment aboard fighter planes, the better to swoop and pursue the enemy. Dowding, fretful about the threat of night bombing, and at how little might be done to intercept planes in the dark, took part in a practical experiment, a test flight in a Battle K9208. It was all a little awkward: the pilot, young Mr Bowen and the Air Chief Marshal, all sitting snugly next to equipment glowing with cathode ray tubes. Yet the planned demonstrations, at 15,000 feet, were a success. The only smudge on the day, as Bowen recalled, was an exchange between Bowen and the pilot about the hair-raising landing: Bowen expressed in rather strangulated terms the opinion that the pilot was on course to overshoot the runway. The pilot, forgetting that their illustrious passenger could hear everything, replied: 'Not bloody likely, with Stuffy in the back.'[11] Dowding took the shocking landing – and the impertinence – remarkably well: as all three men left the (safely landed) aircraft, he turned to the pilot and said graciously: 'I always say, the most important thing is to land the right way up.'

The First Lord of the Admiralty, Winston Churchill, was fascinated and paid a visit to Bawdsey Manor in the early summer of 1939. Having been guided through the intricacies of the recently established Chain Home and coastal radar systems, he was invited to inspect the onboard technology at the back of a Battle K9208. Some manoeuvring was required to get him into the plane; he had to hand over his cigar to a man standing nearby and forsake his homburg. Once he was safely inside, the plane was piloted around the airfield, while Churchill gazed at the cathode-ray tube machinery. Later, in the officers' mess, when offered tea, Churchill, looking horrified, instead requested brandy.

The pace of preparation was acquiring a level of hysteria. Nevertheless, in the space of just a few years, these young scientists had delivered to Dowding a system that a previous generation would have considered impossible. In the summer of 1939, it was still very rickety; the stations in the Thames Estuary, the preposterously prominent maze of masts towering above the Isle of Wight, had almost been extemporised, using bits of equipment that were sometimes brand new and sometimes cannibalised from elsewhere. Yet if there seemed to be an element of making it up on the hoof, this was not reflected at the nerve centre of Fighter Command's operation. The secret core of Britain's defence system was an establishment that very quickly developed a quirky and unique life of its own.

Chapter Five

The Secret Under the Hill

The journey from central London on the Bakerloo Line didn't take long; Stanmore was at the end of the line, about half an hour from Piccadilly Circus. Then, from Stanmore station, you would take a fairly hefty hike (or bus ride) up a steep leafy hill to the summit of that London ridge. The estate of Bentley Priory was, and is, a terrific vantage point; from its Italianate tower could be seen in the far distance the jumbled church spires of the City in those days before skyscrapers dominated the view. There were stockbrokers working in the Square Mile who, as war drew closer, would find themselves being enlisted from their mahogany-filled offices and up to the great house on the hill. One of the quirks about the Dowding system – the means by which the intelligence from radar was harnessed – was that men versed in labyrinthine financial dealings would have an innate knack for this new, strange and complex work.

'When the Filter Room was first formed,' says former WAAF officer Eileen Younghusband, herself highly adept at the complexities of the field, 'they had scientists doing it. But the scientists were too slow. Why? The scientific mind! They'd work it out but then they'd say "It can be that, but could it be that?" Whereas we had to think and make the decision come hell or high water.

'After that, they brought men in from the stock market,' she continues. 'Because in those days on the stock market, the dealers were on the balcony looking down at what was happening below. Profit or loss. Life or death. The same sort of quick decision. They had a bit of maths too of course, dealing with figures all the time. These were older men. Quite a bit older than us, probably twice our age. Mid-thirties onwards!'

Fighter Command had moved into Bentley Priory on 14 July 1936. Those who worked there were beguiled by its history. The property had once been the home of the Austin Canons. The Reformation brought a succession of new deed holders, ending up with James Duberley, an 'Army clothier'. But by 1788, a more aristocratic flavour came to the estate; it was acquired by John James Hamilton, the Marquess of Abercorn. And it was at this period that the house which we still see today was summoned into being. The Marquess engaged architect Sir John Soane to rebuild and reimagine the house. The elegance of the exterior was matched within: a graceful staircase of Portland stone, apartments with large windows, a great skylight to flood the house with sun on brighter days, plus a new gallery which the owner filled with valuable paintings and sculpture. The Marquess himself – 'tall and erect and muscular, with an air of grace and dignity and with a dark complexion, more like a Spaniard than an Englishman', as one admiring contemporary described him[1] – was a product of nearby Harrow School, and a very active social and political animal. He has a form of immortality – the playwright Richard Brinsley Sheridan characterised him as the theatrically overblown romantic lead Don Whiskerandos in his comedy *The Critic*. The house began to attract the most eminent names of the day, from Pitt, Canning, Liverpool and Wellington to literary sensations William Wordsworth and Sir Walter Scott.

But like many other grand estates, Bentley Priory went into a gentle social decline. It was embraced by Victorian commerce: the house was bought by hotelier Frederick Gordon, with the aim of turning it into a fashionable establishment. But the hotel – possibly because it was both insufficiently close to and insufficiently far away from London – never attracted many guests. By 1908, it was sold again, and in its new incarnation became a girls' boarding school. This, too, failed. By 1926, it had been acquired by the Air Ministry.

The steady drumbeat heralding the approach of war in the mid to late 1930s saw the main changes being carried out to customise the house for its coming role. Dugouts were constructed, and at the very beginning of 1939, work began on the secret subterranean Operations Room. 'The average depth of excavation was 42 feet (13 metres), some 58,270 tons of earth were dug out and deposited on and around the building and there were 6,400 tons of un-reinforced and 17,100 tons of re-inforced concrete employed in the building.'[2]

Dowding had been brooding on what would become his 'System', a web of fast-paced communications relayed to all fighter stations and fighter pilots, the centre of which would lie at Bentley Priory. Dowding nominated the Priory's ballroom as the nerve centre, at least at the beginning; it was here that a vast map would be laid out, depicting an area from the far north of Scotland to the French mainland. The map would be set at waist height, constructed in such a way that operatives could lean across it. There was to be a balcony level, reached simply by means of wooden stairs on the side of the room; from here, senior officers would be able to look down at the map and take in the wider picture of aircraft formations.

Special markers for the maps were made. As soon as information about aircraft positions came in, the markers would be deployed; and the intelligence was then to be disseminated to the fighter squadron bases. There was to be a bank of telephones and teleprinters. The General Post Office, then responsible for Britain's telephone network, had made assiduous enquiries about Dowding's needs. Its scientists, based just a few miles away from Bentley Priory in Dollis Hill, seemed more alert than many in government to the cold shadow creeping across Europe. In technical terms, Dowding's system was impressively innovative.

There were later additions, such as the specially devised clocks, which were both inspired and aesthetically pleasing. As well as the normal features of a clock face, there were 24-hour numerals, plus colour-coded triangles at five-minute intervals: red, blue, yellow. These would be used for allocating colours to the markers on the mapping table, indicating the time that an incoming formation of aeroplanes had been detected. 'Electric clocks of the "slave" type and a colour change apparatus receiving half-minute impulses on a telephone line from a master clock in the local GPO were also installed,' reads one Bentley Priory memo from the time. 'The colour change apparatus was fixed to the operations table as an aid to the Plotters who could thus observe when to change the colours of the counters without having to lift their eyes from the table.' The precision was dizzying. 'Experiments were carried out with counters of various colours,' runs another memo, 'to determine the colour that could be seen most clearly from the Control Room.'[3] Orange had the edge over yellow.

Building work began on the temporary ground-floor Filter Room and the Operations Room. At this time, one wholly unexpected source of conflict broke out: it was with the Priory's next-door neighbour. Almost as soon as work began to prepare the estate for war, a widow called Mrs Anson, living at the adjacent Bentley Manor, on Stanmore

Common, started a letter-writing campaign highlighting a range of grievances. It started with what she regarded as intellectual theft. Remarkably, despite the secrecy, she had caught local chatter about operations being sited underground. This provoked her first furious fusillade of letters to the Air Ministry. The charge was plagiarism; the widow claimed that as far back as 1936, she had offered the RAF 'use of her crypt' in order to make their work bomb-proof. Outraged that the idea was being put to use next door, she demanded financial compensation to acknowledge that the idea was hers.

Just as war was declared, Mrs Anson stepped up her own conflict, starting the battle of the driveway. She had originally offered it for sale to the Air Ministry; perhaps the Air Ministry had other matters on its mind, for no immediate response was forthcoming. At some point in the weeks before September 1939, some anti-aircraft brigade workmen had – perhaps rather peremptorily – parked their trucks on her land and built a concrete hut, with the workmen being billeted on the land for the duration; the purpose of this hut was to house a huge number of cables – obviously vital for telecommunications to and from the Priory. The widow was a patriot who had no objection to the principle; rather she took issue with the method. It says a lot about the nature of officialdom at the time that Mrs Anson's increasingly shrill accusations – which were eventually to elicit responses from 10 Downing Street and Buckingham Palace – were dealt with so formally and patiently (if, as we now see in the correspondence, with flashes of comic exasperation) at a time of national crisis.

The widow made a financial claim for the then colossal sum of £10,300, in order to compensate her for the loss of land that she had planned to sell for 'offices, a hotel or a country club'. A memo circulated within the Air Ministry proposed a course of action. '[It] is probably pure conjecture on her part and although she refers us to her solicitors, there seems very little chance that her claim could be substantiated,' wrote the official, M. Murray, to Bentley Priory in October 1939. 'We take it that there are no grounds on which you would be prepared to abandon this site at this stage and it would therefore seem adequate to play the ball back into [her] court by simply telling her that her property has been requisitioned and that compensation will be paid under the Compensation (Defence) Act of 1939.'[4] It was imagined that Mrs Anson would acquiesce graciously. However, the very idea of requisition only added a splash of paraffin to her flames of fury and her correspondence began to travel to some extraordinary corners.

In one letter to the Air Ministry Chief, Sir Archibald Sinclair, she turned her fire on the Secretary of State for Air. 'On Bentley Manor, I have a huge mortgage,' she wrote. 'Sir Kingsley Wood knew this but as I am a widow, he STOLE my land ... and built a cable house for 250 cables. And broke the contract for sale. He knows about this contract.' But very much worse was the effect upon her nerves. She wanted it to be known that at one point during the construction of the cable hut, several workmen popped in and out of her house. She would never have let them in if she had known what the result would be. They left her cushions reeking of 'tobacco juice and onions'. The result, she said, was that the cushions had to be burnt.[5]

She turned up the heat in other ways. One letter was delivered directly to Buckingham Palace (and received a polite reply from the King's Equerry); the Air Ministry catalogued several personal letters to Sir Kingsley Wood, as well as letters to MPs Rhys Davies and Sir Reginald Blair. The Labour MP Clement Attlee (shortly to become Deputy Prime Minister) was also drawn into the affair. After corresponding with her, Attlee wrote to Sir Kingsley Wood and the Air Ministry in the spirit of investigating Mrs Anson's incandescent woes.

As the war progressed, Mrs Anson's rage intensified. Further hostilities broke out when Fighter Command realised that they would have to negotiate with her in order to requisition her home for WAAF accommodation. The story demonstrates how seriously war bureaucrats took their requisitioning, even when dealing with those on the dotty spectrum. It illustrates too how deadly serious they were about money; for there was no suggestion that they would negotiate with Mrs Anson, even for the sake of a quiet life.

Such colourful sideshows failed to dilute Dowding's focus. In conditions of great secrecy, in the days before war was declared, those in the Filter Room now began rehearsing how best to collate the information coming from the various links in the Chain Home Command. The key phrase was Plan Position Filtering; and they were also observing very closely how individuals were using radar, and how effective they were proving to be at it.

Just a few miles west, a similar subterranean operations room was built at the base of 11 Group at RAF Uxbridge in 1938. Each group was responsible for a different sector of the country – for instance, 10 Group focused on the southwest, 12 Group the Midlands and Wales, while 11 Group oversaw RAF stations throughout the southeast, with Fighter Command at the centre of the web of communications and commands. Though functional, 11 Group HQ was yet supremely elegant, with suggestions of art deco in the railing details, and the glow of bronze and polished wood vying with the colour-coded clocks and the illuminated panels. In the period before and just after the outbreak of the war, this would be the domain of Keith Park.

Jim Griffiths worked at Bentley Priory in those pre-war days, when he held the rank of leading aircraftman. He recollected that in the months before the conflict, the establishment had a notably friendly atmosphere: 'The only time we ever saw any of our officers in uniform was when they were going on a staff visit, Armistice Day, King's Birthday or other such occasions; normally they came to work in lounge suits. Looking back, I can only say that at Bentley Priory, we were an extremely happy set of people.'[6]

Air Marshal Dowding requisitioned a west-facing ground floor room as his office; except for desk, chair and telephone, it was notably sparse. From here the command radiated outwards – was delegated – to group headquarters and bases across the country, from the suburban fringes of London to the bleak coastlines of Scotland. The delegation of control was crucial.

Largely due to financial considerations, plus manufacturing difficulties with the aeroplanes, the fighter force was not up to the capacity that Dowding himself had been pressing for. Nonetheless, the pilots were established with several new boons that their immediate predecessors had not enjoyed: proper functioning radios; enclosed cockpits; and proper, surfaced, hard runways, as opposed to smooth (and often slippery) strips of close-cut grass. Some RAF stations had the prized social uplift of easy access to London. Hornchurch was an easy drive in from the east; North Weald a fast railway journey into Liverpool Street. Quite frequently, pilots would take the opportunity to entertain young lady friends in the West End and ensure that they returned to their stations before they could be missed.

Back at Bentley Priory, Dowding did not sleep in the big house; instead, he took a nearby property, a villa called Montrose, living a life of almost Victorian simplicity there with his sister Hilda. Widowed since 1920, Dowding in some ways behaved as though he was very much older than his years.

War was not the only reason that Dowding needed both preternatural determination and thick skin; for in the corridors of Whitehall, Air Ministry manoeuvrings and rancorous office politics were threatening to undermine every aspect of his work. Even the security of his position was called repeatedly into question, and sometimes in the most wounding ways. Possibly because of his demeanour, and the nickname 'Stuffy', his nominal superiors might have imagined that Dowding was too insensitive to be hurt. But this wasn't the case.

Yet, whether his superiors agreed or not, the system he had started to build in 1936 would prove beyond vital. It wasn't just the ingenious 'black magic' of radar, as some older air force figures had it; Dowding was also organising for the comprehensive defence of the capital. He was in charge of the anti-aircraft guns; the sun-bright searchlights that before long would be crisscrossing the sky in great triangles of light. There were the faintly comical barrage balloons – vast, bulbous, silver and glittering – that in time would resemble floating metallic elephants under moonlit skies. There was the all-important human element too: the Royal Observer Corps, dedicated men armed with little more than binoculars, watching the skies as closely as any subsequent UFO enthusiast.

Indeed, in the wider story of Fighter Command, the Observer Corps never seems to get much recognition. Formed during the First World War, it was originally comprised largely of police constables in London. They were under instruction to keep watch for Zeppelins, and when they spotted any, to phone through the positions of the craft. The idea was so effective that it was then put into operation around the country, and particularly in coastal areas. At first, it was purely a police matter. By 1917, for the sake of tidiness, the Royal Flying Corps took over responsibility, under Major General Ashmore, though policemen were still used; the observation posts dotted around the coast were now linked more closely with anti-aircraft gun emplacements and searchlight stations. Naturally, after the war, the Corps dwindled away to practically nothing; but the idea of it remained firmly with the new RAF hierarchy. And so, by the mid-1920s, as part of a review of the defence of the realm, a fresh Observer Corps was formed.

It was made up this time of specially enlisted special constables; in other words, eager civilian volunteers. They had to be trained not merely to detect incoming craft, but also to distinguish between friendly and enemy planes. Out in the vast flat silence of the Kent marshes, new recruits were tested; the trials were a success, and Observer Corps stations were established in Kent and Surrey. The motto of the organisation: 'Forewarned is forearmed'.

Soon there were observation stations across the south coast, and in the Home Counties too – though not nearly enough to have been of real use if some military catastrophe had overtaken the nation in those years. By the mid-1930s, the RAF understood the need for expansion of the Corps – and by 1936, it moved with Dowding into Bentley Priory.

Within the Corps, there was a fresh emphasis on providing cover not just for London and the Home Counties, but also for the great industrial cities of the Midlands and the north; German bombers would clearly be determined to try and paralyse the country's wartime production lines. There were also moves to integrate the Corps more closely with the Dowding system.

The observation posts themselves were structures of the purest simplicity. Whether out on moorland or placed on top of London office blocks, they were basic wooden huts, sometimes a little elevated from the ground. There was not a chance that they would also function as shelters from bombing raids; they could barely shelter the volunteers from the weather. Nonetheless, they would be manned by the recruits, who had been issued with binoculars and would bring their tea flasks. Lacking portability, straightforward telephones were clearly impractical for such outdoor work, so the observers had to use specially designed 'magneto' phones in order to ring through to HQ. These were cranked by handle in order to generate sufficient voltage to ring bells on the same line and alert the operators. These telephones could be worn on the chest, by means of a harness, and came with headphones.

Posts were also equipped with a wondrously complex-looking device – part astrolabe, part giant compass set – known officially as a 'Post Plotting Instrument' but popularly as a 'Micklethwait' after the man who designed it. This involved a sighting bar, a fixed pointer and a fixed map, and enabled the user to roughly work out the height of a sighted aeroplane and then, by means of its horizontal bearing and vertical angle, to get an idea of the aeroplane's position. Such data, when phoned through on the magneto, would be collated and added to data coming in from the radio direction finding; and so it was that with different sources and angles, finer, faster, more accurate calculations concerning the enemy's position could be made.

Neville Chamberlain's flight to Munich in 1938 – and the general, nationwide sense that this would be the trigger for the war – led to the Observer Corps staging a dress rehearsal at the same time. Using various flights and different possible scenarios, the volunteers were put through the paces of what a German 'gas attack' might look like, and it was possible to gauge from this the strengths and weaknesses of the organisation. At around that time, thirty-eight million gas masks had been distributed to the population, while everyone had seen the cinema newsreel footage of the Spanish Civil War and the nightmarish destruction of Guernica on behalf of Franco's fascists by German and Italian bombers. Franco's forces had initially sought to deny that they were responsible for the razing of the town, claiming that their enemies had set buildings ablaze while retreating; but incendiaries stamped with German manufacturing marks were found. It was a dress rehearsal for Blitzkrieg. Millions of British cinemagoers, watching the images of destruction, were told by the voice-over: 'this was a city, and these were homes, like yours'.

There was also the Japanese bombing of Shanghai; W.E. Johns, creator of fictional flying ace Biggles and editor of *Popular Flying* magazine, wrote searingly of the slaughter:

What have these poor devils of Chinese done, whose mangled remains I saw being forked into carts like so much manure? It is a pity the Japanese bomber pilots cannot be shown what they did but that I fancy, is the last thing the Japanese government would permit. Nor, would our own government allow our bomber pilots to see it.[7]

The gas masks alone evoked a thrill of atavistic horror. Everyone believed that the fate of Guernica would be visited upon Britain. Which is why the Observer Corps stood out; keeping watch in ramshackle structures through the night put them as firmly on the new front line as any soldier. Yet even after the declaration of war, the Observers were still essentially citizen volunteers.

They were paid; but they had to do a great deal of hard work in return for it. Class A observers agreed, in writing, to undertake forty-eight hours of observation work a week, for the hourly sum of 1s 3d (paying out a maximum of £3 a week). Class A observers were – at least at the beginning of the war – expected to be over the age of thirty-five. 'They must have good hearing and eyesight (glasses are no bar to members of the centre crew),' reported *The Times*. Class B observers were volunteers who agreed to twenty-four hours' observation a week. Head observers – the men who worked at centres such as that in Maidstone – received a bonus £1.

The job was exacting; and those carrying it out were justifiably proud of their ability to swiftly distinguish between different sorts of planes at any hour of night, let alone day. Like many volunteers, though, they sometimes found their pride being a little squashed by the authorities, who perhaps made the mistake of seeing them simply as enthusiastic civilians. Indeed, the exact status of these vital men was much later to become a source of friction, especially for those who had, some years previously, served in the Air Force. Air Chief Marshal Sholto Douglas wrote to the Chief of the Air Staff, Sir Archibald Sinclair, in November 1940, as London was nightly battered and the Corps kept faithful watch on the incoming raids:

> I wonder if the Air Council realise what a blow it is to the higher ranks of the Observer Corps to be told that they are not allowed to wear their Wings on Observer Corps uniform? There is definitely an atmosphere of gloom, if not mutiny on the question. The Observer Corps uniform, for good or ill, bears a close resemblance to that of the RAF. The senior officers of the Observer Corps are, almost without exception, retired Air Force Officers with a distinguished flying record. Most of these learned to fly prior to 1941, and in fact are pioneers of the flying Services ... It seems perhaps absurd that so small a question should have such an

81

effect … but I can assure you that it does. It … goes deeper than logic.[8]

Sir Archibald went a little further in his response. As well as the token gift of '100 pairs of binoculars' to the Corps, he also announced, the following year, that the entire body had received a terrific honour: it was henceforth to be known as the 'Royal Observer Corps'. 'For some time,' ran one newspaper report, 'there has been a certain amount of dissatisfaction at what the members of the Corps regarded as official recognition. The new title will no doubt give much satisfaction to watchers, plotters and tellers alike.'[9]

In 1942, there was to be a further innovation: women volunteers were allowed to join men in their little lookout posts. Vera Charlton was in the northeast of the country, near Durham, and she joined up as soon as she could. She recalled: 'The look-out post was built of cement. It was a small square building about eight or nine feet high with wooden floors and corners, and wooden things to stand on to look out. There was also a dugout with a wooden stove to heat things on, a shelter with a tiny little window and a Browning rifle. You had to learn how to fire that and how to fix bayonets – my father taught me how to as he was good at it.

'We also had training lessons in the Odeon cinema in Newcastle on a Sunday when there were no shows on. The RAF would provide training films where an aircraft would appear on the screen for just a few seconds, and we would have to describe what it was. It was a sort of test, really, and there were also written tests on RAF procedures. In time I got my first class certificate but there was also an even higher grading, which was called the master test. For the master test, fifty aircraft would appear on the screen, one after another, and we had to correctly identify 95% of those aircraft … It wasn't easy, but if you did pass you were given a little, pale-blue Spitfire badge to sew onto the sleeve of your battle dress.'[10]

Another key aspect of Dowding's meticulous organisation was the deployment of anti-aircraft artillery. These gun emplacements are – in some parts of London – still marked on the maps. In 1938, the anti-aircraft corps was under the command of Major General Alan Brooke; even though it came under the auspices of the army, it answered to Dowding in Fighter Command. The divisions were based around London, but also with a heavy presence around Britain's docks and ports and working rivers, from Hull and Liverpool to Plymouth and Bristol. Not every emplacement was armed with an anti-aircraft gun. Some only had searchlights. There was constant anxiety – as throughout the entirety of the armed services – about whether what they had was enough.

There was also a great deal of extemporisation: where sites for anti-aircraft guns were chosen, it was quite often up to the poor soldiers themselves to make the locations work. Not only would they have to construct the emplacements for the guns, they would also have to build all the other necessary facilities, including living quarters and wash blocks.

At the time of the Munich crisis, anti-aircraft troops were under more pressure than anyone; for if war was declared, it was held as a truism that the first of Hitler's bombing and gassing attacks would begin at once.

In some places, troops were billeted in local houses; in others, they were forced to live outdoors in tents. The work was extraordinarily unglamorous, entailing as it did taking aim at the sky with big guns or big lights. Many of the recruits, it was found, were not even quite up to that, for various reasons; and they had to be moved into other roles. Only later – when the war was under way – would it become obvious just how valiant the men who did this thankless job were. Along with the fighter pilots, it would be they who stood directly first in the line of fire.

In the months before the war, London's population grew accustomed to the sight of the fixed big guns, dark green, pointing up at the clouds from vantage points such as Primrose Hill to the north, One Tree Hill and Hilly Fields in the south and the expanses of Wanstead Flats to the east. The King was given a tour of Woolwich Arsenal, and he looked on with apparent approval at a new generation of anti-aircraft guns.

In 1938, a curious war rehearsal took place in west London, which seemed to carry a flavour of the old Hendon pageants, even though this one was not open to the public. On a patch of open ground opposite Olympia, near Fulham, there was a full demonstration of Air Raid Precautions (ARP) for senior Air Force personnel and various ministers and civil servants. As an enthusiastic reporter from *The Times* wrote:

A scene was staged to represent Kensington High Street. Newsboys dashed through a group of people on the pavement shouting that war had been declared. A raid followed, and air-raid wardens, motor cycle dispatch riders and others were soon at their posts. Gas masks were issued and after a bomb explosion, a decontamination squad dealt with the poison gas.

And all the while, the mighty anti-aircraft guns were aiming into the heavens. Fighter Command knew where the fight would be, at least to begin with; not in the skies over Berlin, but above the streets and parks of London.

The Spartan life of the anti-aircraft gunner crews was conveyed to the readers of the *Manchester Guardian* in the summer of 1939, when escalating tension had resulted in greater numbers of guns popping up all over the country. This emplacement was just outside Manchester:

> The Territorials manning these guns are enjoying no holiday. The sites, for one thing, are not chosen for their natural beauty. In any case, each man has a day's work to do. They rise at 6.30am and do half an hour's physical drill before breakfast. From 9 to 1 they are at practices with their guns. They have a 'target' plane which flies around while they sight it and work out its height. They communicate by wireless with the pilot and are thus able to check the accuracy of their calculations.
>
> Each station has huts (wooden, on brick bases) for messing, cooking, stores and offices. Officers and men sleep under canvas, the tents have wooden floors and each man gets three blankets and a ground sheet. These defences, and good food, enable the men to resist the damp and carry on their exacting work with evident success and cheerfulness ...

There was even a primetime prewar television programme – which in 1939 would have gone out to an audience of at most 20,000 people – devoted to the marvel of anti-aircraft guns. The documentary, sponsored by Fighter Command, featured an imaginary raid on Alexandra Palace, the north London base of the BBC's new television service. In a production clearly intended to demonstrate that London was completely covered, the black and white pictures showed 'one of the latest anti-aircraft guns ... Its accompanying searchlight, with a penetration of three and a half miles (five and a half kilometres), swung round as the sound locator indicated the positions of the attacking bombers. The predictor – the "brains" of the gun – revealed not only the position of the planes but the fuse which must be used so that the shells … might work their greatest havoc among the invaders … the entire demonstration came over on the screen with scarcely a hitch.' The optimism was to be applauded.

Chapter Six

We Are At War

Neville Chamberlain's announcement, delivered in weary and mournful Received Pronunciation, was broadcast on the morning of Sunday, 3 September; the majority of households had wireless sets, and the majority of people gathered around them to hear the long-anticipated news. For some weeks, Douglas Bader – now working for the Shell Company and earning a good living – had been petitioning his old RAF contacts. Some, most notably Air Marshal Sir Charles Portal, had been cautiously encouraging; it was a given that Bader could not have been allowed anywhere near a fighter plane during peacetime. But a time of war might make all the difference. Others, however, would not think of it.

Bader had been down in the country with his wife and in-laws that weekend; he apparently heard the news while washing up the breakfast dishes. Instantly, he went off to write another letter to Sir Charles Portal. When he returned to work on Monday morning, his boss at Shell informed him that he was on the list of indispensable workers who could not be called up. Bader furiously registered his instant objection, and began an even more intense letter-writing campaign.

The Royal Air Force now comprised some 175,000 men – officers and ground staff – and around 8,000 aeroplanes. As war was declared, No. 1 Fighter Squadron was readied to be sent to France. The first reconnaissance mission was sent up: a Bristol Blenheim piloted by Flying Officer A. Macpherson. He was the first British pilot to fly over enemy territory in war; the mission lasted almost five hours, and was gruellingly tense. He and a naval observer had been detailed to photograph German naval ports, and to work out the disposition of enemy warships. This brave flight resulted in a Distinguished Flying Cross for Thompson. Back in London, the air-raid sirens sounded. Reactions were surprisingly mixed; in the event, the fighter squadrons had no need to scramble. What had set off the alarm was a French aeroplane that had not reported its flight plans.

But the false alarm was paradoxically rather a good thing; for it demonstrated that even a single aircraft would be spotted and plotted in Dowding's system. That day is now recalled vividly by Gladys Eva, who was swiftly drawn thereafter into the WAAFs, and to Bentley Priory.

'I'm a Wimbledon girl,' says Mrs Eva, who now lives in the lush Dorset resort of Sandbanks. 'War was declared and I was the first in the queue to get in. And the thing I could do was drive a car. I didn't know anything about the air force.' This was despite the fact that her brother had already signed up and was flying with Coastal Command. The idea – until that point – had not captured her imagination. 'Up until the war, people really didn't talk about aeroplanes very much. There weren't many about and you rarely saw one. I just said to my father, "I want to get in as a driver."' She had very recently passed her test (indeed, driving tests had only been introduced in 1936). 'The only job I saw advertised was with the army, but they only wanted people with seven year licences at the beginning, so I was out.'

Until the beginning of the war, the technical work at Bentley Priory had been carried out by a mix of scientists and City stockbrokers; technical finesse and a certain native speed and wit with mathematics was required. Did young Gladys Eva – nineteen when war was declared – have any inkling of where the tide might be taking her? None whatsoever. 'I left school when I was sixteen,' she says, laughing. 'I hated school.' She had left in 1937 and was very practical: she trained to be a hairdresser in south London and, as she says, 'put the toot into Tooting'. But the fact was that 'I did very little between leaving school and getting into uniform.'

Most accounts of Chamberlain's broadcast on that Sunday morning, 3 September 1939, emphasise the solemnity of families and loved ones gathered around the radio; plus the electric shock of alarm in London when that very first air-raid siren sounded almost immediately. Gladys Eva recalls not so much solemnity as blackly comical chaos. 'We were all saying, "Where are the gas masks?" Because we thought the Germans would be over the top of us. Everybody thought that. Even someone like my father, who was a very well-read man.' With this, Mrs Eva laughs. 'After about ten minutes of us sitting there, my father said, "I've had enough of this, let's go down to the club and have a drink." So we all landed up at the club. And of course there was no bombing for quite a while. Well, he [Hitler] wasn't any more prepared than anyone else. He hadn't got anyone to put up in the air.'

The question of preparation, however, seemed a little fraught on both sides. Had the Germans really decided to attack in those first few hours of war, would there have been enough air power to fight them off? The official history of the RAF commented, of the situation just one year beforehand, 'We cannot judge whether Fighter Command had sufficient forces at its disposal or whether those forces were sufficiently equipped to carry out the tasks of air defence ...' On top of this, when it came to the other defences – the anti-aircraft guns, the Observer Corps – there had been 'an unavoidable catalogue of deficiencies in every department'. By the time war was declared, those deficiencies had been smoothed out – but the fact remained that this was a completely new form of war. A few Zeppelin and Gotha raids would be as nothing to what the world had witnessed being rained down in Guernica during the Spanish Civil War.

There had been production delays too. As the official history points out, they only started making Spitfires in any numbers around the time of the Munich crisis; the factory lines began speeding up in 1939, but this did seem to be a textbook case of leaving it until the last minute. Building new planes was one thing; getting the fighter pilots accustomed to them was another – although, according to Geoffrey Wellum's beautiful and haunting account, man and machine very swiftly melded. On his very first flight in a Spitfire, he recalled his initial apprehension; then, as he prepared to launch into the sky, the sensation changed – the plane, he wrote, 'has come alive with feeling'. The Spitfire seemed to radiate personality: mischievous and impatient and ready to dominate rookie pilots. But after just a few minutes of flying above the cloud, Wellum was infused with a sense of the sheer beauty of it, the 'grace and form' of the wing. And he felt himself almost to be in a dream. Harrowing, terrifying days lay ahead; but Wellum conveyed seductively how the small cockpit could make the pilot feel as if the plane was somehow a natural extension of himself.

The very physicality of flying made it intensely attractive to those who were used to taking risks in their sport. One such was Roger Bushell – later much better known as one of the leaders of the daring break from a German PoW camp upon which the 1963 film *The Great Escape* is based. Born in South

Africa in 1910 and brought up amid great wealth, but educated at Wellington, a rather austere English public school, and then at Pembroke College, Oxford, Bushell was heedless when it came to outdoor pursuits. He was the captain of the Oxford and Cambridge skiing team – one remarkable 1930s photograph shows him in mid-jump during a competition in Canada. He also became close friends with Max Aitken, the son of newspaper proprietor Lord Beaverbrook, who was an equally enthusiastic pilot. Bushell was quick-witted too; law was his speciality and he became a barrister. Indeed, throughout the 1930s, accounts of the cases that Bushell was involved in peppered the newspapers: the successful prosecution of a Dagenham clerk for murder in Epping Forest in 1936; the defence of an Irish labourer in a case of a Paddington bar brawl that ended up with one man dead; even the prosecution of a west London test pilot for flying an 'autogiro' or early helicopter in a manner that would cause unnecessary danger to the general public. 'This was a disgraceful piece of bad flying,' declared Bushell for the police, 'extremely low and dangerous.'

But Bushell was able to inhabit two worlds: the fusty panelled chambers of Lincolns Inn Fields and the wild, wide world high above. The RAF had pulled him in early – Bushell had been flying for the service as an auxiliary for 601 Squadron since 1930, when it was still very much the province of rich, well-connected young men. In October 1939, he went to RAF Tangmere with the reformed 92 Squadron and became one of the first to fly missions as a night fighter. His later exploits at Stalag Luft 111, masterminding the break-out, also give a sense of the cussed bravery he showed in the cockpit. When the British were pulling back to the port of Dunkirk in May 1940, Bushell's squadron was moved to RAF Hornchurch near the Thames Estuary; it was during that harrowing evacuation, with Fighter

Command seeking to protect almost half a million men from German dive-bombing attacks, that Bushell was brought down and captured.

Elsewhere, younger pilots such as Anthony Bartley – born in India in 1919 and educated at Stowe public school, he joined the RAF in 1939 – were drawn in by a straightforward love of flying, coupled with a fascination for the technology that was making this war in the air possible. However, he, and other pilots in turn, attracted attention (and visits to air bases) by figures from a more glamorous realm. As well as going on to receive the Distinguished Flying Cross, Bartley came to know actors such as David Niven and Rex Harrison, who were themselves mesmerised by the possibilities of flying.

It was by no means all glittering rich kids; some of the RAF's finest pilots had more rugged hinterland. Alan Deere – who, many pointed out, looked the archetype of the square-jawed hero of the clouds – was born and brought up in New Zealand, and educated at technical college. Like so many men of his generation, the evolution of flight – the possibilities offered by new technology – was utterly hypnotic. But his life experience was wider than skiing with chums and Belgravia cocktail parties; at one stage, in order to support himself as a young man, Deere took off into the New Zealand countryside to work as a shepherd. In 1937, he wrote to the Royal Air Force, applying to join. Having been accepted, he was a flying officer by the autumn of 1938 and was then posted to RAF Hornchurch. He was to inspire awe for the number of times that he gave death a swerve after having been shot down; and also for maintaining such an appearance of good cheer after each terrifying near miss. In his quieter moments, Deere must have had an extraordinary sense of his own mortality, and of the fragility of life itself.

For others, there was an element that seemed more spiritual, and for whom the Spitfire had its own sort of animal vitality. Richard Hillary, who was to become one of the most renowned – and later most haunting – Fighter Command pilots, recalled how, at a moment of crisis in the air, his plane 'quivered like a stricken animal'.[1] Hillary had the sensibility of a poet; what had drawn him towards the Royal Air Force, as opposed to the sea, or an infantry regiment? Like Roger Bushell, he had a colonial background. Born in Australia, but educated in the bosom of the English establishment (Shrewsbury School, Oxford University), the physically robust and good-looking Hillary had joined the University Air Squadron at the time of the 1938 Munich crisis and had swiftly trained as a fighter pilot. He was a thinker, one who laid great store on the crucial role of the 'creative imagination', as he put it. He also labelled himself as one of those who would 'dearly love to be creative artists but are not'. He had an admiration for his sometime RAF predecessor, the late T.E. Lawrence, and there is a sense too of a highly self-conscious man being pulled towards a destiny that he cannot escape. During his days studying at Oxford in the late 1930s, Hillary got into an argument with a pacifist and explained to him why he would be gravitating to the RAF:

> In the first place … I shall get paid and have good food. Secondly, I have none of your sentiments about killing, much as I admire them. In a fighter plane, I believe, we have found a way to return to war as it ought to be, war which is individual combat between two people, in which one either kills or is killed. It's exciting, it's individual, and it's disinterested. I shan't be sitting behind a long-range gun working out how to kill people sixty miles away. I shan't get maimed; either

I shall get killed or I shall get a few pleasant putty medals and enjoy being stared at in a night-club.[2]

Hillary was being deliberately ironic; the disfigurements that he was to suffer later got him more than stared at in night-clubs. And others, including the author and political philosopher Arthur Koestler, who championed his writing, were to focus on his apparent fatalism. Yet the common factor between such wildly different figures as Hillary, Douglas Bader, and indeed the austere Hugh Dowding, was individualism. Added to this, for the pilots, was the ecstasy of flying itself:

I shall never forget the first time that I flew really high, and, looking down, saw wave after wave of white undulating cloud that stretched for miles in every direction like some fairy city. I dived along a great canyon; the sun threw the reddish shadow of the plane on to the cotton wool walls of white cliff that towered up on either side. It was intoxicating. I flew on.

A little later, when training in Scotland, Hillary had to undergo the extreme anxiety of learning to fly at night, but despite his occasional panic and disorientation in the thick blackness, losing sight of lights, there were still moments of eerie and silent beauty:

Below lay the flare path, a thin snake of light, while ahead the sea was shot with silver beneath a sky of studded jewels ... I was released, filled with a feeling of power, of exaltation. To be up there alone, confident that the machine would answer the least touch on the controls, to be isolated, entirely responsible for one's own return to earth – this was every man's ambition.[3]

94

Back in London, the outbreak of war had given a shot of ferocious energy to young magazine journalist Patricia Clark. She was finding irksome career obstacles, and was to vault them in the most unexpected way: 'I had had the best part of a year working as a very junior editor on a woman's magazine, after I left Germany where I had been at school. And I had a row with the editor, Mr O'Connell.'

When she handed in her notice and told him she was joining up, he replied, 'You can't do that, it will ruin your career. You have a promising career, you're doing very well. You could end up being editor of *Woman and Beauty*.' Her response: 'No, I'm going to join up and do my bit for the war.'

Having made this impressive declaration, Mrs Clark knew that she could hardly hang around. In her lunch hour, she left the office and went walking and thinking. 'I had just passed my driving test,' she says, 'and I was mad keen to drive anything anywhere. So I thought, I know what I'll do. I'll join the army and drive an ambulance. I'll drive it in France and rescue wounded officers from the trenches, like my mother did with my father. Having read all her stories, I had this romantic idea that under gunfire, you rushed and rescued the man of your dreams. So this was my intention. But blow me, I couldn't find an army recruitment centre.

'I was walking back towards the office near St Paul's and I thought, I am not going to go back to that office and eat humble pie, there must be something.' On her way she passed Adastral House in Kingsway, the headquarters of the RAF. 'I thought to myself, They must have ambulances, they get wounded airmen. I might as well drive an ambulance for the air force, why not? So in I went. It was a huge great place, I think it must have once been a ballroom. On the walls leading right up to the end were opticians' charts. And at the end of this vast room was a platform with benches on which people were seated. On the platform were two men, each one with optician's boards, big letters down to small letters. And there were people moving up along the sides, one by one: "You've passed, you haven't passed, you're in, you're out".' It was, says Mrs Clark, a 'conveyor belt system'.

'I thought, piece of cake. Joined the nearest to me. My turn. Got down to the last two. Failed the eye test. So I said, "Look, I can see if I've got my glasses on, I can see those easily."'

'No,' was the reply, 'you can't have glasses in the Air Force, dangerous if you get shot at.' Mrs Clark was told to go home. But her indignation was at molten levels. 'I'm not going to be flying an aeroplane, I thought, I'm going to be driving a car and I can wear my glasses in a car. How can I get round this? So I put my glasses on, slipped over to the queue on the other side of the room. While I was moving up it, I memorised the little lines on each board. All I had to do was remember that the board beginning with a big A was the one which had certain letters on it. So I now sailed through the test. "Fine, you're in," they said.'

For Gladys Eva, the process of getting into the most esoteric of WAAF sections was less guileful, and was based on a piece of pure serendipity. 'I scoured the paper every single day,' she says. 'One night – I always wish I'd kept it – there was a little advert at the top of the *London Evening News*: "Women required for WAAF special duties – no qualifications required." Well, I hadn't passed an exam in my life – I was always playing bridge.'

Next morning she rang up and a woman said, 'We're interviewing tomorrow – if you come up to HQ, it's a free for all.' She found herself waiting for several hours among almost 130 others. 'My name was called, in I went.' She was expecting to be asked where she lived, where she had been educated. Instead they asked, 'What are your hobbies?'

'Well, that suited me – I played all sports. Outdoors. And all card games. They said, "Yes, you'll do."'

Another woman who was to prove highly effective at Fighter Command – Eileen Younghusband – recalls her own feelings when first confronted with the technicalities that were to dominate the next few years of her life.

'I go mad when I see films talking about Bentley Priory and it just shows the Operations Room,' she says now. Mrs Younghusband is speaking specifically of the best-known image – that of young women pushing markers around on a map, like croupiers in a casino. 'All those girls are doing is pushing on the end of the stick the final elements that appear.' But where had all these elements been drawn from? A more frenetic and urgent area: the Filter Room. Here, women like Eileen had to bring order to a maelstrom of different signals.

The complex and extremely rapid job of the filterers – who knew exactly where all the radar stations were – was to evaluate the full range of readings and extrapolate from them more accurate positions and bearings. It was a combination of fast thinking with iron nerve and confidence, because any mistake – even being just a few degrees out – could easily result in pilots' deaths.

Women like Eileen Younghusband and Patricia Clark underwent gruelling and stringent training: partly this was mathematical, partly to ensure a nimble response, and partly to instil icy courage. The authorities had to know that they were psychologically – as well as intellectually – up to the job. In essence, the filterers had to draw order from the chaos of cathode rays and the physical sightings of incoming planes telephoned in from countless watching posts. This is where mathematical confidence and alertness was needed; the ability to think instantly in terms of height and speed and direction, and to transform a fast-approaching formation of bombers into a geometrically accurate impression.

Once they had established to their own satisfaction the presence and position of the enemy, they would lay 'a new track' down on the table before them. As soon as any radar station reported or 'plotted' an enemy signal, 'the filterer nearest – sometimes there would only be two on the table – or up to four on busy nights – would put a counter down – a little cone with a knob on the top. That was to signify a new track. And once she got two plots, she'd got a direction. But it wasn't necessarily correct placing till you got two stations reporting.' Circular plots indicated the planes' position, while numbered triangular plots gave the estimated number of aircraft. Square plots marked the planes' estimated height.

There would also be varying data from other sources, including that from Observer Corps operatives in fields and on cliff-tops. 'Once you got that first counter, you'd call out to the raid orderly, who had a big tray with little metal plaques. They were magnetised and each had a number, and I think they went from one hundred to two hundred. The filterer would say to her, "New track," and she put the next number on. There would be no other information initially. Once the filterer had more information appearing, she would add [with new counters] the estimated number of aircraft, estimated height – and constantly those figures had to be changed. First, because aircraft lost height. And also because more radar stations picked them up and you got more accurate readings. It was a constant reassessment.' Once the process was complete, the information could be sent through to the Operations Room, where WAAFs were on hand, using the complex system of coloured markers to note positions on vast maps of England.

There were other refinements too. For British planes, Mrs Younghusband says, 'we had IFF [Identification Friend or

Foe] signals and Broad Identification Friend – the SOS – and that was an even wider extra bleep. All our aircraft had IFF built in.' This was obviously so there would be no difficulty differentiating them from the enemy. IFF had been introduced a little earlier in the year; each plane – whether from Fighter, Bomber or Coastal Command – was fitted with a device that would show up on radar screens as friendly identification. 'But the pilots didn't always put it on,' says Mrs Younghusband. 'Either they forgot, or they thought Germans had got it as well.'

Nor was the system perfectly formed at the outbreak of war. It took a certain amount of guile on the part of Dowding's deputy, Keith Park, to iron out the labyrinthine complexities. Wrote Vincent Orange:

> At Bentley Priory, Park ... introduced a second table on which could be displayed a clean – 'filtered' – plot once queries had been settled. Only this filtered plot should be passed to the main table. Dowding rejected the idea of a second table when Park suggested it, so he secretly set it up in the basement at Bentley Priory and had power lines installed or reconnected to suit. For some time, all that Dowding noticed was that his 'general situation map' seemed to be much more readable and his Operations Room far more quiet and well regulated. When Park judged the time right, he unveiled his basement secret and Dowding was convinced.[4]

And then the purer, 'filtered' information would be fed to the Operations Room, where, in calmer circumstances, the young WAAFs known as plotters could move counters on maps with certainty. The system, when described on paper, sounds ponderous: but in reality, it moved with tremendous speed.

———

There was another quiet, non-technical revolution; instead it was a philosophical one. It was the very idea that instead of middle-aged men filtering the co-ordinates and performing feats of instant trigonometry, this was work that could be carried out by women. The Air Ministry was at the forefront of this thinking; there was some initial disquiet at Bentley Priory about the idea. There were concerns that, first, an Operations Room would be much more vulnerable to attack than a number of other places, and that it would be wrong to place women in such obvious positions of jeopardy. Then there were questions about reliability; could women be trusted to stick with the work? Would there not be the chance that they would bow out for all sorts of personal reasons?

Such sexist anxieties would have made young women like Eileen Younghusband snort with derision. Nonetheless, how was it that Mrs Younghusband appeared from the start to have such an affinity for the work? There were three factors: the first was her education at Southgate County School in Enfield, north London, which was, she says, 'excellent ... I took matriculation at fourteen and a half.' Having passed her core exams, including maths, she had the time for a much more practical education – allowing her to work on the second factor that made her so suited to Fighter Command. 'I did one whole year of Commerce at the end before I left school at sixteen. It was a fabulous education. I learned book-keeping and accountancy before I was sixteen.' The third factor was a very strong family element. Mrs Younghusband's father had been in the Royal Flying Corps, while her cousin Eric had already signed up as a pilot, receiving his training at the grand establishment at Cranwell. Mrs Younghusband felt very strongly that this had to be her direction.

And rather like Patricia Clark, she had, as a girl, seen something of the darkness that was gathering in Europe.

After leaving school in 1938, Eileen started work with a new company called the School Travel Service, which was set up to run continental trips. Her French was in need of improvement; and so, as a teenager, she took herself to France and managed to get a job as a nanny and governess to three young children in a small town. After the 1938 Munich crisis, it seemed obvious to her – as it was to many others – that it would be sensible to return to Britain. The farewell to her French family was heartbreaking; the rail journey that was to follow haunts her still. The train was packed with Jewish refugees. Mrs Younghusband recalls how, the closer the train got to the coast – and to the prospect of the ferry – the more her fellow passengers visibly started to relax: 'I can see them unwrapping their things, the closer we got to the port.' This intrepid young woman was still a shade too young to join up, but the RAF was to influence the course of her life.

As the war started, the image of the new generation of young RAF pilots was carefully burnished in the newspapers; possibly not with cynicism, but with the journalists' ardent desire to have confidence in these men. As *The Times* put it:

> If all the facts could be set forth, this one would be a story of a strangely romantic quality. Romantic in the devotion of an industry to a task of a magnitude such as it had never contemplated before; romantic in the harnessing of science to the peculiar and urgent needs of air defence; romantic in the sense that the nation has thrown up in surprising numbers young volunteers physically fit in every respect, and moved by a spirit of earnest endeavour, disguised under a light and even flippant manner ... These young men have not to be seen in the mess, or tearing along the roads in their

motor cars, or playing violent squash, but at work in their aircraft.

Technology and spirit; an intricate country-wide web of innovative radar, combined with squadrons – particularly those ringed around London and the Home Counties – twitching with readiness. And back at Bentley Priory, Air Chief Marshal Dowding was now set to see if his architecture of command would work. The sky was instantly expected to blacken with bombers. That they didn't might now be described as a fantastic stroke of luck.

Chapter Seven

Dress Rehearsals

From the night skies above Germany fluttered the snow of leaflets; millions of them. In the air, this was one of the first offensive acts of Britain's war, on 3 and 4 September 1939. Hamburg, Bremen and the Ruhr were targeted. The leaflets, in German, offered a blunt message. 'Warning! From England to the German people!' it began, printed in gothic script.

> The Nazi regime has, in spite of the endeavours of the leading great powers, plunged the world into war ... You cannot win this war. Against you are arrayed resources and materials far greater than your own. For years ... by means of an incredible system of secret police and informers, the truth has been withheld from you. Against you stands the united strength of the free peoples, who with open eyes will fight for freedom to the last. This war is as repulsive to us as it is to you, but do not forget that England, once forced into war, will wage it unwaveringly to the end. England's nerves are strong, her resources inexhaustible. We will not relent. Pass on [this leaflet]

The response from Hermann Goering contrived to sound amused, though the threat at the end was dark: 'If the

British aeroplanes fly at tremendous height and drop their ridiculous propaganda on to German territory, I have nothing against it. But take care if the leaflets are succeeded by one bomb. Then reprisals will follow and will be carried out as in Poland.'

Goering's statement also inadvertently suggested that Germany was not invulnerable to attack. Indeed, the British raid, involving bombers, served a double purpose, according to Major F.A. Robertson, writing for the *Manchester Guardian*: 'A gratifying feature … is the ineffectiveness of German Anti-Aircraft defences. The millions of leaflets strewn about the countryside are evidence which proves to every German that our machines had it in their power to drop bombs and that the German defences were powerless to prevent them.'

From the point of view of Britain's defence, these first nervy days of the war were also making something else quite apparent: that the Luftwaffe was not about to launch an all-out attack on Britain. To do so at that stage – before their invasion of the Low Countries and France – would have required quite a flight: first the German pilots would have to cross the Low Countries, then the Channel, and then fly seventy or so miles up through Kent and the Thames Estuary to target London. Their time and fuel supplies would be limited, and their vulnerability to defensive British pilots great, given the huge distances over which they would then have to return. Not that there was any relaxation in Fighter Command; if anything, the lack of activity increased the nervousness.

This was manifested most sharply – and tragically – on 6 September 1939 in what became known as 'The Battle of Barking Creek'. In fact, the incident in question took place in the skies above the Thames Estuary and the watery marshes of Essex and Kent. It was a misunderstanding sparked by a false 'plot' which suggested an incoming formation of enemy planes. RAF Hornchurch, on the easternmost edge of London, was base to 74 Squadron, led by the formidable and hugely skilled Adolph 'Sailor' Malan. The confusion of the day was recalled by pilot Samuel Hoare:

A false plot had been spotted over on the Essex coast … This aircraft was reported as unidentified and initially three Hurricane fighter aircraft were sent off from North Weald aerodrome to investigate. Well this started the ball rolling, the three Hurricanes were then unidentified by the RDF station, I suppose through lack of communication …

The RDF station then had one unidentified aircraft plus a formation of three, so the controller at No. 11 Group decided he should send off a flight of aircraft to investigate further; so six aircraft went off to investigate the three.[1]

Those Spitfires took off from RAF Hornchurch, and leading them was 'Sailor' Malan. For all these pilots knew, this was it: the first engagement with the enemy. What unfurled was a horrible farce. British fighter planes were chasing one another across the wide skies of the Essex and Kent coasts, Malan and his pilots in unwitting pursuit of the men from North Weald. There was an extra element of jeopardy: as they flew close to the naval dockyard at Chatham in Kent, the guns on the ground opened fire, the men down below as well as the pilots above apparently unable to distinguish between enemy and friendly aircraft. As Wing Commander John Connell Freeborn recalled: 'We were quite a bit away behind the first section of aircraft and were trying to catch them up, when Malan sounded the "Tally-ho!" over the R/T, seeing these supposedly enemy aircraft … Our section went in and we shot down … two unidentified aircraft which turned out to be Hurricanes.'[2] According to other accounts, Malan had spotted right at the last minute that their prey was British, and had shouted down the R/T that the attack should stop. If he did so, then the order was heard by neither John Freeborn nor fellow pilot Paddy Byrne.

The Hurricanes were shot out of the sky. The first flying fatality of the war – a victim of friendly fire – was Pilot Officer Halton-Harrap. Later, the original 'unidentified' plane that had started the entire incident turned out to be a Blenheim coming back from a reconnaissance patrol; it too was shot down mistakenly, by anti-aircraft guns. But the tragedy of the Hurricanes was even more extraordinary; it was not as if the planes were revolutionary new designs that the pilots could not have recognised. What it illustrates is the edginess of the fighter pilots, twitching for the battle to begin.

Having shot down the Hurricanes, the pilots flew back to RAF Hornchurch. 'We looked for Malan,' recalled Freeborn, 'but he was nowhere to be seen.' Having returned safely, Malan had already left base; he was called back. Freeborn, however, was met upon landing by a squadron leader who told him that he and Paddy Byrne were to be placed under immediate and close arrest.

Freeborn, a very young man, was now desperately worried to find himself facing a court-martial. 'But our Commanding Officer,' he said, 'was a hell of a nice chap and he said "Sir Patrick Hastings is Intelligence Officer at Fighter Command Headquarters. Go and see him."' Freeborn did so, having been specially released to make the journey to Stanmore. Sir Patrick met him there and announced that he would act as defence barrister. Roger Bushell of 601 Squadron, of course, also had a distinguished background in law, and he was pulled in to support Hastings. The following month, the case was heard at a specially convened General Field Court Martial at Bentley Priory. There did not seem to be very much argument; on the recommendation of Sir Patrick, who argued that 'this young man should not be condemned for his actions', the case was dismissed.[3]

A matter of greater concern for Fighter Command was the way that the incident illustrated the vulnerable nature of the new Chain Home System. Although the scientists and technicians were constantly making tweaks and adjustments – in the archives are blueprints and memos concerning every last corner of the operation, together with requests for new parts and different equipment – there was no precedent to work from, no established rules to follow. This was an entirely new sort of conflict in terms of speed and technology; everything had to be extemporised. And this to an extent went for the pilots as well. They may have had radio transmission equipment, but it was not yet wholly reliable.

Indeed, for the young men of RAF Hornchurch, taking off in the lemon light of dawn from the mist-enshrouded marshes, heading upwards and tensed with every nerve and synapse to face the sinister approaching wings of the enemy, the war to come was as much about the instincts and skills that they had acquired through extraordinarily hazardous training. It is one thing to theorise about tactics; but for a young pilot thrown into a whirling dogfight, possibly in and out of cloud, the sky swarming with aircraft both friendly and hostile, the mathematical calculations would only go so far. Find your target, fix upon it, hunt your target down.

In those first days of war, fighter squadrons were sent out to France too, and newspaper correspondents returned admiring dispatches immediately. 'The men are in fine spirits,' wrote an embedded reporter of one squadron for the *Manchester Guardian* on 24 September 1939, 'and enjoying the novelty of the conditions in which they are living … most of the men are in billets in towns, villages and farmhouses; the people have done everything possible to make their guests at home … There is no shortage of food and the men can enjoy a variety of choice fresh fruit … Chicken and goose appear on the menus.' Not for such heroes the dreary round of bully beef and hot sweet tea; there was an undercurrent of class bias in the suggestion that for these young men, fresh fruit and goose were no less than they would expect, in sharp contrast to the urban lads being conscripted for the army.

In the midst of this flurry of preparation, this national tensing of the muscles, the King paid his first visit to Bentley Priory on 6 September 1939, and caught his first sight of the radical – almost futuristic – arrangement of the Operations and Filter Rooms. Bentley Priory's location was a matter for the Official Secrets Act; even the wealthy Metroland commuters who lived in the nearby town of Stanmore had no idea of the establishment's true purpose. 'When the King arrived … he was welcomed by the Air Chief Marshal, Head of Fighter Command,' noted *The Times*. 'The King wore the service side cap, and carried his gas mask in a khaki container over his shoulder.' No one had quite discounted the possibility of those poison gas attacks coming. It would be some weeks before the general public felt blithe enough to abandon their own gas masks, and then much to the chagrin of officialdom.

The royal visit must have conferred a sense of vindication on Hugh Dowding; for all the constant tension within the Air Ministry as to whether it was better for Britain's fighters and bombers to go on the attack, here was the King, inspecting the Dowding system, with its ringing telephones, colourful flashing lights and the slick choreography of the filterers and plotters. Dowding had responsibility for one of the more psychologically difficult tasks to achieve in any war: the bestowal of a sense of reassurance, an unswerving confidence that the defences and the fighters would be more than enough to see off any German aerial attack.

But again: had the Germans launched a serious heavy attack, would Fighter Command have been ready that autumn? Despite the radical brilliance of radar, the system itself was still new. As Vincent Orange wrote:

> There were still gaps in the coastal coverage and stations could not report aircraft flying below 1,000 feet [304 metres]. Group and sector controllers were to bear in mind these limitations in the system: range and position were accurate to within about one mile; height was accurate to within plus or minus 1,000 feet [1.6 kilometres} in the Thames Estuary and plus or minus 2,000 feet [610 metres] elsewhere; up to three aircraft could be accurately counted, but more than three could mean as many as nine and more than nine ANY number over nine.[4]

In other words, whenever fighters, from Biggin Hill to Debden, received the signal to sprint to their aeroplanes, take off and intercept the incoming enemy, there would still be uncertainty about exactly what they would be facing up there in the clouds, and in what numbers. But as Dowding himself wrote, 'RDF is very capricious and unreliable but it is better than nothing, as being the best evidence we have of what is going on over the sea.'[5]

In the curious silence of the 'Bore War', a reconnaissance crew based in France managed in early October to get themselves into jeopardy beyond the Siegfried Line – the German line of fortifications and tank defences, built in the First World War, which stretched from the border with the Netherlands to that of Switzerland. Though not a part of Fighter Command, these pilots were nonetheless to give the public an unwitting preview of what was to come. The planes were flying, as the reporter from *The Times* wrote, 'in the most strongly defended part of the Saar. Anti-aircraft batteries put up fierce barrages but our aircraft went through it successfully.' However, on the line of the horizon, the Messerschmitts materialised. What followed was a harrowing struggle for survival. Three British planes had to make a forced landing. As the reporter continued, starting now – consciously or unconsciously – to take on the tone of Captain W.E. Johns:

> The squadron leader's machine alone was left, but he flew on to finish his job. The aircraft by this time was in a sorry way. There were 80 bullet holes in the fabric; the ailerons and rudder were damaged; both petrol tanks were burst and flooding the inside of the fuselage with petrol and fumes ... from the starboard tank, petrol poured through a bullet hole each time the aircraft banked; but by stopping the hole with a handkerchief, the pilot was able to save enough petrol to get home.

And after an excruciating landing – followed by the crew beating flames off one another's clothing – the pilot declared: 'Old Hitler gave me a bit of a headache but that was nothing to what we will give him.'

Skirmishes over enemy territory were one thing; but in mid-October 1939, Fighter Command was to receive its first proper test. Just days before it came, Sir Kingsley Wood, Secretary of State for Air, had been moved to announce in Parliament that inactivity was as fraught for pilots as action. 'The intensity of the operations of Fighter Command ... depends largely upon the activities of the enemy,' he said. 'Instant readiness is demanded and the strain imposed has been as great, if not greater, than if active operations were in progress.'

Obligingly, out of a dazzlingly bright sky, came the enemy. On the afternoon of 16 October 1939, over the wide and grey Firth of Forth, dropping close to the vast red metal exoskeleton of the Forth Railway Bridge, swept twelve German bombers. Their target was the Rosyth naval base. There was something especially incongruous about an attack taking place just after lunch, at half past two on an unseasonally sunny day. According to the official report put out swiftly afterwards, the German bombers were met instantly with RAF fighters; the bombers failed to inflict any serious damage on the shipping below; and four of the German planes were downed. An eyewitness reporter in nearby Edinburgh was on hand to log a helpful account, published in *The Times* the following day, of the reactions of locals to this unexpected German incursion:

> Ideal weather conditions prevailed with the sun shining from a blue sky when shortly after two o'clock, the muffled bark of anti-aircraft guns was heard in the centre of the City of Edinburgh. The shell bursts were plainly visible high around the city … Citizens were puzzled by the absence of any air-raid warning – but the sight of German aircraft being hotly pursued by RAF machines above the house tops put all doubts at rest … Citizens climbed on to roofs and other vantage points to watch through binoculars.

Not everyone seemed impressed; the observer was also keen to record some unlikely nonchalance in the city's business quarter:

> Citizens basking in the sunshine in Princes Street Gardens hardly bothered to lift their eyes from their newspapers and even when pieces of anti-aircraft shell

casing were picked up, there were no traces of undue excitement. One businessman reading a book near the Scott Monument looked up for a moment and after remarking: 'The RAF lads will look after them,' resumed his reading.

Quite so; and this was the Spitfire's first active engagement of the war. The hostile Junkers had been intercepted by pilots from 602 and 603 Squadrons, based in Drem and Turnhouse. The following day brought another small incursion: a formation of nine German bombers went for the more northerly naval base at Scapa Flow, damaging one destroyer. A Heinkel was brought down on the island of Hoy. Small though both of these raids were, they had an immediate – and secret – impact. 'The raids on both places in October,' states the official history of Fighter Command, 'exposed their vulnerability and from October 28th, the Clyde became the main fleet anchorage.' This, of course, was on the west coast, just outside Glasgow, and faced towards the Atlantic; little use for a naval fleet that was supposed to be defending the nation's eastern coastline. A great deal of hurried work was put into the base at Scapa Flow to fortify it more heavily against future attacks.

And what about protecting the shipping itself, as opposed to the bases? The first of the long convoys were beginning their hazardous voyages, carrying not just food imports, but crucial supplies of materiel. Could they be escorted by fighter pilots, who would see off any Luftwaffe aggression? As the official history states:

It was pointed out that Fighter Command could not provide effective protection for shipping except when it was routed to close inshore, and even then there might not be sufficient warning for fighters to reach a convoy

112

or group of ships before the initial attack was made.
Accordingly, it was recommended, and later approved,
that four squadrons of fighters should be formed for
the sole duty of providing close escorts for shipping
passing between the Firth of Forth and Southampton.

These squadrons were soon urgently needed; the Luftwaffe
was fast to spot how nakedly vulnerable the lines of shipping
were. Air Chief Marshal Dowding agreed to move some
fighter squadrons near the coast.

He was also thinking about the vulnerability of the air
force itself: the ever-pressing need for more planes and
pilots, and for more skilled men to train those pilots. Then
there was the tempting target of British plane-making
factories, many of which were in the industrial Midlands,
within striking distance of the Luftwaffe. Direct bomb hits
on those would instantly cripple Britain's defences, leaving
her open to invasion. The plane-making factories were not
about to be relocated to the far west coast. Not for the first
time, Fighter Command was being painfully stretched and
pulled in all directions.

The year turned; and in the first harrowingly cold days of
1940, that freezing winter when London was dense and grey
with coal smoke from millions of homes, and when warming
light was craved on murky evenings, Fighter Command was
anxious to let the citizens know that any German bombers
would be looking for the tiniest chink of illumination. 'It has
been determined that London can never be completely
blacked out,' ran one report, though adding that if the
regulations were followed properly, 'it will be impossible for
enemy pilots to ascertain their exact position.'[6]

Observer pilots had been up there in the dark; they came
back with an extraordinarily poetic vision of the darkened

city. Although it was now difficult to pinpoint particular streets – masked car headlamps had stopped long routes like the Edgware Road glittering for miles – there were unexpected lights elsewhere. 'The flashes from tramcars and electric railways catch the eye of the observer overhead,' ran the report, 'but ... they would be little use guiding pilots to the City. One observer described London from the air during the blackout as resembling the vault of the heavens on a starlit night with a "few diamond necklaces scattered about". The diamond necklace effect is made by railway marshalling yards.'

There were other illegitimate glitters: silvery railway lines picked out by the uncovered lights streaming from windows of houses backing on to the railways; properties that the wardens could never see around the back of, and at whose owners they could therefore never do the necessary shouting.

The Spitfires were getting plenty in the way of dress rehearsals. On the night of 13 February 1940, a Heinkel raider was detected in the mouth of the Thames Estuary. Three Spitfires were sent off in furious pursuit. 'When the raider saw them, he at once began a long twisting dive towards a patch of cloud far behind him,' went the breathless report in *The Times*. 'The three Spitfires followed, firing in turn as they dived. As fast as the raider eluded the fire of one, another was ready to take up the attack. Although visibility was very poor throughout the action, several bursts of fire took effect. When last seen, the enemy was heading eastwards, into cloud and darkness.'

Among the young fighter pilots waiting impassively on the ground for the telephone call signalling that he and his men were to sprint for their planes was Peter Townsend. Since the start of the war, he had been posted and re-posted up and down the country. Come February, he was moved from the sylvan West Sussex base at Tangmere – fresh with its new asphalt runways and superb pilot facilities – to a rougher and readier prospect just outside Newcastle at Acklington. He and his colleagues found rudimentary quarters and a pervasive, uncomfortable east coast cold. But it was from over the granite grey waves of the North Sea that German Heinkels were making their nervy incursions, alternately threatening and infuriating. Townsend lost good friends in the individual skirmishes that were to follow; he himself successfully brought down a Heinkel near Whitby.

A spell at Wick near Scapa Flow in the bitter wastes of northern Scotland was to follow. Townsend later recalled that it was in this period that he crossed a shadow-line; he told his son that somehow, earlier, in his encounters with the enemy, the idea of killing had not even skittered across his mind, for he could not bring himself to imagine killing men who shared so exactly his love of flying. Skirmishes, he said, were regarded more as an insanely dangerous form of sport than as the cold and pitiless pursuit of other aircraft in the hope of making them and their pilots fall thousands of feet to their deaths. But in Scotland, in that gelid spring of 1940, the change had stolen over him. The innocence perhaps had been an illusion. Now, he said, it was more of a killing game.

One night, Townsend was out on patrol in his Hurricane. There had been a great deal of anti-aircraft fire; he knew how easily collateral damage was inflicted. And there came a point when, over his radio, Townsend's local controller told him to abandon his nocturnal search for enemy planes and return to base.

Townsend deliberately disobeyed; he switched his radio off. Flying through the silent dark, he refused to give up, and eventually he sighted tiny lights. He had a Heinkel ahead of him. The young man who had simply wanted to share his passion for flying was gone; now, as Townsend

115

recalled, he was utterly remorseless. He had the advantage very quickly, firing upon the plane that simply could not get away in time. He watched as the dark was dazzled with flames, seeing the plane and its crew plummet into the sea below. Townsend felt no anguish, or indeed emotion of any kind. When he finally returned to the base, it turned out that his Hurricane was peppered with bullet holes. He had been a very short distance from plunging into those waves himself.[7]

In the early stages of the war, prospects for petrified German pilots, whose crashing planes would bring down village telephone wires, were – according to the accounts of the time, at any rate – more favourable than they became during and after the Battle of Britain. During the Phoney War, young Luftwaffe pilots who had survived such crashes were sometimes taken, catatonic with shock, to farmhouses, where they were given cigarettes and tea before being formally taken prisoner.

Despite the best efforts of Fighter Command and ARP wardens, the public seemed unstoppably drawn to putting themselves in danger in order to witness the rare and spectacular dogfights. This was a problem even at night. In late April 1940, an engagement between Fighter Command and the Germans took place off the south coast. The authorities felt obliged the next day to post warnings in the newspapers: 'It has been reported that during the air activity off the south coast on Saturday night, a considerable number of persons pulled up blinds and opened windows to see what was going on without troubling to extinguish lights,' complained the man from the Ministry. 'The Ministry of Home Security issues an urgent warning on this subject, as such action … is attended with great danger from the point of view of national security and is also punishable by heavy penalties. It has also been reported,' the ministry continued with greater gravity, 'that many persons when advised by the police to take cover actually became abusive.'

This was neither the first – nor, certainly, the last – time that such an exasperated public statement had to be issued. How many schoolboys in the southeast and around air stations like Biggin Hill would soon be spending afternoons gawping up at the sky at the first suggestion of anti-aircraft fire? But it was true: there was danger involved. 'It should be borne in mind that fragments from anti-aircraft shells and machine gun bullets from aeroplanes may come to earth at considerable distances from the points at which they were fired,' warned the Ministry.

Coming events cast their shadows before them; the occasional skirmishes on the Thames Estuary and along the Kent coast were giving the fighter pilots their chance not merely to master the technology of the new Spitfires and Hurricanes, but also to try and find a way of controlling fear. Shattering and traumatic though the summer to come would be, the preceding weeks had more sick, silent tension about them for many pilots.

Chapter Eight

'Interesting Work of a Confidential Nature'

The gravity of war was now pulling increasing numbers of women into the air force volunteers, and into RAF stations around the country. In the immediate aftermath of the Dunkirk evacuation, in June 1940, RAF Hornchurch was to receive a visit from His Majesty the King, there to distribute Distinguished Flying Crosses. And it was a WAAF typist who – with quick wits and a deep blush – contributed a hook from her underwear to enable one pilot to fix the decoration on his uniform. The need for ingenuity, combined with good humour – plus the ability to listen to men who were trying to make light of the horrors they had seen – seemed to be understood implicitly by all recruits.

For a few, the good-looking pilots themselves were a draw; the inducement, if only subconscious, to sign up for the WAAF. Other young women had more serious aims. There was a preconception – quite wrong – that the only jobs open to women in the Air Force were the most basic. To serve as a cook, or a messenger, or a driver, carried no shame or stigma; quite the reverse. Any young woman volunteering for such roles in any of the services was lauded for her patriotic spirit. But there were many women in 1940 whose ambitious hearts were set elsewhere. Especially those with pilot relatives; such girls were acutely aware of the daily jeopardy, the extraordinary risks, that Spitfire and Hurricane pilots took even during training flights. They had seen mortal injury and death. These women knew what the pilots – and their families – were facing.

The compulsion to join up, to show solidarity with these friends and loved ones, was powerful, but so was the desire to carry out a role that would make a real difference. This was the case for Patricia Clark, and for Eileen Younghusband too. Then there were many who perhaps sensed in the social earthquake of war that they might have a chance to contribute far more than women had been able to in the past.

The newspapers were not certain initially what to make of the idea of young girls in such masculine redoubts. 'The first official inspection took place on Saturday afternoon of WAAF personnel at a modern operational station in a Fighter Command somewhere in England,' ran the report in *The Times* on 11 April 1940. 'Air Vice-Marshal Leigh-Mallory took the salute at the parade and inspected the airwomen, accompanied by the director of the Women's Auxiliary Air Force Commandant Trefusis Forbes.' Katherine Trefusis Forbes had been at the helm of the WAAF recruitment drive, sorting out every rule and regulation, down to the most suitable form of underwear. The report continued:

[Leigh-Mallory] walked between the lines, noting the trim efficiency of the women and the brightness of their buttons and stopped occasionally to speak to some of the older women who had the ribbons of the last war on their tunics. The women formed threes and were a very smart-looking lot ... Before the arrival of the inspecting officer, a physical training display was given by some of the women, trained by an officer who was a teacher of physical culture during the war.

The report also painted an attractive picture of living conditions; nor was that picture a deceptive one. If the training regimes were a little Spartan, the women assigned to Bentley Priory, Bawdsey and other stations found their quarters rather agreeable:

> The women have what used to be the men's married quarters before the war – a little avenue of small villas. They are pleasant little houses in which usually about three women live. Each has a cosy sitting room, a good bathroom, and two to three bedrooms and a little strip of garden, in which the women have planted primroses and tulips.

But the most important aspect – for the newspaper's women readers – was the hint at more satisfying work on offer. 'More ... Special Duties clerks are being recruited,' the report stated. 'The duties of the latter include interesting work of a confidential nature. No special training is needed, but would-be recruits must be responsible people not frightened by a "hush hush" job.'

Like the codebreaking establishment at Bletchley Park, Bentley Priory was actively on the lookout for sharp, fast, strong women. But first – rather like the Wrens who ended up working on the world's first proto-computers – these special WAAFs would have to go through a period of very austere training. For some, life simply couldn't be better.

Gladys Eva was beside herself with excitement when the opportunity arose. Some elements of the military life, such as drill, were impossible to avoid, although even this was a joy to Mrs Eva. 'We were sent to West Drayton – square bashing for a fortnight. I loved it because I'd been a Girl Guide. Loved my school uniform, loved my Guides uniform. And now I loved my air force uniform.'

Before joining, meanwhile, Eileen Younghusband had been given valuable advice about avoiding cooking or driving jobs: 'My cousin Mae went into the RAF. She's a month older than me and that's what they offered her – she became a driver. Well, I quite like cooking, but that's not what I wanted to do. And Mae knew I always came top at maths in school, so she said, "Just tell them."'

'Once I'd enrolled, then I was sent to the basic camp where everyone goes and you were all in it together. There were thirty in a hut. That's where you were kitted out, you had your free-from-infection checks – nits, colour-blindness. You learned how to march, you learned who to salute.'

The sparse induction at West Drayton, an industrial suburb in the western hinterlands of London, was equally instructive for Eileen Younghusband. It was at this camp that her eyes were opened to a wider world than she had seen in the pleasant north London suburb of Southgate. 'There was a prostitute, in amongst us,' she laughs. 'We were issued with black knickers that came down to our knees – we called them the Blackouts – and then they became Twilights when they got to grey. This girl pranced around in her bra and in these black knickers. I mean, she was very funny. But she was a prostitute. She said, "I got fed up with men, so I thought I'd join the air force."'

For those such as Patricia Clark who had enjoyed even more rarefied upbringings, West Drayton proved more startling yet: 'We were taught how to march and given a knife, fork and spoon. We went for an interview to assess where we might now be posted on to. Were we going to be cooks or drivers or whatever? What are your qualifications, they asked. I said, "I haven't got any."'

The recruiter was undeterred, saying, 'I think what we'll put you down for is Special Duties.'

'What's that?' said Mrs Clark.

She was informed, 'I'm afraid I can't tell you. You have to sign the Official Secrets Act before you can be told.'

Mrs Clark said, 'Can't I drive an ambulance?'

Came the answer, 'No – I'm putting you down for Special Duties. Don't argue with me. That's it. Out.'

'Well, I went out,' says Mrs Clark, 'and I thought, Special Duties … I speak German, I speak French … I could be a spy!'

Patricia Clark found herself transported with excitement at the prospect of the adventure that lay before her, even as her speculations grew ungovernably wild. 'I could be landed in France, I could speak to the Germans and I could spy for my country. I settled happily for it – after all, I thought, what else could it have been? Not the cook-house, not typing, nothing like that or it wouldn't be Official Secrets Act. I was thrilled. I was all for adventure.

'So we get down to West Drayton, to this disused workhouse that had been converted. There was a courtyard and the men's building one side, women's the other. All long dormitories.' And the hopes of a glamorous adventure dissolved.

'The girls I was with – there were about six of us – had all come from English boarding schools.' Mrs Clark's own background had been especially sheltered, she says with a laugh. 'Our gardener, and the man who came to mend our radiogram, and the piano tuner, they were the only three lower-class people that I had ever spoken to.' Now, all of a sudden, her group of girls found themselves surrounded by working-class men from the ranks.

'And here were we, these six girls, being whistled at from across the courtyard. It was frightfully exciting and quite dangerous! We weren't quite sure what was going to happen.

'The following day, after we had settled in, we went downstairs to a big room with a huge table. Round the table were telephones and on the table there were counters. By this time we had signed the Official Secrets Act. And we were told we were going to be doing the very secret work of radar. I sat down at the table and looked at these tiddlywinks – and at that point, I could not have been more upset.' It had become clear to Mrs Clark that her dreams of a career in espionage were not to be fulfilled.

For young Gladys Eva, the whole thing was a little easier because she was something of a pioneer; she had arrived at her posting a little before a great many other women. As a result, there was novelty, accompanied by the notion of being introduced to a technology whose existence she had never even suspected. After drill came the more specialised stuff: a training course at Leighton Buzzard in Bedfordshire. 'That was where you were taught how to plot,' she says, referring to the new skill she was about to acquire. 'And that was in a church hall because at that stage they hadn't built any special premises in the air force area to teach in. I picked it up like fun.' What she was learning – on an extemporised table in a draughty hall – was the art of accurately noting on a map the positions and velocities and heights of aircraft.

'There were six of us,' adds Mrs Eva. 'It was quite physical because the table's quite big. We were doing everything with our hands, so we were right across the table. Plots were coming from all over the place. At the beginning of our time, the doctors decided it wouldn't be good for our health to do an eight-hour watch at night. But then they realised it was even worse to do a four-hour watch because it broke your sleep in the middle of the night. And they thought that wasn't good. So we did eight-hour watches. It was quite tough when it was busy,' Mrs Eva adds with light understatement.

And it was an exclusive club – a club destined for Bentley Priory – that she found she had joined. 'There were not very many others – they didn't want many for the Filter Room.

When we joined up, there was only one Filter Room, and that was at Bentley Priory. Very soon, of course, they were popping up all over, but right at the beginning ...' And what a prospect it was: this new world of vast maps, instant trigonometry, flashing coloured lights, telephones, teleprinters, men and women engaged on a variety of tasks that initially seemed mysterious and esoteric.

The speed and intensity of the work meant that it was important to have pressure valves. Eileen Younghusband recalls such off-duty moments: 'At nearby Bentley Manor, which was our house – if you were new there, you put your foot in the cold fireplace ashes and then you were held upside down, lifted up, and you pressed your foot on the ceiling ...' The footprints on the ceiling was a running joke. As were the saucy adventures of fictional WAAF raver Lottie Crump, whose exploits were the invention of an incoming generation of WAAFs. Lottie's role was to tantalise Bentley Priory's male filterers, regarded by the WAAFS as pitiably old because 'they were in their thirties'.

'The men believed everything we told them,' laughs Mrs Younghusband. 'We were always asked: "Why does Lottie Crump never come on duty?" And we'd either say she was ill or give some other excuse. That she had had some incredible accident in the bath with toy boats. And they believed us. It's those sorts of stupid things that we did, as a way to unwind.'

Yet the tension was ever present. For the fighter squadrons – from Duxford to Tangmere – the spring of 1940 was coiled and edgy. This anxiety was amplified in the higher reaches of command; it was in April 1940 that the term 'lack of moral fibre' began to circulate. The Nazi invasion of Norway – and the humiliating trouncing of the British in that operation – would have been one factor; the universal expectation of an imminent Nazi invasion of England was another. 'Lack of moral fibre' was deemed to be apparent when pilots reported sick or simply refused to fly. Senior commanders were at pains to differentiate such behaviour from 'flying stress' or 'aviator's neurasthenia', which had identifiable physical symptoms such as severe gastric upsets. There had been occurrences in Bomber Command of crew members apparently refusing to fly again. It now seems quite clear that this would have been a form of shell shock, and the authorities knew this too; but in desperate times, such things could not be admitted out loud.

The calculated phrase 'lack of moral fibre' came to be feared among fighter pilots as well – because anyone suspected of such a thing would be packed off immediately to an 'Assessment Centre' and stripped of rank and privileges. In other words, it was the 1940 equivalent of being handed a white feather; an accusation of cowardice.

The pressure did get to a few men. It is surprising that it didn't get to more. Even during training, the young pilots were required to become inured to death and mutilation. Nor was the end likely to be quick; just the long stomach-quivering drop from the sky, or the flames enveloping the cockpit, scorching the hands and the face, destroying the eyes, roasting the flesh beyond recognition. Trainee pilots frequently witnessed their fellows crashing, the inexplicable moment when their machines somehow bucked from beneath their control. They witnessed the hacked bloody bodies, or indeed bodies that had split apart on impact after a fall of thousands of feet when scorched parachutes failed to open.

Quietly, everyone knew that any airman might succumb; according to some pilots' accounts, there was the even greater fear of that airman turning out to be themselves. The problem was particularly acute in Bomber Command, where some crew members had no control over the way the plane was flown; they were required to perform other functions in a craft that might disintegrate around them. For fighters in single-seater aircraft, there was at least a sense of being in charge of one's own fate, the possibility even in crisis of escaping. But fighters suffered too.

We might now recoil at the granite pitilessness of high command when it came to identifying traumatised pilots, picking them out and packing them off. Yet at this moment of national crisis, there was also another unanswerable, abiding fear: that their fear could be contagious. Even Air Vice Marshal Keith Park, now promoted to head 11 Group in Uxbridge, said that there was a 'necessity for the speedy handling of such cases ... it is essential that any such cases be removed immediately from the precincts of the squadron or the station.'[1]

The cult of Douglas Bader – it is not going too far to describe it thus – expressed in some ways the unconscious determination to see this fear blotted out. Here was a double amputee who had suffered not merely in the aftermath of that 1931 crash, but also in the unspeakably painful days and weeks after the surgery: the damaged nerves, the roaring phantom agonies from nerves no longer there; then the further pain of adjusting to new, artificial legs. There was the ordeal of learning how to walk in a new way, the balance completely changed; and the further ordeal of regaining a full sense of masculinity, being able to talk to women without constantly fearing what they would think of his crippled state.

But, even more important, here was a man who simply wrestled the darkest fear to the ground without a second thought. Nothing would stop Bader in his determination to become a fighter pilot once more. By implication, any pilot – unhurt or whole – who did not share his determination was a lesser man.

Yet even before the Battle of Britain, fear in a fighter station could be as pervasive as the mist on a winter moor. Pilot Geoffrey Wellum quietly encapsulated this in his references to the mess after a mission, as the men sat around, waiting for the telephone to ring with the order to set out into the skies once more. Wellum noted the silence, as well as the outbreaks of blustery bonhomie. He noticed that one of his fellow pilots – sitting deep in an armchair, seemingly too absorbed in his book to join in the sporadic, strained conversation – never turned a single page of that book.[2]

According to Lord David Cecil, in his essay 'The RAF':

So dangerous a life inevitably leaves its mark on the nerves. The airmen preserve a rigid appearance of imperturbability and good spirits; but one soon begins to realise that they are living in a state of tension. The newspaper picture of the laughing aviator, carelessly risking his life, is not really a flattering likeness. It is no compliment to a man to say that he is too insensitive to know when he is in danger. Anyway, it seemed to me a false picture. Going down to the airfield with a group of men about to start on night operations, one notices that through the mask of self-control, their eyes gaze out serious and preoccupied.[3]

The bluff heartiness was a recurring leitmotif stretching back to the First World War; and in contemporary accounts of epic, extraordinary beer-drinking, we catch a glimpse of the effort to beat back the darkness. Even the aware, sensitive (and comparatively teetotal) Geoffrey Wellum was brisk on the subject of death: the training comrades who had lost control and had been incinerated in their cockpits; the pilots failing to eject as their planes spiralled out of control. The expression 'gone for a Burton' originated with the RAF; the light way of announcing that a comrade was no more. The phrase had been an advertising line for Burton ale; only pilots could mordantly conflate the act of going out for a beer with death. And yet, even with such studied nonchalance, how was it possible for pilots to get a decent night's sleep after a stretching day or night in the sky? The author Roald Dahl, as a young man, was a fighter pilot for the RAF in Africa. Of the experience of fear, he wrote that:

> [It] creeps closer and closer, like a cat creeps closer stalking a sparrow, and then when it is right behind you, it doesn't spring like the cat would spring; it just leans forward and whispers in your ear ... At first it whispers to you only at night, when you are lying awake in bed. Then it whispers to you at odd moments during the day, when you are doing your teeth or drinking a beer ... and in the end it becomes so that you hear it all day and all night all of the time.[4]

For some fighter pilots, the outward signs might include a shaking hand (one recalled how a friend of his would hold cups or glasses at an angle so no one would see the tremor), violent stomach upsets or constant facial spasms. Occasionally it was even more direct: a pilot refusing point-blank to get into the cockpit. But as well as that straightforward fear, there was an invidious extra layer of dread: the idea that the authorities might spot your fear and haul you out of the squadron, labelling you a coward and a man who would let all his friends down. This was the double cruelty of the idea of 'lack of moral fibre': men were forced to violently quell their most natural fears because of the even more unendurable fear of disgrace.

All of which enables us to place those legendary fighter pilot drinking stories in a rather more understandable context; the squadron leader, for instance, based at a rural station who, upon his return from a mission, would clamber into his car and activate a loudspeaker system attached to the car roof. He would drive through the country lanes and when he came within three-quarters of a mile of the squadron's favourite pub, he would announce into the loudspeaker, 'Three pints of bitter and two gins, please,' thus ensuring, to save time, that his refreshments were already lined up when he arrived at the bar. In some accounts, the drinking stories – the rural taverns, the cheerful after-hours lock-ins, the beer and whisky, the enormous quantities consumed – make you wonder how these men could possibly function before dawn the next day. Many of them must surely have been still drunk come first light. Perhaps for some that was the best way to approach the next day's flying.

And what of grief? Close friendships were formed during training. What would be the impact when a good pal was killed? Said Wing Commander Athol Forbes: 'When a chap doesn't come back, we don't grieve over him. If we did that, we'd go completely nuts in no time. We just think he's been posted to another squadron in a hurry and hasn't had time to say au revoir.'[5] Which is almost a romantic way of looking at it. For young Geoffrey Wellum, instead of pretence, or indeed remembrance, there was something rather more oppressive and chilly: perfect silence.

Also, according to Wellum and many others, there was a huge amount of superstitious observance – although, interestingly, rather less religious observance. The superstition came in the form of little mascots, charms, and even images painted on the outside of the plane. One pilot had an image on his aircraft of Hitler being booted up the backside. There were men who flew with souvenirs from their girlfriends, including silk stockings. Others were more traditional, carrying St Christopher's medallions. Some squadrons had charms lucky enough to cover all men. At Biggin Hill, 609 Squadron's mascot was a goat, christened Billy de Goat. Billy was even promoted: starting out as flight sergeant, he made squadron leader, and was permitted in the mess, where he was allowed the occasional slurp of beer. He was also occasionally allowed to enter the office, where it could be claimed truthfully that he had eaten any particularly irksome paperwork.

The days were fast coming when the character of these young men, and of the young women working alongside them, would be tested in a way that nothing could have prepared them for. And Air Chief Marshal Sir Hugh Dowding, in those days – before the battle that was to define him – would have to withstand vicious attacks from many on his own side. The time for the system that he had so diligently constructed – this high-tech web of radar and observers, superbly skilled young pilots and sharp-witted young women – was at hand, and the nation's future was their responsibility alone.

Chapter Nine

Blood Runs Hotly

The walls had been closing in on Air Chief Marshal Dowding since the beginning of the war. Not only were other services and sections of the air force making demands upon resources that he felt should have been devoted to building up Fighter Command, but in the spring of 1940, there was also constant pressure to send pilots to France. The feeling in the Air Ministry and the War Cabinet was that the British had to do all they could to bolster the French forces. For Dowding, though, there was a biting anxiety that he had not yet sufficient pilots or planes to look after British interests, let alone French.

Some months earlier, in October 1939, he had written an impassioned plea to his colleagues in the Air Ministry:

> The best defence of the country is the Fear of the Fighter [sic]. If we were strong in fighters we should probably never be attacked in force. If we are moderately strong we shall probably be attacked and the attacks will gradually be brought to a standstill. During this period, considerable damage will have been caused. If we are weak in fighter strength, the attacks will not be brought to a standstill and the productive capacity of the country will be virtually

destroyed ... I must put on record my point of view that the Home Defence Organisation ... should receive priority to all other claims until it is firmly secured, since the continued existence of the nation, and all its services, depends upon the Royal Navy and the Fighter Command.[1]

Nevertheless, during the eerie months of this twilight war, French demands and British fears had coalesced; six fighter squadrons were flown to bases on French soil. That winter, when the snow fell heavily and the hard frost gouged ruts into the frozen earth, there were limits even to the amount of training that could be done. Yet there were suggestions throughout this time that more fighters would be needed. The Air Ministry wrote to Dowding:

We must face facts, one of which is that we could possibly lose the war in France just as much as in England. And we must therefore anticipate the possibility that we could not in fact refuse to come to their assistance any further if they really had their backs to the wall. If we had not done something in advance to enable us to come to their assistance in such a situation, the result would be, I am sure, that we should have to send over aircraft but they would be in no position to operate at all effectively when they got there.

When the Germans launched their assault on Norway in April 1940, Dowding's Fighter Command was being stretched in other directions too; there was to be greater protection both for the bases in northern Scotland and for shipping in the Channel and the North Sea (this defence of fishing boats gained fighter planes the nickname of 'kipper kites'). A great deal was being asked of the Hurricane and Spitfire pilots already. And although extra squadrons were being added, it was never easy to find sufficient properly experienced officers to train them.

In the pre-dawn darkness on the morning of 10 May 1940, the citizens of the Low Countries – and in particular the inhabitants of Rotterdam – woke in dread at the noise of successive hollow booms, the shaking furniture, the nightmare sense that some giant was approaching out of the night. The Germans had launched their Blitzkrieg, demonstrating the lethal effectiveness of the Luftwaffe. This was the event the dress rehearsals for which had been witnessed by the world during the Spanish Civil War.

For Britain and France, the war had now started in earnest; and the calls for further fighter squadrons to be sent to France intensified. Some soldiers of the British Expeditionary Force who marched over the border to Belgium recalled being cheered by the sight of a Hurricane taking on a Junkers, and winning.

On that same day, 10 May – the day that Winston Churchill took over as Prime Minister from Neville Chamberlain at the head of a National Government – the HQ of the British Air Forces in France issued this statement to the newspapers:

> In the course of today's operations on the Western Front, the Royal Air Force has been constantly in action. Our reconnaissance aircraft have been operating over a wide area. Enemy troops have been attacked by our bomber squadrons. Wherever German bombers have been encountered, our fighter squadrons have engaged them. Reports indicate that in the course of these combats, numerous enemy aircraft have been destroyed.

This pathological public optimism was maintained even as it became swiftly and horrifyingly apparent that the German armies were starting to scythe through France. On 16 May – a day that would turn out to have the greatest significance and impact upon Dowding's career – it was cheerfully reported that 'our fighter pilots had a good day. There was no lack of targets and attacks were pressed home from dawn to dusk. A formation of six Hurricanes attacked 25 Messerschmitt 110s and shot down five ... the morale of our pilots and crews could not be higher.' And a statistic was deployed that would be repeatedly echoed throughout the coming weeks and months: 'The daily toll inflicted on enemy aircraft is working out at more than three to one in our favour.'

The French still wanted a great deal more from the RAF. Not only had Churchill been Prime Minister for a mere matter of days, he could not have been thrown into the job at a more precipitate moment; he had flown to Paris and the pressure from his opposite number Paul Reynaud was intense. Reynaud wanted ten more fighter squadrons to be sent over to help in France. In fact, it is still worth asking whether extra numbers of British fighter planes might have helped in the face of what seemed an unstoppable and inevitable German advance. And even if there was not much practical effect, might the impact upon morale have made a difference? In other words, had the French felt more fully supported, might they have avoided collapse?

Yet at this crucial point, with promises being made to the French by the War Cabinet – promises of which Hugh Dowding was not yet properly aware – he issued the first of a series of explicit pleas for the strength of his home defence not to be diminished. His initial salvo was in a letter, dated 14 May, to Air Marshal Peirse: 'I want the Fighter Command to pull its full weight in this battle, but I want it to do so by shooting down Germans in this country and not by being used as a reservoir for sending reinforcements to France.'[2]

Later that day, Dowding learned that the War Cabinet had approved the plan for ten more of his squadrons to be sent over the Channel. His response can be read as a cry of distress and passion, even though his language and manner were measured. He asked that he be allowed to address the War Cabinet in Whitehall, in person. Permission was granted.

There are those who see Dowding's intervention as the moment that the course of Britain's war was decided. It was unusual to have such a figure speaking out personally, as opposed to simply trusting to his superiors. What gave the situation an extra twist of poignancy was that for those superiors, and for those around that War Cabinet table, Dowding was a man who seemed to be on perpetually borrowed time – on one occasion his retirement had been coldly announced to the evening newspapers by his superiors without his knowledge, and then equally dismissively deferred. On 15 May Dowding wrote a memo to the Under-Secretary of State for the Air Ministry which repeated the points he had made to those men:

> I hope and believe that our Armies may yet be victorious in France and Belgium, but we have to face the possibility that they may be defeated. In this case, I presume that there is no-one who will deny that England should fight on, even though the remainder of the Continent of Europe is dominated by the Germans ... Once a decision has been reached as to the limit on which the Air Council and the Cabinet are prepared to stake the strategic existence of the country, it should be made clear to the Allied commanders on the continent that not a single aeroplane from Fighter Command beyond the limit will be sent across

the Channel, no matter how desperate the situation may become…

I believe that if an adequate fighter force is kept in this country, if the fleet remains in being, and if Home Forces are suitably organised to resist invasion, we should be able to carry on the war single-handed for some time, if not indefinitely. But if the Home Defence Force is drained away in desperate attempts to remedy the situation in France, defeat in France will involve the final, complete and irremediable defeat of this country.[3]

Ahead of his appearance before the War Cabinet, Dowding had written to Keith Park on 15 May, possibly in search of reassurance:

We had a notable victory on the 'Home Front' this morning and the order to send more Hurricanes was cancelled. Appeals for help will doubtless be renewed, however, with increasing insistence and I do not know how this morning's work will stand the test of time; but I will never relax my efforts to prevent the dissipation of the Home Fighter forces.[4]

And Dowding, after his speech to the War Cabinet and his careful memo, prevailed; but was he right? The German troops – some hardened to the edge of psychopathy by their experience of raging across Poland, certainly gave the impression of terrifying confidence as they smashed through small French towns and tiny villages. Yet it was quite a different matter in Berlin; the sheer audacity of the push past the Maginot Line that sent the tanks rolling into the French countryside was viewed with some nervousness by a few in German High Command. And there would come a point when this advancing spearhead would have to stop, regroup and refuel. The supply lines might have been vulnerable. There was indeed an Allied fightback on 24 May at Arras; such a thing was not inconceivable. If perhaps the Allied soldiers had not witnessed traumatised refugees being sadistically picked out by diving Stukas, but instead had seen those Stukas being engaged by more Spitfires, might there have been a different view of the Wehrmacht as a whole?

Operation Dynamo – the evacuation of the British Expeditionary Force – from northern France was initially a secret so well kept that even Members of Parliament were unaware that it was under way. In the warm blue amethyst evenings of late May, a flotilla both impressive and deeply eccentric was gathered at Ramsgate and at the mouth of the Thames Estuary. The hundreds of thousands of Allied soldiers trapped in the port town of Dunkirk, and on the wide exposed beaches outside it, would clearly need an extraordinary number of vessels to get them clear and back across the Channel.

The bulk of the carrying was to be carried out by naval destroyers; but in order to transport these crowds to the larger boats out in the deeper water, little ships would be needed. Those doughty Thames barges, flat-bottomed skoots and elegant Thames yachts were to become a perfect synecdoche for Britain itself. But they were going to have to sail through fires, for those fine blue days also made conditions murderously easy for the Luftwaffe.

Douglas Bader, by now back in the cockpit with 12 Group at Duxford, recalled through his biographer, Paul Brickhill, the curious and alarming nature of those days. As 'dawn glowed in the east', he was told: 'Patrol Dunkirk, chaps, 12,000 feet [3,660 metres]. Take-off as soon as we're refuelled.' Bader replied: 'What the hell! What's happening over there?' The officer shrugged. 'Haven't the slightest idea. Something about evacuating I think.'[5]

They saw how, 'out from the Thames estuary, from Dover and the bays little boats were swarming, slowly converging, heading south east till they stretched across the sea in a straggling line, trailing feathers of foam, yachts and tugs, launches, ferries, coasters, lifeboats, paddle steamers'. Then, moments later, Bader saw the men on the beaches, thousands of them 'like ants'. There followed a dogfight with a Messerschmitt.

The ensuing days perhaps mirrored the anger that the soldiers felt below; in Bader's account, it was difficult in the air to find a fight tangible enough to take on. Flying out from Hornchurch, down the Thames and then across the Channel to France, he was aware below of the burning seaside town, the flashes of heavy artillery from the surrounding countryside and, even at the height of 910 metres (3000 feet), the heavy, thick smell of burning oil. The Messerschmitts at which Bader tried to take aim 'flicked across in front like darting sharks, winking orange flashes in the noses as they fired'. Bader fixed his sights on one, and saw another go down. 'The heady joy of the kill flooded back as he slid out over the water towards England,' wrote Paul Brickhill. 'A glow of fulfilment. Blood runs hotly at the kill when a pilot wins back his life in primitive combat.'[6]

Just a few days before, back in the lanes of England's Home Counties, Bader had been pulled over for speeding; he received a letter telling him to attend a magistrates' court in Stevenage. Bader had written to the court authorities with savagely civil sarcasm, asking that his case be deferred while he undertook his flying duties. The court was having none of it; in his absence, he was fined £2 10s. Bader, now luminous with rage, wrote a cheque to the court and sent it along with a letter apologising that he could not have been there, but that he was attending to another matter at Dunkirk. The story illustrates the way that ordinary life went on with ruthless stolidity in Britain even at a moment of extreme national crisis.

At Fighter Command, the nature of the emergency of the German invasion had meant an extemporised response. At 11 Group headquarters in Uxbridge, Keith Park ran up against the most obvious logistical difficulty; Dunkirk was quite a distance away to be covered by short-range fighters, and the time they spent over the town before they had to return and refuel would necessarily be limited.

As soon as Dynamo was under way, the fighter effort was co-ordinated at the station at Hawkinge on the Kent coast, very close to Dover. Staff at Hawkinge reported back to Keith Park. This was Fighter Command's first serious engagement with the enemy. Park knew of the unique and terrible stresses that were placed upon pilots even in quieter periods; at the start of an entirely new kind of conflict, he had to ensure that the men had all the support they could get.

He was thinking in physical as well as psychological terms; for as great as the mental effort and focus of flying in combat was the strain imposed on clenched muscles and limbs. His idea, according to Vincent Orange, was that there would be short periods of heavy duty for those in the air and their support crews on the ground; these would be followed by long periods in which the pilots would be able to enjoy the most comfortable surroundings possible. They would fly in the mornings and in the afternoons; consideration was given to lunch and even to tea. Pilots would take off from their permanent bases, but when returning to refuel they would land at forward bases closer to the coast.

Meanwhile the Luftwaffe attacked northern France with demonic ferocity. Roads out of small towns leading towards the coast were choked with frantic refugees, who were picked off from above by German pilots almost as a macabre form of target practice.

The Air Ministry and the army wanted continuous daylight patrols above the beaches of Dunkirk, with fighter planes deployed in strength; but such an arrangement was logistically tricky. Either they had continuous patrols or they had fighter planes out there in great numbers; but there were not enough planes to put on continuous shows of strength. This might be one of the reasons why aggrieved soldiers imagined that the RAF was simply abandoning them to their fate; compared to the relentless attacks from the Germans, the British simply seemed to be almost invisible. Yet the fighter planes were up there, and it has been recorded that they did an effective job of protecting the harbour of Dunkirk to the extent that hundreds of thousands of Allied soldiers were able to use it for embarkation.

Midway through this extraordinary crisis, Keith Park himself flew across the Channel over Dunkirk to see conditions first hand. He concluded from his observations – and after having spoken to other pilots – that the best way to counter the Stukas was not a continual presence over the area (difficult to manage because of the need for constant replacement planes while the others went back to refuel) but fighter planes flying in twos and sometimes fours, the better to engage the enemy directly, in order to draw their focus away from the beaches and the vulnerable soldiers below.

The fact that so many Allied soldiers were successfully rescued from Dunkirk (Churchill and the War Cabinet had anticipated that only 45,000 would escape) was therefore tangentially thanks to fighter pilots high above. But now Dowding and all at Bentley Priory, along with everyone else in the country – from the War Cabinet downwards – were expecting a full-scale German invasion of British shores. Ever the optimist, Keith

Park was 'exhilarated' by the prospect; the dangerous days of Dunkirk had given him an opportunity to see how his defensive procedures worked in action.

And it was now that Winston Churchill made that extraordinary, immortal speech in Parliament, remembered chiefly for its declaration that 'we will fight on the beaches'. In fact, this speech – reproduced in *The Times* on 5 June 1940 – was longer than many now think, and included a lengthy passage concerning the RAF and Fighter Command that encapsulated a certain incongruous romanticism. The imagery was quite deliberate: 'May it not be,' he asked rhetorically, 'that the cause of civilisation will be defended by the skill and devotion of a few thousand airmen? There never has been, I suppose, in all the world, in all the history of war, such an opportunity for youth. The Knights of the Round Table, the Crusaders, all fall back into the past – not only distant but prosaic. These young men, going forth every morn to guard their native land, and all that we stand for, holding in their hands these instruments of colossal and shattering power, of whom it may be said that "Every morn brought forth a noble chance/And every chance brought forth a noble knight" deserve our gratitude.'

The line of poetry that Churchill quoted was from Alfred Lord Tennyson's *Idylls of The King* – specifically, the moment at which Sir Bedivere cries out over the dying form of King Arthur. Chivalry, death and the possibility of future resurrection (Arthur was the 'once and future king'); this vision of warfare was a dimension apart from the nightmare of the First World War – it was cleaner, purer. Nor would Churchill be alone in envisaging Fighter Command in these terms.

The fighter pilots were prepared, as still yet more young men went into training. But what of the nerve centre of the operation? How prepared for this defining moment were the young men and women of Fighter Command?

Chapter Ten

Alert

The people of Britain were nerving themselves for full-scale invasion. There were some who dreaded sleeping; they had recurring nightmares about the Nazis making land. The men of the Local Defence Volunteers – often armed with whatever items they were able to scrounge, including antique cannons from local museums – were, in June 1940, being joined by the returned soldiers, who had been forced to leave their weaponry behind on the French coast in order to make the mass evacuation possible. Yet the events of Dunkirk had somehow been a national adrenaline shot; even the omniscient sounding Ministry of Information had been caught on the back foot by the wave of exhilaration that had greeted the spectacle of the rescued soldiers. Though the German attack was expected, there was something quite new in the air.

For the squadrons of Fighter Command, there was the ever pressing need to get more young pilots trained. The backgrounds of the new recruits differed from those who had been there for some time, and who often had previous flying experience, but recruits who survived training still displayed an almost innate ability to fly in harmony with their machines; to sense and react to what a Spitfire could and could not do in the air. It was a striking combination: a form of balletic grace combined with cold, ruthless aggression – kill or be killed.

There is a photograph from the time, utterly arresting and haunting: it simply shows a young fighter pilot curled up in an armchair, by a fireplace, in an officers' mess. He is in full uniform, clearly ready to fly; and he appears to be asleep, his legs over the side of the chair and his hand near his mouth, giving an initially disconcerting impression that he is sucking his thumb. It is, though, equally disconcerting how very young this man looks. There is an extraordinary innocence and youth about the way that he is arranged in the chair. And we also get the impression that he is not sleeping at all; that his eyes are shut and relaxation is being feigned because if they weren't, then he would be pacing up and down furiously, racked with tension. This is a portrait of a boy who will shortly be required to vault into the heavens, piloting complex machinery and facing savage jeopardy. You cannot help thinking to yourself: what if that had been you at the age of eighteen?

All around these youngsters was woven an intricate web of support; not merely from the experienced ground staff, working with laser-sharp focus to ensure that the planes – and the pilots – were in peak condition, but also from the men and women around the country who were listening closely to the enemy over the airwaves. Just a few weeks previously, at Bletchley Park, a young codebreaker called John Herivel had brilliantly found a way to crack the Luftwaffe's Enigma codes, the means by which the most secret information and battle orders were conveyed between commanders and pilots. Partly Herivel's work was based on psychological insight into the Enigma operators and how they might set up their machines each day. From that point onwards, Bletchley Park was able to read much of the Luftwaffe's secret traffic, relaying intelligence directly to Bentley Priory.

Added to this was the work of the Y Service; large numbers of Wrens, members of the Women's Royal Naval Service (WRNS), based in small coastal stations, eavesdropping on radio communications between Luftwaffe pilots. As the war intensified, some of these women found that the work had a curious intimacy to it; they came to know, from their voices, individual German pilots. Some of the pilots knew very well that their radio conversations were being monitored, and they seemed not to care very much. A few sometimes addressed remarks directly to the young women they presumed were listening in to them. As the daily dogfights started claiming their inevitable victims, the Wrens of the Y Service found themselves listening to familiar pilots 'screaming and cursing' as their planes went down in searing flames. A few Wrens recalled how – despite themselves – they found these moments deeply upsetting. The information provided by Bletchley and the Y Service was not always useful on a day-to-day basis, though it had proved invaluable beforehand in revealing the buildup of Luftwaffe forces and it also provided an in-depth picture of great strategic value, from key Luftwaffe figures to technology, all of which was stored in cross-referenced card file indexes. Nonetheless, combined with radar and the work of the tireless Observer Corps, it offered Dowding and his lieutenants at Bentley Priory the assurance that the enemy was being monitored as closely as possible, and that each scrap of information held out the possibility of keeping ahead of Goering.

Indeed, as the pilots of Tangmere and Hornchurch and North Weald and Biggin Hill flew increasingly hazardous sorties – now piercingly aware that the enemy no longer had to fly long distances in order to strike at the land beneath them – their work needed ever higher levels of accuracy from those working on the ground in order to be genuinely effective. The women of Bentley Priory had pilots' lives in their hands when they calculated at top speed the positions of the innumerable aircraft massing to assault. But how ready were these women?

Twenty-year-old Gladys Eva was at Bentley on the eve of the Battle of Britain, filled with fizz and a profound excitement. 'It was quite extraordinary,' she says. 'They had literally only just that day opened up the underground Operations Room. So everybody was there: medics, boffins, all there trying to work out how it was going to work. But the medics were the most interested: they were worried about us WAAFs. We had to have tests – eyes, blood, everything – because they were very concerned about the effect it would have on us. But we were tough. There was a job to be done and that was that.'

This was also no time for girls from a sheltered background to be delicate. 'We also had lectures on VD and syphilis and I had never heard of anything like that!' says Mrs Eva, roaring with laughter. 'I was under the chair, honestly. I thought, What am I hearing? I jolly soon learned, I tell you.'

And she immediately fell in love with the atmosphere of Bentley Priory and the structure of Fighter Command. 'I was fascinated, of course. We had such an interesting time. It was early on and the boffins were still working down there in quite large numbers. You would always have two or three of them down there with you, trying to work out if they had got the whole system right.'

There was a lot of testing; everyone had to be absolutely clear about the sort of operation they were about to embark on. This was a new kind of war; on all levels, the new techniques had to be checked neurotically. No detail was too small to overlook.

'No one really knew about the work,' Mrs Eva continues. 'We were the pioneers.' Even if not every detail was imparted to her, Mrs Eva was well aware that she was working at the heart of something that a decade ago would have been regarded as supernatural agency.

'This radar system was something amazing,' she says. 'On a really fine day, you could pick up the Germans from take-off. It didn't often happen. But I've seen it happen. Then you would plot them, and they would be massing together. And we all knew what was heading for us.'

Nor were the women simply automata to be guided by the rhythms of the new technology; from the start, they took a great deal of initiative and their superiors at Fighter Command were grateful for it. 'We did two or three days learning how the system of radar worked,' says Eileen Younghusband, 'and how it was used. Superficial, in a way, but enough to give us a picture. They gave us varying tests. Then we were separated out. Some of the people who were manually dextrous and perhaps not so good on other things became radar operatives, because their role was going to be manual. Anybody who was good at maths was immediately put in the Filter Room. And then the rest went into the Operations Room.'

There was one other extremely important requirement: precise diction. At Bentley Priory – and other Fighter Command stations – clear Received Pronunciation was regarded as being literally a matter of life and death. 'At Bentley, you had to speak what was then called the King's English. Because imagine the radar operators talking on a telephone line to a filter room plotter. They would be giving all the salient information. They would say "Stand by, new track" and then give the actual position – estimated 50-plus [miles, 80-plus kilometres] and 10,000 feet [3,048 metres] ... And if that man had had a broad Geordie accent and the girl this end had a Welsh accent and she had to say "Could you repeat that?" – the information would probably be half a minute late and it would go on the table with the wrong number.'

Meanwhile, Patricia Clark's initial dismay at the first sight of her work – the very idea that she would be 'playing tiddlywinks' – dissipated very fast. 'As I got to know what it was all about, it was a different matter altogether. It was exciting and I loved my work. I was never at a stage where I wished I wasn't doing it.'

Mrs Clark had less pure interest in the scientific side; she was more interested in grappling with the practicalities. 'We went off for a fortnight during training to Bawdsey Manor, where we were told about the Dowding system and I don't honestly think I took an awful lot of it in. I wasn't awfully interested in the background – only in what we were doing, not how we came to be doing it. The seriousness of the situation didn't really evolve until after Dunkirk probably, when I realised how crucial the whole thing was.

'There wasn't a lot of incoming flying the first year that I was involved, because everything was going on over there on the continent. But there was the excitement of being on duty – and then all the enormous education in what went on in the big wide world. Then there was Dunkirk: then the flying started ... I also had friends, two cousins, who went into the Air Force, killed fairly early on in the Battle of Britain,' she says quietly. 'We all had friends who were involved in active duty. One chap who went to Dunkirk had his arm blown off. So one was very much involved in the war.'

The fall of France had brought expert exiles: Polish airmen, among whom were some who had tried – with very limited numbers of planes – to hold off the German invasion of September 1939. Their ideas on air defence were interestingly similar to those of Air Chief Marshal Dowding; like Fighter Command, the Polish had used a system of 'ground observers alerting a central control point, which in turn was in radio communication with flight commanders on patrol'. What they lacked, however, was Dowding's secret ingredient: radar. On top of this, they had but a fraction of the air power of the Germans.

After Poland had been brutally overrun, many pilots had decided to continue the fight by travelling – often by circuitous and hazardous routes – to France. As the Germans then swept through the Low Countries and across the Maginot Line, the Polish flew and fought bravely, though again in planes that had little of the nimbleness or versatility of British fighters. And now, in that moment of summer when Britain was caught in breathless suspension, a squadron of Polish pilots was formed, first coalescing in Blackpool. Commanded by a British squadron leader, Ronald Kellet (together with Canadian Flight Lieutenant John Kent), 303 Squadron was pulled together with some fine Polish air veterans.

Initially there were obstacles, not least of which was the language. Kent later recalled:

> We were not only faced with the problem of forming and training the squadron in a normal way, we also had to teach rudimentary English and convert the pilots on to our aircraft, which were Hurricanes. This presented more problems than one would normally expect, as some of the pilots had never flown aircraft with retractable undercarriages. Also, throttles worked in reverse direction, few had handled constant speed propellers, the air-speed was indicated in miles per hour instead of kilometres and the altimeter registered feet instead of metres.
>
> All this led to some interesting situations, as one can imagine. Furthermore, our tactics were different and they had never heard of radar or interceptions

controlled from the ground. I was amazed and very favourably impressed at how rapidly the Poles mastered these complexities – both pilots and ground crews.[1]

The squadron was moved into the southeast, 11 Group's area of command, and set up base at RAF Northolt on the western fringes of London. Issues of language – for all Polish pilots across the country – were dealt with smartly by the RAF, and manuals were specially issued with Polish translations. It was clear at first that Fighter Command – although welcoming its new recruits – did not quite know how to slot the Poles in with the other squadrons. The lack of English and the question of how they might handle formations and complex orders from the ground was only one element; there was also apparently concern about the Poles' morale.

Such qualms were understandable but also a lamentable underestimation of this fresh intake. The Polish pilots had seen their country, their communities and their families fall under the shadow of both German and Soviet subjugation; many had fought their way through an increasingly unstable eastern Europe in their efforts to get to France and then to Britain. Their desire for vengeance was volcanic.

There were a great many Canadian and Australian pilots too; and among them some Americans. Officially, since the USA was a very long way from joining the war, these men had no business or right to be flying with the Royal Air Force. The numbers can therefore only be a guess. The RAF itself has identified eleven American pilots who flew and fought in that summer of 1940, but there might well have been many more. Some crossed the border from America into Canada and signed up with the Air Force there.

Despite the extra recruits, Fighter Command didn't have enough pilots; it didn't have enough planes. Its aerodromes in the southeast were almost pitiably vulnerable. Radar was a boon, but was also skittish and by no means some magic wand to wave.

And yet despite the weaknesses, which were apparent to everyone, those young pilots – alongside the super-alert ground crews and the sharp young women of Fighter Command – set their faces to the coming battle with extraordinary verve, their fear masked by the beguiling optimism of youth.

Chapter Eleven

The Sky was Black with Planes

If you have ever flown across America, coast to coast, and looked out of the aeroplane window, you will have seen how extraordinarily vast and empty that country is; just a few minutes to the east of Los Angeles, you are crossing desert that seems to stretch away without limit. The reverse is true for Britain; from the air, there is almost always something to be seen below.

For the Luftwaffe in 1940, there was even more than there is today in terms of potential targets: vast industrial plants, sprawling factories turned over to the war effort, the dark bulks of riverside power stations, lines and lines of glittering rails leading to railway marshalling yards filled with coal and with food for the cities. For those German pilots now based near the coast of northern France, a short hop across the grey Channel would bring them to Dover, to Ramsgate, to Deal. Pilots a little further south in France could look easily at the mighty docks of Southampton, and at Portsmouth. For German pilots carrying out reconnaissance missions, a surprisingly short journey would take them far inland, to counties like Berkshire, Oxfordshire, even as far northwest as Cheshire. In the summer of 1940, Britain was rich and replete with potential bombing targets; and that was even before the cities and the towns and their civilian populations were taken into account.

Also there for the picking was the enormous amount of cargo being transported back and forth in convoys, through the English Channel and up the east coast of Britain. At this moment of national crisis, the Cabinet and Fighter Command were left to second-guess what the German plan might be. Certainly there would be a sustained attack from the air, with a view to invading, or forcing the country to capitulate and seek terms. The question was: what course of action would the Luftwaffe decide upon? Were there to be swarms of paratroopers, as in the Low Countries? A sudden lightning strike on British airfields and bases, disabling the capabilities of the fighters? A sustained assault upon shipping, endangering the country's food supplies? Or a campaign of bombing so relentless that the net result would not merely be a huge death toll but also exhaustion and badly damaged morale among a sleep-deprived workforce?

Churchill had given the battle a name before it began; in the aftermath of Dunkirk, he told the people that they would now be facing a 'Battle of Britain'. It is generally held that that battle began on 10 July 1940. The initial assault was upon shipping and the towns of the south coast. The Air Ministry was very quick to reinterpret the attacks. 'The greatest damage on the German Air Force since bombing raids on this country began,' ran the communiqué. The newspapers were beguiled and so too, it seems, were eager English onlookers. 'There were air fights all day long, mostly off the south and east coast of England,' reported *The Times*. 'They began soon after dawn … [there were] Spitfire pilots patrolling the Kentish coast … three British fighters attacked one formation of Messerschmitt 110s.' A nameless pilot was quoted describing another attack as being like 'a cylinder of circling enemy aircraft'. The report described how the pilot 'climbed to the top of the circle, then did a spiral dive down towards the centre, attacked a Messerschmitt and a Dornier … and put them both out.'

Though one might have expected newspapers to place emphasis on German losses, the fact was that the Luftwaffe was by no means invulnerable. There had been a number of losses throughout the Battle of France, and it was taking some weeks simply to put machines through repairs and obtain the supplies required to begin an attack on Britain in earnest.

Later, Dowding observed: 'I wouldn't like to differentiate between the material and aircrews of the Luftwaffe and the Air Force … In technical skill and in courage we could claim no superiority over the Germans, although there was of course a very great difference in spirit. I don't think that any higher degree of skill and courage could possibly have been expected.'[1] But there was one serious difference, certainly as Dowding saw it; and that was the nature of the authorities that they answered to.

Dowding and Fighter Command had already demonstrated that their voices were heard; the plea of 15 May to the War Cabinet to conserve forces for the fight to come would not have been mirrored in German High Command. In other words, Goering and the Luftwaffe had no choice but to accede to the whims and desires of Hitler, and Hitler alone. The forthcoming invasion of Britain would not be a matter for debate in German High Command. But this element – the caprice of an already notoriously capricious dictator – made Hitler's next moves very tricky to anticipate. At the time, Dowding said: 'It is difficult to prophesy the exact sequence of events in an attempted invasion; but it appears at least possible that the enemy might not launch any seaborne attack in heavy ships or barges until he had established a pied-à-terre somewhere on the coast by means of troops, guns, and even tanks, transported by air.'[2] He foresaw that German paratroopers might aim to capture one of the British air bases near the sea. Then carriers could sail in with more troops and more weaponry, under cover of more air attacks, frenzied in their ferocity.

There were two fearful examples: the pulverising of Holland a few weeks beforehand, and the Nazi invasion of Norway just weeks before that. Dowding noted that once the Germans got a foothold, however precarious it seemed, they were apparently incredibly difficult to 'dislodge'.

On 10 July, there was a fearsome assault upon shipping in the Channel. The captain of one boat gave this eye-witness account:

> Hundreds of bombs fell all around. It was just like a shower of hail. Some of the raiders were shot down in flames. Through my glasses [binoculars], I saw the tails fall off two of them as they crashed into the sea, chopped off by machine gun bullets from British fighters. More German aeroplanes then flew over us and they were attacked by Spitfires and Hurricanes. The sky was black with planes.[3]

They had been so since before dawn; that was when the first of the German craft started reconnaissance and meteorological flights, the length of England's south coast and further afield. According to the official history, a Spitfire caught and destroyed a Dornier over Yarmouth, on the east coast, at 5.20 a.m. on 10 July. The Dornier had been spying on shipping; several hours later, a convoy in the vicinity was attacked. Further south, the pioneering radar system picked up a build-up of German planes in the region of Calais. Just twenty minutes later, that formation of planes was swooping in on a convoy sailing past Dover. It was defended by six planes from 32 Squadron. 'We claimed the certain destruction of seven of the enemy at the cost of one pilot,' states the official history, 'while the convoy only lost one four-hundred-ton ship, a ludicrously small return for so great an effort on the part of the Germans.'

But further west along the coast, the positions were reversed; a German plane, flying alone, managed to slip across the water and bomb the harbour at Falmouth in Cornwall with devastating results. One vast ship was sunk outright and several others went up in an inferno. It was concluded that the new radar system had its weak or blank spots; this part of the southwest was clearly one of them.

In early July, Dowding had expressed misgivings about the idea of Fighter Command having to devote men and planes to the defence of shipping; he was looking forward to when the convoys would be routed around the north of England and Scotland. On that first day of the Battle of Britain, Dowding and Keith Park must have felt their hearts to be the weight of anvils; so too must the young pilots of 11 Group who were expected to meet head-on a force whose size they could not calculate. It was those pilots who were most directly in range, and on whom the responsibility disproportionately fell.

Spitfire pilot Geoffrey Wellum was among those who had been relocated closer to the front line in the sky, down at the Biggin Hill base in Surrey. In his memoir, he wrote of those days: 'This must be England at her most endangered, and her most dangerous. She is alone. Nobody else in the whole world to help her. Taking tremendous punishment, her back to the wall, but dishing it out too. We can only go forward. Can't go back any further. Bloody Nazis. Someone has got to stop them.'[4]

An island under siege: that feeling, shared by the majority of the population, was acutely heightened for the pilots.

Lying on their beds and trying to sleep – imagine trying to sleep in those circumstances, knowing what the next day is going to bring – they would often hear the distant drone of a German plane high above and their anxiety would be intensified further. A soldier on the ground was one thing; you could defend, attack, know roughly which way he would move. But the freedom of the air meant that the realm above was so much more difficult to defend.

Those early days of sustained German attack also put a huge strain on the brand new system installed at Bentley Priory – the Operations Room and the Filter Room. 'It was very, very physical – and you had to be pinpoint perfect,' recalls Gladys Eva. 'There was never any room for a mistake. Particularly when you were telling [marking down co-ordinates]. If you put a counter half an inch out of line, you were putting the whole shoot out. It was very particular. Mentally you were tired by the time you went off watch. But I never wanted to go off. I loved it.'

Mrs Eva's recollections about accuracy were echoed throughout the Air Ministry. Interception was a lickety-split business; if the timings were out, the fighters would be too late to stop the enemy from raining fire down on their targets. But all sorts of complications were thrown in for women such as Gladys Eva and the staff of the Filter Room; first, there had to be a built-in time lag from the time the planes were first registered by the new radar system. Then a certain amount of intuition was needed when it came to calculating the height of the planes. The Spitfires wanted to get above them; but often, the Germans would swoop in low and – counter-intuitively – begin to climb the closer they came to the British shore.

For the women and men hoping to interpret the distant echoes from the atmosphere, training only went so far; they needed the real experience that would bring more instinctive responses. Imagine if their timings erred towards the premature, indicating that the Germans were approaching faster than they actually were. The young Spitfire pilots might be launched into the air too early, causing confusion when trying to get a bearing on the enemy and creating problems with the planes' limited fuel supply; there was only so long they could stay in the air without having to come back down again. There were other difficulties: the system might detect traces of enemy planes, but the significance of their flights and their routes still required correct interpretation. The enemy was canny, sending up decoy flights to trick fighter squadrons into staying up in the air before being hit with another force flying at them from out of the sun. The mathematical co-ordinates could only reveal so much; the rest would have to come from a kind of sixth sense borne from experience. On the ground, pilots were starting to overestimate the heights that they would need to climb to, their aim to literally stay on top of the enemy.

The German focus sharpened in July 1940; and it sharpened on the shipping. Protected by circles of fighters, German bombers delivered murderous attacks on convoys and other shipping in the Straits of Dover. They were also working in conjunction with the German navy; pilots high above would send details of convoys on to E-boats, the sleek German fast-attack vessels.

In other words, it was an almost impossible proposition for the pilots of 11 Group. On the other side of the Channel, the Germans had absolute freedom over when, how, and in what numbers they would launch their attacks over the sea; squadron leaders and the personnel of Bentley Priory could only, at best, second-guess them. It was also the case that 11 Group was formidably outnumbered; not only were the Germans frequently high above them, but in daunting numbers too. The pilots could see with their own eyes just how many bombers and fighters they were attempting to fight off; the scale of the enemy's forces compared to their own. Yet they were to go up continually, day after day. The biography of Douglas Bader lays great emphasis on his aggression; a similar attribute, found within all the pilots of 11 Group and running counter to their insouciant public image, helps to explain their persistence in carrying on the fight against such odds, although different accounts and memoirs suggest that it came in the form of icy cold-bloodedness as opposed to hot temper.

In the pilot logbooks one can now examine in the archives – so carefully and formally printed, bound in black or blue leather, with names embossed on the cover in gold, and columns inside for 'aeroplane type and number', 'time', 'height', 'course' and 'remarks' – can be found reports of this incessant daily activity. We see a little of that studied brevity, yet also flashes of surprising boyishness. In one pilot's logbook – that of H.R.L. Hood from Manston, detailing days in late July 1940 – we see that he has been taking his Spitfire up over Kent between three and five times a day; that he has been on 'interception patrol' and 'convoy patrol' and occasionally on interception between Manston and Hornchurch. Then in one day's entry, amid these clipped 'remarks', we see two little hand-drawn swastikas – one with a leg going the wrong way, showing then as now how oddly difficult swastikas are to draw from memory. These represent the two German planes that he succeeded in shooting down. 'Shot down one '87 and one 09' is his only comment. A day later, we find him back up in the air, on three sorties, once more on patrol.

Another logbook, that of W.E. Coope, carries on its cover one man's proud progress through the RAF: the titles 'Flight Officer', 'Flight Lieutenant' and 'Squadron Leader' have each been scrubbed out in turn, and underneath them on

158

this palimpsest is the title 'Wing Commander'. Amid the flights and missions marked 'secret', there are occasional glimpses of human frailty; the entry for one period in 1940 does not deal with flights taken but makes a very quick nod to 'hospitalisation' for 'jaundice'. Of course in strict terms, pilots were not supposed to keep diaries; yet looking through a logbook now – all those meticulously recorded sorties, and the time they took – it doesn't take too much imagination to peer between the lines, to envisage the daily task of conquering the most understandable fear in the world in order to get out back among the clouds.

The dogfights over the roiling waters of the Channel quickly brought home another advantage that the Germans appeared to enjoy; when their bombers were shot down, they were frequently able to rescue the pilots, quickly picking them up and sailing off in E-boats. It was different for the British, at least at first: when either a Spitfire or a Hurricane was hit, and was forced to plunge into the water, the plane would tip over nose first – and sink almost immediately. This was a further terror in store for the pilots; if not death or mutilation in some nightmare inferno, then drowning in black, freezing waters, your body never to be seen again. Many pilots were unable to stop imagining the idea of sinking to the bottom of the sea and staying there forever, forgotten. The early days of the Battle of Britain led to changes; the navy and coastal stations were made ready to launch boats to swiftly retrieve any pilots who might have managed to get free of their planes before that final plunge.

Yet what were the aims of the Luftwaffe? What were the aims of the Führer himself? On 19 July 1940, as German planes locked on to their shipping targets with increasing confidence, and by night laid mines in the waters, Hitler gave a speech to the Reichstag, reported in the *Manchester Guardian*, in which he sought to portray himself as the voice of reason, and Churchill as the blood-stained warmonger in cahoots with Jewish financiers:

> Believe me, gentlemen, I feel a deep disgust for this kind of unscrupulous politician who wrecks whole nations and states. It almost causes me pain to think that I should have been selected by fate to deal the final blow to the structure which these men have already set tottering. It never has been my intention to wage war, but rather to build up a state with a new social order and the finest possible standard of culture.
>
> Mr Churchill ought for once, perhaps, to believe me when I prophesy that a great empire will be destroyed – an empire that it was never my intention to destroy or even harm. I do however realise that this struggle, if it continues, can end only with the complete annihilation of one or the other of the two adversaries. Mr Churchill may believe that this will be Germany. I know it will be Britain. In this hour, I feel it to be my duty before my own conscience to appeal once more to reason and common sense to Great Britain as much as elsewhere ... I am not the vanquished seeking favours but the victor speaking in the name of reason.

On the same day, the Air Ministry reported an epic battle in the skies above the south coast as the Luftwaffe made another determined attack on both shipping and harbours. 'Spitfires, Hurricanes and anti-aircraft guns all helped to beat off the enemy ...' ran the report. 'In the second action, which took place in the afternoon, more than 50 German bombers and fighters attempted to raid a south coast harbour. Six patrolling Hurricanes swept up to engage the enemy. Three, however, were immediately attacked by twelve Messerschmitts and the other three Hurricane pilots counter-attacked. Three Spitfires chased two other Messerschmitts.' The report glowingly detailed the German planes that had been shot down; nor did it shy away from the obvious fact that the British pilots were at all points heavily outnumbered.

The Spitfires were also flying through atrocious Channel weather; on 24 July, they brought down twelve German bombers in very heavy rain. The relentlessness of the German attacks, it is suggested in the official history, was only partly to do with the harassment of shipping, and perhaps more to do with wearing Fighter Command down; day after day, awake in the pre-dawn darkness, all of this might have been expected to start sapping the mental strength of even the most committedly aggressive fighter pilot. There was a double futility about fighting in rain and cloud: the enemy's aims blurred by horrendous conditions, the defenders knowing that palpable hits in thick billowing cloud would be reduced. And for the defending pilots, the added hazard of knowing when to call it off, and try to reach home.

It was not just the southeast corner of the country that seemed to be acutely vulnerable in those opening days of the battle. Dowding had fears for the southwest too: the industry and ports of south Wales, as well as the great bases at Plymouth and Falmouth. He arranged for heavy anti-aircraft guns to be moved to the region, and also ordered the deployment of more vast barrage balloons as a further line of precaution. And more balloons were ordered for Dover, and for the coastline around. Ever since the Dunkirk evacuation, Dover had been recognised as being of key strategic significance, both as a focus for the Navy and as a possible bridgehead for the enemy.

Towards the end of July came the first inkling of official disquiet with Dowding's approach to the defence of Great

Britain; the first sense in the corridors of the Air Ministry and of Whitehall that the thinking had to be altered. Some had begun to question the use of coastal airfields; 11 Group, whose pilots had been shouldering so much of the weight of responsibility, were still based at the inland stations of Croydon, Biggin Hill and Hornchurch, making only occasional use of coastal stations such as Rochford in Essex and Hawkinge in Kent. Dowding's superiors were puzzled: why couldn't the fighter squadrons be more permanently sited on the coast? That way, surely they would be faster to meet and intercept the enemy.

Perhaps this was so, although it has been pointed out that once the Germans were flying over the Channel, it wouldn't have made a great deal of difference in terms of timing. There was another consideration: for the Germans, the coastal airstrips made exceedingly tempting and relatively accessible targets. The advantage of being stationed a little further inland was that the pilots' bases were less vulnerable. It might take a few minutes' more flying time to meet the enemy, but at least they knew that they would have a runway to return to.

There was another element to the whispering campaign against Dowding, and this was to do with the debate that dated back to the 1920s. Should Britain not have been taking the air fight to the enemy? A couple of weeks earlier in July 1940, Churchill had declared as much to War Cabinet colleagues: 'There is one thing that will bring him [Hitler] back and bring him down and that is an absolutely devastating exterminating attack by very heavy bombers from this country upon the Nazi homeland. We must be able to overwhelm them by these means, without which I do not see a way through.'[5]

Many in the Air Ministry agreed, among them the 67-year-old Lord Trenchard, former Commander in Chief of the

RAF. He had retired from the service some years back, and had been persuaded in the 1930s into taking control of the Metropolitan Police. With the outbreak of war, Lord Trenchard was eager to offer his expertise to the Air Ministry, and he, like others, watched Air Chief Marshal Dowding with dissatisfaction; this complex defensive network was getting Britain no further towards winning the war. Trenchard was among those who thought it would be better if Dowding was removed from his post. The fact that the two men had worked closely and with mutual regard some ten years before was neither here nor there. This was a philosophical and existential dispute: mere survival versus total victory. Trenchard's belief in the bomber, and in much more aggressive tactics, chimed with that of Churchill.

The Luftwaffe was growing bolder; one sortie in late July saw bombers flying from more southerly points on the French coast, and crossing Britain. Birmingham received its first bombing raid. Liverpool attracted German attention. A bomb was dropped on a munitions factory in Hatfield in Hertfordshire. Another difficulty faced in those early days by the Filter Room was sometimes the sheer numbers of planes being tracked; if in sufficiently large numbers, with different targets, the tracks would end up in a labyrinthine state. With time would come the experience to unravel the larger picture through intensive analysis, but in a wholly new kind of conflict, never before experienced, skilled extemporisation was key. Dowding, for instance, arranged for squadrons from the north of Scotland and north of England to be drafted down south, and for less successful fighter planes like the Defiant to be moved to quieter regions.

So in one light, the cavalier treatment of Hugh Dowding in terms of job security is almost blackly comic. Just as Britain's fight for its very existence was under way, the Air Chief Marshal of Fighter Command had no idea whether he was about to be forcibly retired. He also knew little about the extent of the talk against him in very senior circles. Back in March 1940, Dowding's superiors had extended his contract of service to 14 July 1940. At the beginning of July, with all nerves taut for the coming conflict, Dowding not unreasonably tried to find out whether he was about to be given the push, or whether he was to be granted yet one more postponement. Quite apart from any feeling of personal slight – though he would have been hardly human not to have felt resentful – Dowding knew that any changeover might also mean a fundamental change in approach, one that would affect all of his pilots.

Dowding got hold of the Chief of the Air Staff, Sir Cyril Newall. There was what is sometimes described as a full and frank exchange of views. Dowding had demanded of his superior on the telephone, 'If you want to get rid of me, then get rid of me, but don't do it in this way.'

Newall then wrote to Dowding; given the nature of the times, the climbdown was hardly wholehearted:

> I am writing to ask if you will again defer your retirement beyond the date which I last gave you of July 14th. Under present conditions I should be more than loathe [sic] for you to leave Fighter Command on that date and I would be very glad if you would continue in your appointment as Air Officer Commanding-In-Chief until the end of October. If, as I sincerely hope you will be, you are willing to accept the extension, an official letter to this effect will be sent to you in due course, and I will also write to you regarding your successor.[6]

It was hardly a ringing endorsement; Dowding was swift to write back. Again, this was partly pride (the shabbiness of his treatment went beyond conventional rudeness into something bordering on contempt) but also, more pointedly, conviction that he knew how Britain's air defence should be run:

> Apart from the question of discourtesy, which I do not wish to stress, I must point out the lack of consideration involved in delaying a proposal of this nature until ten days before the date of my retirement. I have had four retiring dates given to me and now you are proposing a fifth. Before the war … I should have been glad enough to retire; now I am anxious to stay, because I feel that there is no-one else who will fight as I do when proposals are made which would reduce the Defence Forces of the Country below the extreme danger point.[7]

He was referring to those squadrons mooted for France, back in May. A smoother diplomat might have made an effort not to bring up old rows; Dowding on the other hand was direct in citing what he clearly considered a personal triumph – thwarting the will of the Air Ministry and the War Cabinet to ensure the safety of the country. It is not difficult to see how such an attitude would cause answering resentment. There were those in the Air Ministry younger and, as they would have seen it, more modern-minded. Dowding was a man of the last war. In Sir Cyril Newall, moreover, he was up against a gifted office politician. Word reached the Secretary of State for Air, Sir Archibald Sinclair, who wrote to Dowding in treacly tones. In turn, Newall got to hear about this correspondence, and wrote to Dowding again: 'I can understand that you feel that you have not been treated with the consideration you would wish, but I must ask you to put this down to the stress of events in recent years, of which we are both only too well aware. May I ask you to accept my sincere apologies.' But there was a postscript which revealed that Newall had been seriously needled by the suggestion that Dowding, and Dowding alone, knew how best to defend the nation. Newall wrote that he was

> unable to agree that there is no-one else who could resist as you do proposals to reduce the defence forces of this country below the extreme danger point ... Only last month, I was glad to have your support at the Cabinet when the question of sending fighter squadrons to France was under consideration. I must point out that the policy of the Air Staff has consistently been directed towards conserving our Air Defence Forces in the face of the various conflicting aims that have right or wrongly been made upon them.[8]

This was the point at which Dowding levitated with rage; indeed, the resentment never really appeared to leave him. For of course, he had stood quite alone in that session of Cabinet, making his impassioned case for not sending any more fighter squadrons over to doomed France; there had been no loud cries of 'hear hear' as he had presented his checklist of reasons to the Prime Minister. Yet again, though, a more skilled diplomat might accept that, just occasionally, this is how one's superiors behave.

By the end of July, the precise meaning of the German tactics was still a matter of debate. The attacks on shipping had been relentless and yet, according to the official history, simultaneously ineffective. But cunning Luftwaffe decoy tactics were effectively deployed to boost coastal bombing raids, drawing fighters into unnecessary action while elsewhere, larger numbers of the enemy were homing in on their targets; in early August, for instance, RAF fighters made contact over Dorset with huge numbers of Messerschmitts that had flown over from Cherbourg. There followed an epic and terrifying battle in the air – but the Luftwaffe's aim that day was to exhaust its foe. That battle was actually intended to draw fire away from an even larger German bombing party that was making ineluctably for the Dorset harbour of Portland.

'The railway line at Portland station was blocked, a submarine school was hit, two oil tanks were set on fire, two small destroyers were slightly damaged and there was a good deal of damage to private property,' records the official history. Yet, even here, the bombing raid was not counted as being especially effective; the formation of bombers and escorting fighters was fought off by 213 Squadron. Later that day, there were German attacks on tankers off the coast of Norfolk, and a concerted effort to destroy the barrage balloons and defences of Dover. On that day, 11 August, British losses were heavy: twenty-five pilots killed or missing, twenty-eight aircraft destroyed. On a day-by-day basis, such losses would be impossible to sustain.

At about the time when he was wondering if he was about to be fired, Dowding had been invited to spend the weekend at the Prime Minister's weekend house, Chequers, in the Chilterns. It was there that Winston Churchill gave him an assurance that he very much wanted him to remain on the active list. As the Luftwaffe assaults began, the Prime Minister naturally took an avid interest in the nerve centre of the RAF's defensive operation. He visited Bentley Priory, and was there in the Filter Room as the news came through of the heavy losses suffered by a squadron of Defiants. According to Dowding's biographer, Churchill was grave and also concerned about the heavy loss of aircraft, as well he might have been. To this, Dowding's response was at once correct yet also an indicator of how perhaps he might have frayed the nerves of those close to him. He reportedly told Churchill, 'That may be so, but what I am conscious of is that so many of my men have died.'[9] The insult was unintentional. But it is also an illustration of a kind of leaden quality in Dowding; admirably straightforward, quite without side, but also slow to read the mood of others.

The rate at which fighter aircraft were being lost was also a matter of vehement concern for *Daily Express* proprietor Lord Beaverbrook, whom Churchill had appointed as Minister for Aircraft Production just a few weeks before. Although factories had been allocated for the work of producing fighter planes, the assembly lines, even after Dunkirk, were still sluggish; Beaverbrook, whatever anyone thought of him (and there were plenty who could not abide him) was renowned for an abundance of energy. He turned to Vickers Supermarine down on the south coast, and in doing so went to war with the Air Ministry. He wanted Supermarine to take over the slow production process at a Nuffield-owned factory in Castle Bromwich. The aim of the Air Ministry was to ensure that the Castle Bromwich production line was heavy on the new generation of bombers; the prevailing view was that defensive fighters were not enough, and that Britain had to have ample means of launching pre-emptive attacks. But sardonic Beaverbrook was at one with Dowding: for the moment, it was the fighters that were needed most. For if the Germans managed to get a sniff of air superiority, then there would scarcely be a chance to launch any kind of attack at all.

The desperate battle for the survival of Britain was properly under way. Now it was to sweep into a phase of greater intensity.

Chapter Twelve

Nerve Endings

There was always more to bombing than the immediate moment of destruction, or the horror and the stunned mourning that followed. Whether aimed at cities, towns or villages, the explosions reverberated beyond individual death and injury. They marked the annihilation of the familiar, the erasure of memories. A long-standing row of shops or a centuries-old pub might simply vanish with no warning. In once teeming neighbourhoods, there would be bewilderment and even disorientation as people struggled to steer past the fresh wounds in the earth, the cellars suddenly opened up to sunlight. Landmarks that had stood in the closely packed high street for as long as anyone who lived there could remember, vanished as though they had never existed. Bearings were lost, physically and emotionally.

On a broad social level, such destruction is accompanied by a communal hurt; it is an act of elemental aggression against which there can be no immediate, direct reprisal. The bombers swoop in, drop their load, and are already flying away across the moonlit sea as the fires they started reach their height below.

Before the Blitz began in the autumn of 1940, the Luftwaffe were already flexing their bombing muscles. Dowding and his pilots were doing everything possible to fight them off.

But the defence of the nation could not mean the blanket protection of each and every community that found itself underneath the mighty battles in the air.

As summer reached its height, England's extreme south-east, the county of Kent, was becoming better known among military personnel and civilians alike as 'Hellfire Corner'. Towns and villages in the high ribbon along the white cliffs were fast growing accustomed to bombs and bullets. There were, though, outbreaks of neurosis. Local street lighting, for instance, had been modified to what was called 'star-lighting'; the idea was that in the darkness of the night, the lights would be perfectly visible to a distance of about three metres (ten feet), but would then rapidly dim the further one moved away. But they attracted superstitious violence; there were accounts of anonymous locals waiting until the small hours and then going out to stone the illuminations, convinced that the German bombers would easily be able to see them. The authorities had to issue pleas for this nocturnal sabotage to cease.

In the midst of the German assault, an intriguing report was filed by Brigadier General John Charteris exclusively for newspaper readers. Citing American intelligence, he gave voice in the *Manchester Guardian* to the question that the entire population was asking: when would Germany make its expected pounce?

> The reports now being received from the United States of German troop movements towards the Channel coast, of the closing of areas in France and of the collection of barges may betoken the concentration of an invading army and the completion of the last preliminaries before the long-advertised attack on Britain is launched. But there is also the possibility that all these reports originate from the fertile German

Propaganda Office and are circulated mainly as another move in the battle of nerves. If they are meant to have jostled our nerves, they have not succeeded.

There was something unintentionally droll about that 'long-advertised' – there still seemed not to be a completely coherent invasion plan. But the Luftwaffe, as well as luring British fighters up into the air, were proving worryingly proficient at targeting the radio direction finding stations around the coast. At Bentley Priory, the core of the fighter operation was solidly defended; the Operations Room underground, and securely beneath concrete. Around the coast (the same was true for a large variety of listening stations), installations were altogether more fragile. They did not have the luxury of concrete. Dowding himself noted 'rather severe damage and casualties … The operating personnel and particularly the women behaved with great courage under threat of attack and actual bombardment.' Later, Dowding reflected on the often improvised nature of the RDF facilities in the more exposed areas around the coast. Given the frenzy of preparations that had to be made in order to meet the German threat head-on, this was one detail that had to fall by the wayside; there was simply too little time, in the wake of Dunkirk and the moment of crisis that followed, to expend huge amounts of money and labour constructing elaborate premises for each and every one of the stations. Many had to remain in wooden structures.

There was later some criticism that Bentley Priory itself was so well defended when others weren't, to which Dowding replied: 'It was considered that the nerve centre should be protected first, with the protection of the nerve ends to come as soon after that as possible.'[1]

Raids on the RDF stations formed part of a shifting kaleidoscope of Luftwaffe aggression that some in the Air

Ministry found bewildering. In these early stages of the Battle of Britain, some senior RAF figures appeared unable to comprehend Dowding's defensive tactics. Francis Wilkinson, an aide to Dowding, told Robert Wright:

> I think it was that which led him [Dowding] to have at least some of those awful rows with those people at the Air Ministry. Some of them up there simply didn't seem to know what was happening, or understand what it was all about. One day, an Air Commodore from the Air Ministry came to see Dowding. It was right at the time when we were very low on pilots who really knew how to fly. I listened to him in astonishment when he said to Dowding: 'But I don't understand what you're worrying about … you've got plenty of aeroplanes and pilots.' I thought poor old Stuffy would have a fit.[2]

Among those pilots were increasing numbers of Poles, the bond with Britain growing demonstrably stronger as they burned with memories of the German invasion of their own country. In the Scottish town of Perth, the Polish airmen were much in demand in the dance halls. Sometimes, the competition between them and the local men for the attentions of Perth's fair maids grew a little rough; but in time, many unions (and indeed marriages) were formed. Language was an initial barrier; one local woman recalls that taste in food was another hurdle to be jumped, especially when young Polish men were being presented to sceptical Perth parents. It is rather moving now, incidentally, to go and visit the Polish section of Perth cemetery; somehow it is here that one gets a real sense of the wartime impact that these pilots made.

On the part of the RAF, the admiration was mutual. One officer told *The Times*: 'Their strength is rooted in deep religious feeling and a patriotism which is derived from each man's love of his own village and country. Nearly every man bears the scars of tragedy, knowing that his family, if alive, is suffering from a degree of oppression and cruelty such as never darkened Poland before in all its tragic history.' It is instructive to see RAF officers giving such intensely lyrical quotes; a measure perhaps – in an age long before what we know as spin – of the Ministry of Information's long reach.

As August came, it might have felt, nationally, that the country's guard was being dropped a fraction; at the beginning of the month, 10 Downing Street was moved to issue this statement, reported in *The Times*:

> The Prime Minister wishes it to be known that the possibility of German attempts at invasion has by no means passed away. The fact that the Germans are now putting about rumours that they do not intend an invasion should be regarded with a double dose of the suspicion which attaches to all their utterances. Our sense of growing strength and preparedness must not lead to the slightest relaxation of vigilance or moral alertness.

In the more northerly areas of the country, a frenetic training programme for novice fighter pilots was under way. 'We watched an exhilarating mock battle,' wrote one reporter, not disclosing the name of the village or the county, 'delivered by a flight of Spitfires against Blenheims in the guise of enemy bombers. These fighter pilots are in a state of eager readiness to engage the enemy, and we saw what the concentrated power of their eight machine guns means when an aircraft discharged a few sharp bursts, at a rate of 160 rounds a second.' But in some eastern coastal areas, pilots were not so much eager as, in some cases, salivating to fight. Douglas

Bader, for instance, with 12 Group at Duxford, was later to give strident voice to what some significant higher figures were saying: that Dowding was getting the tactics wrong, and that if they weren't changed, the Germans would land.

There was sometimes an acute cruelty about the fates of the fighters. The flamboyant American William Fiske, based at Tangmere, had spent that summer on the attack, even on one occasion forcing a German plane into a barrage balloon. On 14 August 1940, his Hurricane was hit. Despite the flames, the choking smoke, he somehow managed to guide the plane in back to base. Yet he had not reached safety. His cockpit was now glowing red with fire; the efforts of the ground crew to pull him out were Herculean – he was caught in parachute paraphernalia. For a moment, it must have seemed as though he and his team had triumphed. One observer noted that Fiske was burnt around the hands and the ankles. They managed to lift him out of the plane. But the entire effort had been too much for his system. He died, as one observer put it, 'of shock'. Fiske was twenty-nine years old.

In the first few days of August, the Germans were still aiming for shipping. They dived on Dover, trying to shoot out the barrage balloons to make life easier for the bombers coming behind. They attacked convoys near Southampton, picking off straggling ships. The British squadrons always aimed to climb above them, sometimes higher than 6,100 metres (20,000 feet). The apparent discipline of the huge German formations – the fighters ringing the bombers – was reduced during such air battles to a frenzy of chaos. The British fighter pilots swooped; and all was a kind of fractal confusion. The Spitfire pilots would see with icy satisfaction the flames erupting near the tails of the Junkers or Messerschmitts. Sometimes they saw worse; German pilots in stricken planes trapped and panicking in their cockpits, or even jammed, halfway in and out, unable to budge as their planes plunged inexorably.

Then there was the surge of adrenaline when they themselves were hit. Sometimes cockpits would erupt in flames, and pilots, in the effort to ready themselves to bail out, would suffer hideous burns to their hands and their faces. They would then have to plunge these burns into the salt sea below. There were injuries that, if survived, would change lives; and the popular imagination now began to be haunted by the image of mutilated young pilots, and their chances of leading normal lives – dances, romances, courtship, marriage, sex – outside of the war. The public understood very well the potential horrors that each pilot faced every day. The truly astonishing feat is how the pilots – both British and German – learned to overcome the disorientation of these fast, fluid aerial battles; the split-second moment of seeing the enemy emerging from bright sunshine, the climbs and dives to evade fire, the whirling, twirling prospect as one pilot chased another across the sky, trying to keep him in his sights. Training only went so far.

This seemed also to be true of the operation at Bentley Priory, as it would be of the workings of all the Filter Rooms that were later set up around the country. The women and the men, informed of incoming aircraft, had just seconds to make swift, complex calculations to ensure that the fighters were sent up to the right places, at the right time, and at advantageous heights.

'All the plotters and filterers – they had boyfriends, brothers, cousins, husbands in fighter squadrons or bomber squadrons,' says Mrs Younghusband. 'We knew the squadrons operating.' For herself, she recalls particular intensity not just around Fighter Command but focusing on Bomber Command, the men who were making sorties into enemy territory. 'Especially when we were doing the high raid bombing later,' Mrs Younghusband says, 'you knew what squadrons were operating, you knew your husband or your boyfriend was in that squadron.'

The Luftwaffe was now preparing to step up its operations. On 8 August 1940 an extraordinarily intense and focused effort took place to destroy a convoy off the Isle of Wight. This was the first day of an entirely new phase of the air war; a lustier, more brutal, more determined assault. The attack – bombers and fighters flying out across the waters in huge numbers, totalling about 300 throughout the course of the day – began at around 8.30 in the morning. The ships of the convoy were already being escorted by fighters. The enemy dived down at them out of the sun. In the first wave, over sixty German planes attacked; two of the ships were sunk but otherwise, impressively, the fighters largely held them off. But the Luftwaffe was not finished. Several hours later, an even larger force came screaming down from the heavens: over a hundred German bombers and fighters, having massed at Cherbourg, made an even more focused effort on the convoy. Six RAF fighter squadrons roared in and the results, from the pilots' point of view on both sides, was pandemonium.

Then, later into that sunny afternoon, the malignant drone was heard again; the convoy, now near Bournemouth, was forced to spread apart as over 130 German Junkers and Messerschmitts tore into it with explosives and bullets. Throughout, the tally of losses was, extraordinarily, very much in favour of the British. In the morning attack, they lost two aircraft as opposed to the Luftwaffe's nine; at lunchtime, the figures were twenty-seven Luftwaffe aircraft downed against the British five; in the Bournemouth attack, it was another twenty-seven German planes lost and six British. An attack had also been launched on Dover, which necessitated sending further fighter squadrons up; it was later thought that this was possibly a decoy. But again, there were tragic losses, including that of a Blenheim, which had been up in the air in the region on a training flight. The pilot either threw himself into the battle or somehow became ensnared through inexperience.

Then, as twilight gave way to brief summer darkness, the night flights commenced; Germans crisscrossed the country, seeking out the open mouths of estuaries to lay the mines for shipping. There were German planes on other missions; in the northwest, over Manchester, one craft was dropping leaflets. Elsewhere, small and oddly isolated bombing raids were taking place. In Somerset, Crewkerne and Yeovil were targeted, as were a couple of small towns near Warrington, in the northwest. In the green Chilterns, just a couple of miles from the Prime Minister's weekend retreat of Chequers, the town of Wendover and the countryside around took sixteen bombs.

The German air force was flexing its muscles; and on 12 August, Luftwaffe command renewed its focus on the vulnerable, largely undefendable RDF bases dotted around the coastline. These presented too tempting a target not to pick off. Indeed, there were points at which those RDF stations could not quite pick up how many German planes were massing across the Channel – the network, like a modern mobile phone network, had weak spots. When 610 Squadron set off from Hawkinge to intercept those planes that had been detected, it found, at 4,877 metres (16,000 feet), many more than had been anticipated, flying over Dungeness on the Kent coast. Some of these planes slipped away and successfully bombed Lympne airfield. Meanwhile, a little later, 65 Squadron, based in Hornchurch, had set off into the skies to keep an eye on Chatham and the great naval base near the Thames Estuary. But all movements were a little out; the German pilots had other matters on their hands. They went for the RDF stations on the Sussex and Kent shoreline, one by one: first Pevensey, then the station in the pretty little town of Rye, and finally the installation on the edge of Dover. The effects were temporary; within twenty-four hours, all were back up and running. But even in that short time, a hole had been opened up in the defences and – coincidentally – Fighter Command's timings were out that day, which had meant that the bombings had taken place just as relief squadrons were getting ready to fly.

That was just the morning. By lunchtime, a fierce and large attack on the Isle of Wight RDF station, and on the base at Portsmouth, had been launched by a vast formation reckoned to be in the region of 500 Luftwaffe planes. According to the RAF official history, 'The enemy bombers were in formations of seven or eight sections in line astern and layered up, defensive circles being frequently seen.' Spitfire squadrons were already up beyond the clouds to meet them; but in sheer numbers like these, some were always going to get through. And so it was that the RDF station at Ventnor on the Isle of Wight was reduced to charred rubble; and for ten terrible minutes just after midday, Portsmouth came in for fiery bombardment, despite all the efforts of the RAF. The Spitfires and Hurricanes perhaps had reason to exercise a shade of caution here; for the Portsmouth anti-aircraft gunners were in full cry, and bringing down German planes into the sea. In the melee of aerial skirmishes, aiming from the ground cannot always have been easy or completely accurate.

It is also a reminder of how sparse the British forces looked next to the massed might of the German air fleets. Even now, it seems mathematically astounding; small squadrons of Spitfires and Hurricanes taking off to encounter industrial quantities of German bombers, and ignoring the numbers to take them on with extraordinary ferocity. Surprise was part of their armoury; once the defenders had reached a certain altitude, they then dived out of the sun. 'Attacks were carried out on the rear extreme left hand and right hand section of the bombers from astern and from the quarter by the first three sections of the Hurricanes,' states the official history. 'The rearmost Hurricane section concentrated on protecting our fighters from an attack by the Me 109s as they carried out their attack on the bombers. They did this by firing at long range in front of the Me 109s as they dived to attack our leading sections.'

But the relentlessness was another factor; on that one day, the pulses of German attacks, all over the southeast from the Thames Estuary down to Hampshire, had gone on until the early evening, by which time the sun was starting to dip. It has been suggested by the official historian that all this activity had one specific underlying aim; to see just how far the squadrons of RAF fighters could effectively cover so much territory, and for how long. It was not so much a test of strength as a rather chilly analysis; one during the course of which the Luftwaffe lost about fifty-seven planes and a great many pilots, with yet more planes damaged and yet more pilots wounded. On that day, twenty-two British fighters were destroyed; twelve pilots killed. Despite the Luftwaffe's heavy losses, they still had the overwhelming weight of numbers.

Chapter Thirteen

Big Wing

Life for the British fighter pilots was taking on a curious dualism: the familiarity of the base and all the faces there, the comforts of tea, cocoa, corned-beef sandwiches, the cool green grass beneath one's feet; and then the life above – a life of daily, unthinkable stress requiring, from dawn until sunset, unceasing alertness, coupled with the ability to blank out the huge discomforts of G-force, of unheated cockpits, of the noise of engines and guns. To fly alone, for so many hours a day, would be exhausting enough by itself. But add to that the furious concentration, plus the effort to keep mind-paralysing fear at bay, and a quite different order of mental control and willpower was required. Because, of course, bravery is not about not being frightened – only a fool or a robot would not be frightened – but the ability, somehow, to compartmentalise the fear, and indeed the fatigue, shut them away in another room as, for the third or fourth time that day, you don parachute and strap yourself into your cockpit, ready once more to try and shoot men down in flames before they succeed in killing you.

Some time later, in 1941, an *Evening News* headline read 'Methedrine wins the Battle of Britain'. It was not strictly accurate. Benzedrine was the slightly less potent pharmaceutical substance dispensed by RAF medics both to pilots and to WAAFs in filter rooms. (Joan Wyndham, an aristocratic and bohemian writer who had wasted no time in joining up, recalled: 'I really love the clear, cool feeling in my head, and the edge of excitement it gives to everything you do'.) Strikingly, it has since emerged that German Luftwaffe pilots were, in the summer months of 1940, being given a stronger drug. It was called Pervitin; some pilots noted with delight that it made them many times more alert than huge amounts of coffee ever could. It was a methamphetamine, and it became known as 'Pilot's chocolate'. In the short term, certainly, this drug – essentially crystal meth – had an extraordinary effect on Luftwaffe pilots, giving them seemingly superhuman resistance to tiredness and indeed despondency. Rather the reverse; the drug induced a form of euphoria. However, it was not long before the darkness of the drug manifested itself, in inability to sleep and psychotic phases; there were even instances of suicide. And then, of course, there were the horrific side-effects of addiction, from hallucinations to profound depression.

The use of Benzedrine in the RAF was very much more sparing. But it was still about fighting off tiredness, and helping the pilots focus. Of course there were drawbacks, as there are with every drug under the sun; in this case, too much Benzedrine would result in lengthy periods of wakefulness when what the fighter pilot needed after four or five sorties in a thirteen-hour flying day was the precise opposite. Then there were the unpredictable results of mixed intoxicants, such as the uproarious scenes at RAF Hornchurch just weeks before the Battle of Britain began, when one fighter pilot swallowed his allocation of Benzedrine, then mixed it with a great slosh of whisky, which had the effect of making him noisily monopolise the upright piano in the officers' mess for hours.

For all the roistering tales of ale and spirits and pills after long days of fighting 10,000 feet above the ground, however, most pilots would not have had the energy for more than a swift half of beer; instead, they were craving bed, and the merciful oblivion of deep sleep. This is an extraordinary aspect of the Battle of Britain difficult to envisage now; after so many successive days of killing, and seeing one's friends killed, the pilots would wake again just before dawn (a cup of tea prepared for them by their batmen if they were officers) and, in that moment between dream and full awareness, the weight of what they would have to face yet again pressed down on them like a cold boulder. At the height of the Battle of Britain, any sort of rest for pilots in 11 Group was rare. Air Chief Marshal Dowding was intensely aware of the need for these men to have days on the ground simply to repair their stretched nerves, but there were not enough pilots to go around. There were so many young pilots still in training.

By this time, as he explained some years later, Air Chief Marshal Dowding's thoughts on the defence of Britain had crystallised:

There was a distinct difference between the objectives of the opposing sides. The Germans were out to facilitate a transfer of ground troops across the Channel, to invade this country, and so to finish the war. Now, I wasn't trying with Fighter Command to win the war. I was desperately trying to prevent the Germans from succeeding in their preparations for an invasion. Mine was the purely defensive role of trying to stop the possibility of an invasion, and thus give this country a breathing spell. We might win or we might lose the war, or we might agree on a draw – anything might happen in the future. But it was Germany's

objective to win the war by invasion, and it was my job
to prevent an invasion from taking place. I had to do
that by denying them control of the air.[1]

Despite Dowding's rationale, however, it was becoming
increasingly obvious by August that there were those in
Fighter Command who vehemently opposed his defensive
system. For figures such as 12 Group's commander Trafford
Leigh-Mallory, the limits on the numbers of planes that
could be sent up was a source of immense frustration.

Leigh-Mallory had started flying in the First World War,
after which he rose to wing commander and air commodore,
all the while commanding a flying training school and also
acting as air adviser to the Geneva Disarmament Conference
of 1932. But his career, indeed much of his life, had been
shaped in the open cockpits of biplanes flying high in the
abstract skies above the fogs and filthy air of the trenches.

RAF Duxford (now the home of an excellent branch of
Imperial War Museums) was the base of 12 Group; just a few
miles south of Cambridge, and close to the Essex border, it
was within seventy-two kilometres (forty-five miles) of Greater
London and the Thames Estuary and indeed not far from
RAF Debden, which was part of 11 Group. But Duxford's
responsibility and focus was on defending the manufacturing
heartlands of the Midlands, as well as the east coast north of
the capital, stretching up to Suffolk. This became a matter of
some frustration for 12 Group's most famous pilot, Douglas
Bader, based a little further north in Coltishall.

He and Leigh-Mallory had been observing the flight
formation of the attacking Germans; those formidable line-
ups of bombers, with their protective encircling fighters biting
and diving like sharks at the more modest forces of 11 Group.
Not unnaturally – for his belligerence was very clear and
focused – Bader wanted the chance to hit back at the Germans.

He wanted to be able to put together 'big wing' formations – that is, send up larger numbers of planes in each squadron to fight back the incursion. The great difficulty for Dowding was that even before that summer, Bader was held in awe not only by young trainees but by his superiors. Understandably so; to have returned to pre-eminence as a pilot after the long trauma of amputation and rehabilitation was a spectacular achievement. It took a particular kind of man to push on with that kind of willpower. Possibly Bader had an excess of it.

It has been pointed out that Bader's view of aerial warfare was deeply coloured by the exploits of his heroes throughout the First World War. He very much believed in dogfights, with all the acrobatics that they would entail, even though there were those around him who tried to insist that in the new age of the Spitfire and the Hurricane, the nature of such fights was radically different. Now, in another echo of the First World War, where Royal Flying Corps fighters flew in formation during battle, Bader came to the firm belief that squadrons should be sent up in large disciplined numbers to meet the enemy head-on.

The argument against Bader went like this: the invaders themselves liked big formations because the bombers needed protection, and they were working against inflexible time limits; they could spend only so long over enemy territory without running out of fuel, and they had to stick to rigid flight plans in order to guarantee the success of hitting pre-ordained targets. The defenders, by contrast, had the element of flexibility.

The British could – in theory – either match the numbers, or harass and beat back the enemy from a variety of different angles and bases, and with less concern over time as they were performing this defence over home territory. The enemy might have had brute force, but the defenders could outwit and surprise them with unconventional attacks that would seemingly come out of nowhere. And thanks to the coastal chain of RDF stations, there would be warnings in time to get the individual fighters up into the air. Dowding's view of the defenders going up in 'big wing' formations was that all nimbleness would be lost. Such forces would take very much longer to assemble than the individual pilots dashing for their cockpits. And if so many aeroplanes were focusing on one target, who would be left to defend the targets of other German bombers that might have managed to slip through?

But how much time can there ever be for theory when the nation is facing an expected invasion and when – as was the case by mid-August – the enemy is making determined efforts to destroy its air bases? Bellicose and stubborn Bader might have been; but in this moment of extraordinary crisis, wasn't it natural to listen to the born warrior? Dowding later said: 'When I look back on it now, it was asking a lot of any man to think of being able to curb Bader, particularly when he was doing so well in his own flying.'[2]

In the face of the events of 13 August 1940 (and the days that immediately followed), the sheer urge for retribution would have gathered many to Bader's side. The true nature of the German plan, those huge yet exploratory attacks, became clear on what was later revealed to have been termed by the Germans *Adlertag* – 'Eagle Day'. In other words, this was what German High Command regarded as being the real start of the Battle of Britain.

On those days in mid-August (after a badly stuttering start on 13 August for the Luftwaffe, which was hampered by low cloud), the Germans launched a spectacular aerial assault intended to smash Fighter Command into the dust. Those few days would see an estimated 1,000 enemy planes cross the sea in a series of pulses that stretched from Portsmouth to the Tyne. On 13 August, the pale wide skies above the

Thames Estuary were filled with the ominous buzz as the bombers headed for Sheerness. At the same time, a fleet had set course for what it considered an important prize: the Royal Aircraft Establishment at Farnborough in Hampshire, together with the nearby Odiham station. Yet even though German bombers at one point made Southampton a target that afternoon, the fires that they started in several warehouses were quickly smothered.

The Germans made serious mistakes; one wave of attackers was absurdly lacking in synchronisation. A group of Messerschmitts had contrived to get so far ahead of the bombers they were supposed to be protecting that in fact they could do no such thing; then, it seemed, they could barely protect themselves against a counterattack from Spitfires of 11 and 10 Group over the Dorset coast. More waves of bombers came, the aim to strike at airfields from Essex down to the south coast; yet the airfields that sustained the most damage – Eastchurch in Kent, Detling just a few miles away – were the province of Coastal Command. The Royal Aircraft Establishment got away with barely a splinter; Farnborough's airfield was untouched, as was the Odiham base. The fighting was ferocious; from the point of view of the German pilots, it must have looked utterly unhinged.

Over the subsequent days, the ferocity and occasional chaos of the assault was sustained. There were other, less predictable, casualties of war. On 15 August, in Croydon, Surrey, near the aerodrome, a scent factory was hit. The resulting fire and smoke were suffocating. The attack on the aerodrome itself caused local damage. 'Concrete and tarmac were thrown across a road, some pieces as large as footballs being thrown 20 yards or more,' wrote a reporter for *The Times*. 'Windows of many houses on a council estate were shattered and slates were blown from roofs. A double decker bus proceeding towards London was wrecked … There was

right: 'A beautifully proportioned body and graceful curves just where they should be'. Lord Balfour of Inchyre was one of many pilots who rhapsodised about Spitfires, seen here in formation.
© IWM (CH 740)

left: Although much joked about at the time, the striking silvery masses of barrage balloons – here protecting shipping – were a valuable tool in Fighter Command's defensive arsenal and were ubiquitous over London.
© IWM (A 6175)

right: The Luftwaffe over London. On the night of 7 September 1940, Hitler's promised retaliation for an RAF raid on Berlin came in the form of wave after wave of bombers. The pilots of Fighter Command managed to shoot down a surprising number.
© IWM (C 5422)

above: Bentley Priory, on the hilly northern outskirts of London, from which Fighter Command personnel could see London ablaze during the height of the Blitz. In the eighteenth century, the house played host to poets and princes. © Graham Hill/Stanmoretouristboard

below: The first Operations Room was set up in the ballroom; whilst a more secure and hi-tech version, including colour-coded clocks, was being constructed beneath the ground.
© IWM/Getty Images via Getty Images

right: Air Chief Marshal Hugh Dowding (right), architect of the RAF's defensive fighter network, nicknamed 'Stuffy' owing to a perceived dryness of manner, with His Majesty King George VI. In fact, Dowding was much more sensitive – particularly about the welfare of his pilots – than many realised. © Popperfoto/Getty Images

below: The Hornchurch station down on the marshes near the Thames – which on autumn mornings would frequently be shrouded with yellow fog – was to prove pivotal throughout the fight for Britain, and was frequently targeted by the Luftwaffe. © IWM (COL 191)

right: Sir Trafford Leigh-Mallory, who fought with Dowding, championed the theories of Douglas Bader, and rose to become Air Chief Marshal. Despite their profound differences over tactics, both men shared deeper beliefs: Leigh-Mallory and Dowding were avowed spiritualists.
© Popperfoto/Getty Images

above: Douglas Bader, centre, surrounded by 11 Group colleagues. It is possible that his disability – both legs amputated after a horrific accident – stoked his ferocity in the air. He was also, for the time, unusually abstemious in the pub. There is a Douglas Bader Foundation today in London, helping children with disabilities. © IWM (CH 1413)

left: New Zealand-born Alan Deere, one of many pilots from around the world who came to fight for Britain, originally hailed from a deeply agricultural background but set his heart on flying for the RAF. © IWM (CH 13619)

right: Patricia Clark, who worked as a Flight Officer in Fighter Command's Filter Room, was one of a select group of young women. Her rarefied social background made her war career a voyage of discovery and also inspired her later success as a best-selling novelist.

© Patricia Clark

right: Max Aitken, pilot son of Lord Beaverbrook, the Minister for Aircraft Production. Aitken was a skilled and flamboyant fighter who caught the attention of Churchill and was friends with fellow pilot Roger Bushell, later better known as the genius behind the Great Escape. © Popperfoto/ Getty Images

right: Pilot Tony Bartley, who embodied the perceived glamour of Fighter Command; friends with actor David Niven, he was later to marry the film star Deborah Kerr. © IWM (CNA 125)

left: The first eyes and ears to see the incoming waves of enemy fighters were members of the Observer Corps. They were often First World War veterans, and were keen to receive proper recognition. © War Office Official Photographer/ IWM via Getty Images

below: A number of young women volunteered for the Observer Corps, working in hazardously exposed conditions and mastering the calculations of speed and trajectory produced on the 'Micklethwaite', an astrolabe-style device. © Planet News Archive/SSPL/Getty Images

right: With radar in its infancy, navigation could be dicey, especially in the absence of familiar landmarks; some pilots even used Bradshaw's Railway Timetable to identify certain lines to guide them back to base.
© IWM (C 1664)

below: The Operations Room, tracking incoming raids with astonishing accuracy in a pre-computer age, was staffed with skilled operators, from young WAAFs to City of London stockbrokers, all of whom were good with instant calculations.
© IWM (CH 7698)

left: The ground staff at each fighter base became renowned for their forensic devotion; but the pilots were also mesmerised by the workings of their planes.
© William Vandivert/ The LIFE Picture Collection/Getty Images

right: The signal to scramble was sometimes curiously a relief; the hours beforehand waiting in the mess were, even though pilots never admitted it at the time, a source of great tension.
© Jimmy Sime/Central Press/Getty Images

left: During the height of the Battle of Britain pilots found themselves sprinting into action many times a day. That combination of courage and focus, repeated over weeks and months, was an astounding psychological and physical feat.
© Fg. Off. N S Clark/ IWM via Getty Images

a number of casualties, some of which were fatal.' Some victims were trapped in debris and had to be given blood transfusions. The call went out for blood donors.

Foreshadowing the dark autumn to follow, sirens were sounded in the centre of London – and were ignored by many people. Indeed, some Londoners deliberately stayed out on the streets, apparently mad with curiosity to see a proper modern bombing raid. The Air Wardens became frantic in their efforts to make these people see sense. They would not have long to wait.

Elsewhere, in Rochester, Kent, near the Chatham dockyards, houses were hit, with several fatalities. There was damage of strategic importance too; two aircraft works, Pobjoys and Short's, were repeatedly dive-bombed by some twenty German planes. At Short's, pretty much the entire plant was destroyed, along with the planes under construction within. Attacks on the airfields produced mixed results: serious damage was done to Martlesham Heath in Suffolk – two hangars were obliterated, plus the officers' mess, and a few aircraft too. Hawkinge aerodrome took a few bombs, but without any lasting effect; meanwhile, on the Thames Estuary in north Kent, the Eastchurch aerodrome was also targeted, though in that instance, it seemed that more damage had been done to the local railway line.

Over the course of those few mid-August days, it was the range of the attacks that was so breathtaking. In the northeast, houses near Seaham were hit. 'Miners stood on top of a pit-heap cheering and waving their caps when a British fighter engaged a fleeing bomber out to sea and shot it down,' said one reporter. Down in the southwest, meanwhile, 213 Squadron and 87 Squadron, based in Exeter, had the epic fight of their lives over the south coast; waves of some thirty bombers, ringed around with 100 or so fighters. The long days stretched out seemingly without end: the enemy seemingly inexhaustible, sending yet more and more planes across the sea; Fighter Command squadrons up and down the country, but most particularly in the southeast and southwest, equally in combat all day, pausing only to return to refuel; a quick turnaround and then back into what was simply described as 'the melee'.

According to Air Ministry communiqués handed to the newspapers, on 15 August 144 enemy aeroplanes were destroyed or downed; 27 British planes were lost, but eight pilots were later found safe.

A young WAAF called Iris Cockle had just joined up and had started working at Kenley Airfield, just to the south of London. She was to see, close up, on 18 August, just how terrifying and traumatic German raids on aerodromes could be. She recalled: 'During a quiet spell, a male sergeant asked me if I would take charge while he and a few colleagues took a break. Shortly after he left, I heard the ominous tones of the air-raid siren. The next thing I saw was planes of the Luftwaffe hedge-hopping across Kenley, dropping bombs and raking the area with gunfire. I threw myself into my section's dugout to find that I was the only occupant.

'For the next few minutes, I just sat there frozen with fear as the air-raid exploded above me. Then came the deafening silence after the planes had passed over, followed by the sound of a voice. "Hey, blondie," it said, "you'd better get out of there, there's an unexploded bomb on the roof of your dugout." It was a young aircraftman who had stuck his head into the dugout to see if anyone was still alive. I vacated what I thought was my safety zone as quickly as I had entered it.

'When I came up into the light,' she continued, 'all I could see was devastation everywhere. There were great scoops ripped into the ground that had been created by the bombs. Rubble from what were once buildings was scattered everywhere. Vehicles lay on their sides; some with smoke and flames billowing from them. A German plane had buried itself nose down in the ground. Worst of all was the sight of comrades lying either dead or injured.'[3]

Naturally, the coverage for public consumption was relentlessly upbeat. Yet there was also an authenticity about the kind of language that one unnamed fighter pilot used in an interview a few days after the events of 13 August. He was describing one particular skirmish he and his comrades had got into 'far to the south of the Isle of Wight', where 'two separate squadrons of Messerschmitt 110s were flying about in an uncompleted circle at around 4,000ft [1,220 metres]'. 'I was curious to know why they were circling around like that,' said the pilot in the *Manchester Guardian*. 'And we decided to have a crack ... the lad on my left shot down one Messerschmitt 109 which, I think, was intended to be a decoy. It was supposed to lead us down to the circle but our pilot shot him down first when we started on our dive. We broke up the circle quite effectively. All three of us got at least one and I think we must have taken them by surprise ... I flew over another circle of enemy fighters for about five minutes until they had all cleared off.' He gathered some intelligence too. 'Then I went down and saw one of their pilots in the water. He was easy to see for all around him was a big patch of green vapour – a method used by the Germans when they get into the water. It shows their friends where they are. You can see the green vapour from five miles away.'

The day wasn't over. 'While I was investigating this, I was attacked by a Messerschmitt 110 which ... I had overlooked. I skidded round and climbed for him but he broke away to my left. I was still turning and at about 1,000ft [304 metres], I stalled. He was right in my gun sights. I just gave him a quick burst and he heeled over and went straight into the sea and broke up. Then we went home.'

These were also hailed successful days for the anti-aircraft gunners; German bombers were successfully brought down before they could inflict large-scale damage on Portsmouth dockyard and the surrounding areas, though of course some buildings and a railway station were hit. Similarly, on the Isle of Wight, it was not only the RDF station that was hit; several other buildings went with it.

And all of this while Douglas Bader and his pilots of 12 Group were compelled, by an accident of geography, to look on, as fighters to the far north and the far south of them stretched every nerve to bring the Germans down. In fact, some pilots from squadrons in his area were deployed on 13 August, but it is possible that there had been some kind of RDF mix-up; they chased a few German fighters but then turned around as the attack on Martlesham Heath aerodrome became apparent. They were too late; the bombers were already doing their work. Certainly they could be chased off, but the damage was already done. There were these and a hundred other prickling frustrations; the maddening psychological blow of an enemy seeming to act with apparent impunity. 'It was intolerable to Bader that others should be plunging into the fire of battle (not to mention honour), while he was held impotently on the ground,' wrote Paul Brickhill.[4]

'There were not sufficient forces available for a reserve of fighters, a masse de manoeuvre, to be kept back and used only when the direction and strength of the enemy's attack was known,' states the official history. 'Instead, the concentrated formations of German bombers and fighters were being met by squadrons containing no more than twelve, and frequently fewer aircraft. It was rarely, therefore, that the Germans failed to reach their targets, provided that the state of the weather was fair.' The odds across those days, in other words, were quite terrifying: 'The individual fighter squadrons, since they normally came into action independently of each other, were engaging up to ten times their number of the enemy.'

A further difficulty was that attacks made on Kent and the Thames Estuary carried little advance warning, simply because the journey across the Channel was so much briefer. The incoming bombers and fighters also had the inbuilt advantage of height – they were already high above as the Spitfires and Hurricanes climbed to reach them, vulnerable to their firepower. Would it not have been possible to have the Spitfires patrolling those skies? For reasons of fuel, but more pressingly of numbers, the answer was absolutely not. This is to say nothing of the effects of cloud cover, and the ways in which the enemy could use it to slip through and go on the attack.

What makes this period seem all the more remarkable is the apparent coolness of Hugh Dowding, and indeed of 11 Group's Commander Keith Park. The system of delegation – allowing each squadron to react swiftly to a threat without orders having to go up and down the chain of command – must have been wearing on the nerves of not only all those at Bentley Priory, but everyone in the Air Ministry. It is one of the most fundamental impulses: the need to grab and take control. Douglas Bader was giving voice to an anxiety – verging on anguish – that was shared by many above him. Dowding, though, was implacable.

How many pilots and planes could the British afford to lose in the course of this onslaught? The losses had already been grievous and although plane production was now at full tilt, the training of new pilots was by necessity a process that could not be rushed. Were the German supplies as elastic and seemingly infinite as they seemed? Throughout the course of the Battle of Britain, Air Chief Marshal Dowding knew exactly how much responsibility he bore for the entire future of the nation. And even though his own comments seem to suggest otherwise, there must have been moments in the days that followed when he had pangs of doubt about the course he was taking.

Chapter Fourteen

'We Will All Be Here Soon'

German pilots were mapping out the nation. During that summer, they frequently did so on the nights when the moon was full and bright. The blackout below gave civilians a certain level of security, a protective cloak; but, using the glittering threads of rivers, the silver lines of railway steel, the enemy pilots were able to explore the darkened land below. They were seeking out the places towards which intelligence had pointed them: the manufacturing plants, specifically the plane factories, such as the great works at Filton, near Bristol. There was a chilly insolence about such missions, and something curiously as invasive as invasion itself. Naturally, the British were flying equivalent missions over Germany and its conquered territories. Nonetheless, the German sorties carried an extra charge of unease because there was still an essential mystery involved: what were they planning? And the invasion: when? And what form would it take? There was no one in Britain, however, who didn't think that the Nazis would soon be landing.

Brief respite came for Dowding and the squadrons throughout the southeast just beyond the midpoint of August 1940. For a few days, the Germans scaled down operations to a series of scattered incursions. This is not to underplay the devastation caused by the raids: an oil storage depot in south Wales turned into a choking inferno which blazed   for   over a week; a swooping raid in Skegness targeted a naval training establishment and blew away a number of buildings, including 900 huts. But the vast formations of bombers and fighters were, for a brief few days, largely absent from the skies over Britain. In part, the Luftwaffe was regrouping, giving the squadrons based in France a chance to effect repairs and allowing the pilots a brief window of rest. Even throughout those days, though, the people of Britain were never allowed to forget that while they slept, there were killers flying high above them, with bombs poised to drop.

Sporadic nocturnal attacks in the Midlands targeted factories; in the West Country, the bombers homed in on Filton and dropped sixteen tons of bombs, putting part of the works out of action temporarily. And Londoners received a premonition of what was coming to them; Germans explored and targeted the industrial northeast of the city, from Walthamstow to Enfield, site of the vast ordnance works. In the event, factories sustained little damage; instead it was residential properties that suffered. Night-time defence was not a strong element in the work of Fighter Command, though it was not for want of trying. Radar could do so much; but in the velvet darkness, there was little the Observer Corps could have done to help without the vast arcing searchlights, and the very poor visibility made matters impractically difficult for the pilots. The leaders and pilots of Fighter Command nevertheless carried on as though they vastly outnumbered the enemy.

In the lives of fighter pilots, despite their nerve-tautening sorties, there were moments of curious serenity; fragments of time that appeared to stand apart from the frenzied flow. After one messy dogfight above the Channel, towards the end of the day, Geoffrey Wellum, piloting his Spitfire high above the clouds, knew he had to get back to base. But something had chimed in his soul. He wrote:

> The sun is now below the horizon and the whole world in which I find myself is one of purple mistiness. Nothing appears to be alive. I am alone in a strange, still environment. No movement at all. My aeroplane is stationary ... This is a type of peace and tranquillity that, to my mind, is utterly beautiful. It is a shame having to think about the ground and having to get back on it. If only I could go on flying like this forever.

Yet he was also sharply aware of the incongruity: 'A short time ago, I probably killed a man. I was excited and elated, totally taken up with the chase and the kill on a "him or me" basis, and now this terrific sense of peace. What a strange life we pilots lead.'[1]

Another curiosity of those comparatively still days was the way that the German press, at the behest of Dr Goebbels, stepped up reports of a Britain that was held in a desperate stranglehold. 'Conclusive phase of the war begun' and 'Great Britain in thumbscrews' were two of the headlines to appear during this brief Luftwaffe interregnum. Berlin newspapers also suggested that the blockade of the island was complete, and that this was a satisfying fate for a nation that had inflicted starvation on German women and children with a similar 'totalitarian blockade' throughout the First World War. 'The peril to which England has threatened to expose Europe now turns against the island itself,' declared one newspaper. 'England is from this day cut off from the world.'

But the British had other concerns. Indeed, on the same day, the Ministry of Home Security was moved to issue a nationwide plea: could members of the public please stop sightseeing the sites of bombing raids? Not merely the day after, but actually while the raid was in progress. 'It should be realised,' stated the stern communiqué, 'that not only do persons congregating in crowds offer a target to enemy raiders, but that the work of rescue and firefighting may be gravely delayed.'

Air Chief Marshal Dowding kept a semblance of stability throughout this period at Bentley Priory by sticking to a disciplined routine. But was such a thing possible for his deputy Air Vice Marshal Park at Uxbridge? Having command of 11 Group – with its pre-dawn alerts followed by air battles that would run on until past sunset – imposed both terrific physical strain and mental strain, as did the fight to remain free of doubts about his strategy when so many of his superiors were starting to question his wisdom. Park nevertheless stood his ground. On one later occasion, he said of the events of late August 1940:

Owing to the very short warning received of enemy raids approaching England, or the south of England, it would have been quite impossible to intercept enemy formations with big wings before they bombed their targets such as the aerodromes and aircraft factories. At the very best, big wing formations from No. 11 Group, if we had used them, would have intercepted a few of the German raids after they had unloaded their bombs on vital targets, and were able to take evasive action by diving away in retreat under cover of their own fighter formations or escorts. The German escorting fighters, having the advantage of height and being freed from the need to escort their bombers, would have decimated our fighter squadrons.[2]

On top of this, Park knew better than anyone precisely how overstretched his 11 Group fighter squadrons were. In a later interview, he recalled that 'I was a very worried man because I was short of pilots – I was never worried about the supply of aircraft.' The reason for this shortfall was quite simple in Park's view: incompetence and 'bad planning' in the Air Ministry. He remembered that when he was later sent to the ministry's training department, he discovered that no one there had ever quite realised the pressing urgency of the pilot shortage. By contrast, the rate of aircraft production was one of the few aspects of life at that time that gave him solace. The reason? 'Every night at midnight,' Park recalled, he would get a personal call from Lord Beaverbrook, 'asking for the score sheet'.[3] Park would tell him of losses and damage; Beaverbrook passed the figures on to the aircraft production factories.

In August 1940, even during the brief lull, Park was never tempted to underestimate his enemies – wherever they might have been. The Germans were the same as they had been in the last war in the most crucial respects: they were 'very good natural warriors,' he said, 'good fighters in the air.' If they had one fatal weakness, it was that they were 'slow to adapt themselves when set plans were thrown out, either by the weather, or by the enemy suddenly launching surprise action'.

Park, by contrast, had been almost absurdly adaptable, stretching his resources to their thinnest by setting up shadow airfields – emergency bases that could be deployed in the event that the main squadron aerodromes were targeted. He ensured that the shadow bases were properly equipped with all the telecommunications and radios that they needed. 'This wasn't a little game,' said Park. 'We weren't in a position to test out theories.' Indeed, he went further, asserting that if he had followed Bader's theories about formations, 'I would have lost the Battle of

Britain.' It was all about the continued existence of 'London and the Empire'.[4]

And at the time, he knew what was coming. The Luftwaffe had first targeted the shipping and the convoys and the supply lines; then they had tried to make inroads into aircraft production. Next it was going to be an intensified German effort to destroy aerodromes and aircraft and hangars and communications – anything to put Fighter Command out of action. Then the way would be open for the German landings to begin, from the air and from the sea. In other words, Park knew that if 11 Group messed this up, they 'might well have lost the war for the Allies'.

On the morning of 24 August 1940, German forces launched a bombing raid on Great Yarmouth in Norfolk. This could not disguise the steady build-up of forces facing across the Channel towards the country's south coast. There were skirmishes and feints; British fighter squadrons in the air were trying to patrol the vulnerable airfields. But there were a great many airfields, and few fighters. The anti-aircraft gunners at Dover were initially effective against the incoming Germans, but a second raid proved more difficult to anticipate and see off. At lunchtime, the Germans targeted Manston in Kent and caused some damage, though not perhaps as much as they might have hoped. But the day was yet young. In mid-afternoon, about thirty Ju 88s, with their faithful fighter escorts, made their way relentlessly towards London.

They were engaged by 501 Squadron, but as a savage dogfight between fighter planes began, the bombers bulldozed through. Along the Thames estuary; banking to the left; and then, a few miles short of the great docks, banking right – they were making for the Hornchurch base, not far from the vast industrial works of Dagenham.

197

Extraordinarily – and thanks to local anti-aircraft guns – out of 100 bombs dropped on the base, only six landed within its perimeter. The surrounding country consisted of reedy lakes, meadows and marshes. The German bombers turned to make their escape. Defiants and their crews, stationed at Hornchurch, set off in pursuit; according to the official history, the Defiants eventually managed to overtake the bombers, and the rear gunners had the rare and bloodthirsty satisfaction of firing directly into their opponents' cockpits.

But the enemy was not quite finished for the day. It had another large 11 Group station in its sights. Again, there were decoy formations up in the air; the squadrons were being pulled in all directions. But a droning mass of bombers materialised offshore from Shoeburyness in Essex, twisted inland just a little further north, and dived determinedly on the base of North Weald.

On this occasion, they were slightly more effective; although they made little impact on the landing grounds, they destroyed the station's generator house and living areas. It was at this point that Air Vice Marshal Park decided that it was time to take on the limitations of the otherwise excellent radar system. Although, as he recalled in an interview, the system 'could give you the position of the approaching craft', and swift calculations by the WAAFs in the Operations Room would give a good idea of its speed, what it still couldn't do was give an accurate figure of height: 'If you had a reading of 10,000 feet [3,048 metres], then you had plus or minus 2,000 ft [610 metres].' The answer, he thought, was for the pilots to break radio silence upon spotting enemy formations. Radio silence gave pilots the advantage of surprise, enabling them to individually track, follow and attack the enemy from behind or from out of the sun. Breaking radio silence to report back to their squadron bases would alert the enemy to their own positions – but Park calculated that it was better for base, and for 11 Group HQ at Uxbridge, to be furnished with the height and the strength of the incoming bombers as soon as the patrolling fighters had spotted them.

At the start of this new and much deadlier phase of German attack, there were more sinister foretastes of what was coming to London and other cities. One night, Observer Corps volunteers watched a single plane making its way up the Thames towards the capital; it then circled the entire city, almost at leisure. On those muggy nights, a couple of other enemy planes got through too: railway bridges in east and north London were hit, a railway line was put out of action and hundreds of people in Bethnal Green had to be evacuated from their tenements when bombs fell close. And always a sense of the enemy sizing up the territory, stalking around and around, fraying the nerves of those below.

The response was, however, more multidimensional. The weekend's bombing saw the stepping up of 'Spitfire funds', the aim of which was simply to raise money to buy new fighters. Down in south London, for instance, the 'Lambeth Walk Spitfire Fund' injected a note of black comedy. 'Already large boxes are being made free of charge by our local undertaker, Mr Harry Smith, for money to be dropped in by passers-by,' said a local spokesman. Did any of that community have any inkling of what would be coming to their own district in the black months of the winter? Similarly, the East End districts of East Ham, West Ham, Barking and Wanstead opened their own funds. Their proximity to the vast docks made their own vulnerability more obvious. The fund-raising may have provided at least a small psychological boost.

As Air Vice Marshal Park and Air Chief Marshal Dowding contemplated the evolving tactics of the Luftwaffe, a surprising voice weighed in with words both of admonition for friend and foe and encouragement for the RAF. 'This is what comes of declaring war first and preparing for it afterwards,' George Bernard Shaw told the *Manchester Guardian*. 'The Germans have been preparing for the war for six years and their planes are out of date; ours are still being made, and they are newer and faster than theirs ... Meanwhile, we must say what we are fighting for ... People are getting impatient, for no-one knows what our aims are.'

That seemed not quite to be the case; for elsewhere, on 26 August 1940, RAF Bomber Command targeted Berlin, struggling through thick weather across the continent to try and hit armaments factories. There were also raids on the docks at Bremen, and swooping attacks on airfields in Belgium and northern France. It was hardly as if Britain was simply sitting back and taking it. The intensity of attack and counter-attack was to greatly increase.

Intelligence reports gathered from a variety of sources throughout August 1940 seemed to find signs of imminent Nazi attack oddly lacking. There was little indication of a build-up of armaments in Belgium or northern France; less movement of vessels around the northern French ports than might be expected. Yet this in itself may have been a feint. Moreover, why would the Nazis assemble craft that could easily be bombed long before they were needed? This indeed would appear to have been the case when, just a couple of weeks later, Britain found itself once more on official invasion alert (that is, an incursion was expected within three days) with the appearance of around 700 self-propelled barges in and around the port of Le Havre.

Before this, the Spitfire and Hurricane pilots were still heavily outnumbered but continued to counter-attack with extraordinary ferocity. This frequently involved pilots attacking German bombers not from above or from the side, but head-on, a tactic that must have seemed to Luftwaffe pilots verging on the suicidal. The aim of the British was to break up the bombing formations before their escorting fighters could intervene and take the fight elsewhere. Partly it was to do with the improved armour on the German planes; only by flying directly at them could a pilot be reasonably sure that his bullets would meet their mark. There was also evidence that the German pilots were utterly spooked by the tactic and dispersed quickly, as well they might. From their point of view, the British pilots must have looked terrifyingly insane. It is said that Dowding had not previously given his approval for this sort of action; the idea was that Spitfires should take on the fighters while Hurricanes engaged the bombers. With so few pilots, however, and with the battles unfolding at such speed, the tiny squadrons improvised and the terrifying direct assault was the result. By the end of August, the technique had complete official approval.

But the German bombers were now coming further inland, more frequently, crossing the country to find a range of targets from the Liverpool docks to large factories on the outskirts of Birmingham. There were Luftwaffe aircraft flying over Newcastle; Pilot Officer Robert Jones recalled the day in mid-August when his patrolling squadron, running low on fuel, had begun to wonder if the warnings from control had been a 'wild goose chase', when he was suddenly confronted with the terrifying sight of an enormous flight of bombers and fighters – the 'biggest I had seen since the Hendon Air Shows' – which, without even thinking of tactics or techniques, they had to take on instantly. Further down south, meanwhile, in 12 Group, Douglas Bader was increasingly furious about the way that he and his own pilots had appeared to be sidelined at this crucial moment. 'Day after day,' wrote his eager biographer, 'while the fights raged, Bader alternately sulked and stormed in the dispersal hut at Coltishall ... Ops ignored them. He kept railing at the stupidity of keeping them on the ground while outnumbered squadrons had to engage a massed enemy.'[5]

It is hard not to sympathise with Bader's passion: a warrior being denied the one fight towards which he had striven his whole life. Added to this was his own huge experience and charisma; the men in his squadron were inspired. They were not alone: so was his 12 Group commander, Leigh-Mallory. The Fighter Control Officers association now suggests that Bader and his commander had failed quite to take on board the full impact of radar, or the intricate thread of speedy communications woven by Dowding and how it broadly enabled him to deploy fighters to the right places at the right time, as opposed to simply relying on pilots' sense. Those who opposed Dowding were not necessarily to know that some dogfights, rather than being conducted by pilots sticking to principled formations, were ending up as frenzied free-for-alls. Bader's voice was to grow more resonant yet, and he and Leigh-Mallory were to be instrumental in causing Dowding some distress. Even Air Vice Marshal Park started to incline a little towards their point of view: that it might be better to send up more fighters to see off the larger German formations.

For the civilians far down below, these epic encounters in the skies were sometimes difficult to follow; for small children, the falling bombs and the bullets and the constant alien noise triggered profound anxiety. Mollie Mellish was then ten years old and living in Kent. Decades later, she recalled: 'It was during the hop-picking school holiday. On that day, waves of German planes came over from Dover and the Kent coast and I remember standing in the garden looking up at so many planes that it was like a big black cloud. I tried to count the German bombers but there were too many and I had to give up. Then Spitfires and Hurricanes came on the scene, they were dog-fighting with the German planes most of the day. There was lots of machine-gun fire and vapour trails, maybe also the odd parachute of someone was shot down ... It was the worst day, with continuous gunfire noise ...

'The boys in the village, including my brother and his friends were all out looking for shrapnel and shell cases. Some shrapnel found was very jagged and still hot.'[6]

The producers of that shrapnel were making decisions faster than split seconds. Flight Lieutenant Dennis Robinson, based at Warmwell, years later recalled one particularly harrowing engagement, and the way that it affected the course of his life afterwards: 'The first thing I felt was the thud of bullets hitting my aircraft and a long line of tracer bullets streaming out ahead of my Spitfire. In a reflex action I slammed the stick forward as far as it would go. For a brief second my Spitfire stood on its nose and I was looking straight down at mother earth thousands of feet below. Thank God my Sutton harness was good and tight. I could feel the straps biting into my flesh as I entered the vertical with airspeed building up alarmingly. I felt fear mounting. Sweating, mouth dry and near panic. No ammo and an attacker right on my tail.

'All this happened in seconds,' he added, 'but now the airspeed was nearly off the clock. I simply had to pull out and start looking for the enemy. That's what I did, turning and climbing at the same time. As I opened the throttle fully, with emergency boost selected to assist the climb, I noticed wisps of white smoke coming from the nose of my fighter. God, no! Fire!'

Like all other airmen, Mr Robinson had one abiding fear. 'Suddenly the engine stopped,' he continued. 'Apparently a bullet in the glycol tank had dispersed all the coolant and even the faithful Merlin [engine] could not stand that for long at full power. So that explained the white smoke. Blessed relief. The fuel tanks of high octane fuel are situated very close to the pilot in a Spitfire. The dread of being burned to death was one of the worst fears. It drew heavily on any reserves of courage one had. You can imagine by now, my eyes are searching wildly, frantically, looking for my adversary – but, as often happens in air combat, not a single plane was to be seen in the sky around me. The release of tension as I realised my good fortune is something that cannot be described. You only know what it is like to be given back your life if you have been through that experience.

'The problems that still confronted me ... seemed almost trivial in comparison with my situation of a few seconds before,' Mr Robinson concluded. 'I experienced this feeling several times during the battle ... It somehow changed my value system, so that things that had seemed important before never had the same degree of importance again. Maybe that's what generated the anti-authority behaviour among us. It was no good telling us not to do a victory roll over the airfield when we returned from a scrap.'[7]

Morale naturally was central; and airmen were allowed all sorts of latitude rarely extended to the members of other services. Even their entertainment was of a racier quality. The pilots of RAF Hornchurch were on a couple of occasions treated to performances from the Windmill Girls. Part of Vivian Van Damm's *Revudeville* at Soho's Windmill Theatre, the girls were famous for forming 'tableaux vivants' in the nude; the only way that they were permitted to hold a licence for performing – issued by the Lord Chamberlain – was that they stayed stock still on stage. 'If they move, it's rude,' was the dictum. And so the naked ladies would arrange themselves in scenarios such as 'Paris Street Life', with one making the shape of the Eiffel Tower.

There was also music, and comedy too; a dozen or so nude women standing stock still in silence might have been both sexy and slightly uncanny. They had been to the station before, invited by the then commanding officer Max Aitken, Lord Beaverbrook's son; he moved effortlessly in show-business circles. On that occasion, the women had put on a few garments in order to perform some sexy dance routines. In response, the station's WAAF officers staged a walkout midway through the many encores.

Any distraction, no matter how absurd, was eagerly appreciated. And in the meantime, the ever-shifting tactics of the enemy kept the pilots tensed. The German bombers weren't now aiming purely at industrial targets, or even airfields. Another tactic was what they termed 'dislocation bombing', the idea of which was to launch raids over factories and working-class housing, shattering the sleep of the workers below. The bombs that fell across the Liverpool area at the end of August, from the docks to Port Sunlight, were an element of this approach. If the planes hit any targets that could do damage to war production, then that was considered good; equally important, though, was the task of eroding the spirits of the workers, particularly in areas of high trades union membership, for there was always the possibility of fomenting damaging strikes and demonstrations, putting pressure on the government to sue for peace.

Another maddening factor, calculated to increase the psychological pressure, was the requirement for England's towns, from Swansea to Newcastle and over the border in Scotland too, to remain on the highest air-raid warning alert. The eerie banshee cry of the siren would jolt tired populations towards the shelters, their sleep for the night truly wrecked.

When Winston Churchill rose in the House on 20 August 1940, he was keenly aware of the need to bolster not only the exhausted young pilots but also the general public who understood just how much these pilots were doing to defend them. Once again, this speech of Churchill's – reported in full in *The Times* the following day – will live on immortally thanks to one phrase, which came at the core of a long and occasionally florid address. Of course, the Battle of Britain was still raging; and strikingly, Churchill chose first to issue reassurance of a different sort.

'The great air battle which has been in progress over this Island for the last few weeks has recently attained a high intensity,' the Prime Minister declared. 'It is too soon to attempt to assign limits to its scale or to its duration.' But, he went on, Britain's fighter forces were expertly inflicting grievous losses; as a result, brilliant salvage work meant that all sorts of machine parts could be given new life. Churchill was first keen to address a key national anxiety: a shortage of Spitfires. 'The splendid, nay astounding increase in the output and repair of British aircraft and engines which Lord Beaverbrook has achieved by a genius of organisation and drive, which looks like magic, has given us overflowing reserves of every type of aircraft, and an ever-mounting stream of production both in quantity and quality.'

These words were also partly for the benefit of German High Command; there was always the knowledge that such speeches would be pored over. The speech rose and swelled: 'The gratitude of every home in our Island, in our Empire, and indeed throughout the world, except in the abodes of the guilty, goes out to the British airmen who, undaunted by odds, unwearied in their constant challenge and mortal danger, are turning the tide of the world war by their prowess and by their devotion.' There then followed the phrase invoked so often today: 'Never in the field of human conflict was so much owed by so many to so few.'

His speech, though, continued at some length afterwards, mentioning the courage of the bombing crews, and then broadening out to the fallen state of France, to the possibility of new alliances elsewhere, to the prospects in the Mediterranean, and most particularly, reaching out towards the United States of America. 'The right to guide the course of world history is the noblest prize of history,' Churchill said in answer to questions about war aims. 'We are still toiling up the hill; we have not yet reached the crest-line of it; we cannot survey the landscape or even imagine what its condition will be when that longed-for moment comes. The task which lies before us immediately is at once more practical, more simple and more stern.'

There had been airy mentions of a possible invasion, largely for the purposes of dismissing the idea, but Churchill concluded – using a pointedly American image – with his thoughts about the future. 'I do not view the process with any misgivings. I could not stop it if I wished; no-one can stop it. Like the Mississippi, it just keeps rolling along. Let it roll. Let it roll on full flood, inexorable, irresistible, benignant, to broader lands and better days.'

For Fighter Command, those more benignant days were still some way off. This was not a flood with which they could roll; they were having to hold it back with all their might. Back at Uxbridge, Air Vice Marshal Park, having ceded a little ground on the number of planes sent up to fight off the invaders, at last gave 12 Group, together with Douglas Bader, the role – absolutely vital – of defending 11 Group airfields such as North Weald and Hornchurch, while 11 Group pilots took off to meet Germans head-on.

Yet in this murderous world, there were also outbreaks of a weird but genuine chivalry. Pilot Officer Dowling of RAF Hornchurch recalled the day in August 1940 when the crew of a Luftwaffe bomber that had been shot down were safely picked up, arrested and taken back to the station where they immediately 'clicked their heels and bowed'. One of the German crew was a major. It emerged that he had visited Hornchurch as a member of a pre-war delegation. Now, captured, he announced with some bravado: 'We will all be here soon.' Despite the boast – and the potential murderous ill-will in the air – a German-speaking English officer lightened the mood by taking to the camp piano and striking up a popular German tune which the bomber crew could not help themselves joining in with. Naturally, the next day, the prisoners were hauled off elsewhere for interrogation; but that night with their English counterparts gave further evidence of the mutual regard shared between highly skilled pilots.

The latter days of August saw the Germans starting to intensify their night bombing raids. Birmingham, Coventry, Plymouth, Portsmouth, Liverpool and the wider area around Merseyside were the focus of this new phase. And the attacks were heavier; many more high explosive bombs were being dropped. But at this stage, once again, the Germans were not quite succeeding on their own terms; for it appeared that a number of their pilots were failing to locate the Mersey. The Luftwaffe pilots thought that they had hit their targets; this, at least, was what they reported back to their own commanders. However, the result was that bombs fell on Wigan and St Helens, and a large number in the depths of the Cheshire countryside. An aircraft factory at Speke was on the receiving end of a few incendiary devices and several oil tanks were set ablaze at Ellesmere Port.

Then, right at the end of the month, they came for the airfields again. And this was the point at which the jagged schism between Air Chief Marshal Dowding, and Trafford Leigh-Mallory and Douglas Bader of 12 Group was painfully torn open. As Dowding said years later:

> There were occasions when Park was so hard-pressed that all his squadrons were in the air at once. But was it for a squadron commander in Norfolk, in no. 12 Group, with a clearly defined task, to decide whether he should be drawn into some other task? Park could ask Leigh-Mallory to look after some of the north-eastern aerodromes on no. 11 Group if he felt it was necessary, and there were the squadrons standing by for that very purpose. Among them was Bader's own squadron, to be called upon when necessary.[8]

On 30 August, Squadron Leader Bader led his pilots into an assault on a formation of German bombers, and they succeeded in bringing down a few of them. As a result, an exultant Bader made a request of Commander Leigh-Mallory that he should be allowed to take up many more fighter aircraft from several squadrons. Leigh-Mallory could not have agreed more vehemently. It should be remembered that the disobedience was not to spite Dowding; both men were convinced it was about the survival of the nation.

Dowding wanted them to protect airfields in the south-east; and they didn't. The inherent problem of the 'big wing' tactic was that it was fine when directed against a solid, unified formation of bombers; but often the Luftwaffe would send over feints and decoys – fighters without bombers, more waves of bombers coming behind but heading for different targets. On 30 August, as Keith Park's 11 Group fighter pilots were dealing with incursions over the south coast, the key airfield of Biggin Hill in Kent just outside London was targeted; the bombers got through with ease. [T]he attack was one of the most successful that the Germans had so far made against a Fighter Command station. Thirty-nine officers and men were killed and twenty-six wounded.[9] No. 12 Squadron failed to see the attack formation in time. Later that day, another formation of German bombers came roaring up the Thames Estuary and again turned south, subjecting the airfield to another bombing raid. Keith Park's 11 Group requested that squadrons from 12 Group patrol and defend the area around the North Weald base, just on the outskirts of London near Epping Forest. That base was indeed successfully protected; Bader and his fellow pilots launched a bravura fightback against the incomers.

But, the better to intercept the invaders, Bader disobeyed radio instructions from his controller concerning the height at which to fly. The controller had said 4,572 metres (15,000 feet); Bader chose his own co-ordinates. In part, this seemed to reflect his frustration with Dowding's RDF system; very often, Bader had found that the information passed back to him from the controllers concerning the position of the attacking force was either inaccurate or simply came in with not enough warning.

Radar was also incompatible with big wing formations. But this was where Bader and Leigh-Mallory had appeared to completely misunderstand Dowding's system. For this tactic to work, they needed time to assemble, to take off; the time simply wasn't there. The incoming Germans might be over London by the time they got themselves together. Worse: the big wing would then, of course, be picked up by Dowding's radar system; the presence of so many planes in the sky could interfere with the clarity of the readings on enemy planes. Another consideration: such formations would make the work of the anti-aircraft guns much more complex. How were the big guns to discriminate between German bombers and large numbers of RAF fighters?

———

Meanwhile the certainty prevailed that these concentrated attacks on airfields were the prologue to the invasion of England. With air bases knocked out, and the RAF unable to defend from the air, the sky would soon be filled with German paratroopers. At Bentley Priory, the table of the Operations Room had already become almost full with enemy plots in the southeastern corner.

Given that Fighter Command's squadrons contained between them approximately one thousand pilots, the raids of August had seen a frightening number of casualties and deaths. In the days around the end of August and the beginning of September, just over 100 pilots had been killed. As well as the human loss and the suffering, there was now also an alarming deficit of flying experience throughout the squadrons. 'For the whole of August, only some two hundred and sixty fighter pilots had been produced … and these were outweighed by casualties,' states the official history. 'The Command was steadily wasting away.'

The young men were there; but it took time to train them to a level where they might be able to take on the hugely experienced Luftwaffe. The memoirs of so many pilots are filled with the recurring leitmotifs of headstrong young men taking to their Spitfires, imagining that they are flying flawlessly, only to meet with hair-raising near misses – trying to land at night and completely missing the landing grounds, forgetting to lower landing gear, misjudging turns and rolls. The adrenaline gave them a fleeting illusion of immortality; the number of their fellow trainees they witnessed being torn apart in great orange blooms of flame, their planes crash-landed in fields, soon ripped that mirage away. The ground crews were dedicated and among them featured a great many experienced men, but these young pilots needed all the voices of wisdom they could get.

The stories of some casualties haunted the national imagination. One such was the Oxford rower and putative novelist Richard Hillary. On the morning of 3 September 1940, he and his fellow pilots had taken off through 'the yellow fog' that habitually settled on RAF Hornchurch, alerted to an incoming raid of at least fifty enemy fighters. Even in battle, Hillary noticed the beauty of the white clouds, 'like layers of whipped cream'. Over the Channel, they saw the enemy and the enemy saw them. What followed was a vortex of disorientating action; Hillary fixed his focus on a Messerschmitt that was to be his prey and closed in on it, giving it bursts of gunfire. With a huge red explosion the Messerschmitt jerked out of sight, but now Hillary's own plane was rocked by an explosion that shook the control stick from his hand. The cockpit was in flames; Hillary managed to tear back the hood but was then aware of a moment of piercing agony. He lost consciousness.

When he came to, Hillary was falling through the air. In a radio broadcast he made on the subject, he did not dwell on this at all, merely observing that he pulled the ripcord of his parachute. But to have passed out convinced that this was the moment of death, only then to wake flying free through the air; to be suspended between the earth and heaven, completely detached, completely free … Hillary's parachute blossomed and held, and he dropped into the waters of the North Sea. On the way down, he had become aware that he was very badly burnt; his trouser leg was seared off, there was intense pain by his hip, and when he closed one eye and looked down, he could see his horribly burnt lips jutting out like 'car tyres'. His hands had been pretty much melted;

and in the water, he scrabbled uselessly at the parachute release catch. Hillary now contemplated death more consciously, as he floated in his life-jacket in the 'not un-warm' water, and his eyesight went. He knew rescue by a passing boat was unlikely; and as much as he tried to retreat into dreamy abstraction, he remained sharply conscious. At one point, accepting quite calmly the inevitability of his death, he deflated his life-jacket and tried to slip beneath the waves. But drowning oneself is not easy; and as he kept on bobbing back up, that incredibly unlikely boat did pass by, and he was rescued.

His injuries, however, were hideous. In hospital, kept on a constant flow of morphia, Hillary was aware of floating on a 'sea of pain' as his burns were coated with tannic acid (the idea was that the acid, which formed a crust, would protect the raw flesh from further infection; in fact, it had the opposite effect). His eyesight took a long time to return; but he was aware of nurses weeping around him. Hillary one night had a dream or a vision; it was of his great college friend and fellow pilot Peter Pease. Hillary saw him in his plane, a very slight smile on his face, saw the Messerschmitt flying up behind him, and saw Pease's plane plunge to the earth. Hillary was next aware of doctors and nurses around his bed trying to calm him. A couple of days later, Hillary recalled, a mutual friend of his and Peter's visited his bedside and told him the news: Peter was dead. Again, there is a hint, in this and other stories, that flying was almost a halfway house between this life and the life beyond; and that pilots had the ability to see through the clouds that separated them.

Hillary came under the care of a pioneering plastic surgeon, A.H. Micindoe; his reconstruction of the pilot, down to new eyelids, was extraordinary, though there was little that could be done for Hillary's gnarled, crooked hands. After so many procedures, Hillary went to America in the hope of adding his voice to the efforts to bring the Americans into the war; but he was dissuaded from making public speeches for fear that his disfigurements, which could never have been wholly repaired, would instead advertise the horrors of war. He came back to a posting with Fighter Command.

But a man who has felt that power and exaltation, seen the 'fairy city' in the skies above, been through man-to-man combats of Arthurian rigour, when one either kills or is killed; how would it ever have been possible for such a man to stay on the ground? Having tasted the beauty of the skies above, the compulsion to return could certainly be described as addiction. Hillary campaigned in 1942 and 1943 to get back into the cockpit. He was set to work training a new influx of pilots and it was while out flying at night in Scotland that he crashed; both he and his radio operator were killed.[10]

In Hillary's 1942 memoir, he had seemed to suggest that there was such a thing as destiny, and that death might not be far off. But this was not fatalism; for why would such a man ever want each flight to be his last? The reverse, surely, was true: the very thing that appeared to give his life real flavour were those transcendent moments high up among the stars.

In September 1940, squadrons were being called in from quieter areas to give some respite to the pilots based in the middle of 'Hellfire Corner'. But rested pilots – and their repaired aircraft – were still limited in numbers. A number of planes had been battered quite severely and needed proper attention; the same was obviously true for so many of the young crews. At Bentley Priory, intelligence was indicating that the attacks from the air were going to get worse, not ease off. The trend for pilots such as Douglas Bader to disobey controllers and climb much higher than the altitudes they were ordered to – in order, understandably, to have the enemy below rather than above them – was leading, unfortunately, to bombers slipping through far beneath them and destroying their targets before the fighters could stop them.

The day before the start of the Blitz, 6 September 1940, the beleaguered and exhausted denizens of Bentley Priory received a secret visit from the King and Queen. Air Chief Marshal Dowding hosted a special lunch for them in the officers' mess. On that afternoon, the Germans launched three serious raids; Dowding was obliged to talk to the Queen almost incessantly for forty-five minutes about operational matters, largely because the royal party had to be kept in the subterranean Operations Room as the attack took place.

Gladys Eva, who was also there underground in what the Bentley operatives called the hole, remembered the almost dream-like intensity of coming off a shift at midnight, emerging from the well-lit control room into what should have been the dark night sky – and instead seeing a malign orange glow. In the hole, those who worked around Dowding noticed his pallor and his papery complexion; his gnawing fear was that the German attacks on the airfields would continue, that his Fighter Command would be smashed, and that thereafter, the invasion and subjugation of Britain would begin. When instead the Germans switched tactics – and set out to rain the fires of hell down on London and Britain's major industrial cities – Dowding could almost have wept with relief. Because paradoxically, these murderous raids brought fresh hope.

Chapter Fifteen

'Resist Until the Very End'

Thinking back, years later, Lord Dowding said of the start of the German bombing campaign known as the Blitz: 'It brought an intense feeling of relief to me – intense relief. I could hardly believe that the Germans would have made such a mistake. From then on it was gradually borne upon me that it was a supernatural intervention at that particular time, and that was really the crucial day.'[1] At this point of intense crisis, such a sudden blossoming of faith is perfectly understandable. By Saturday, 7 September, when that first thunderclap of destruction broke above London with demonic force, the long-anticipated invasion was understood to be nigh.

Gladys Eva recalls that time in the Operations Room vividly – but as she was eighteen years old at the time, her perspective was rather different. 'We'd been working downstairs, so we knew what they were doing to London once they started to bomb. You would go out of the hole and the whole of the sky would be lit. There were planes everywhere. You could see London easily from Stanmore. And we had been plotting them, so we knew they were over in vast numbers. But I never remember feeling anything but calm. I just loved the work.

'In the Filter Room they soon put me up on the balcony,' continues Mrs Eva. 'It was a responsibility, of course. When you put a plot on the table, you were responsible for putting it in the right place. But when you were up on the balcony, you had to be even more so.' Filter officers from both the air force and Coastal Command would be present, and they would soon know if any queries were coming through from the stations as to the accuracy of the information they were receiving. 'They would all be there because they would want and need the information for different reasons. If you look at a filter table, if you are only an eighth of an inch out, you are a mile or two out. You either had the knack to do it or you didn't. And I was lucky. You didn't have to be clever – I was just able to do it.'

Stanmore might have looked sufficiently far from London – high to the northwest on a wooded escarpment – not to be at paramount risk during the bombing campaigns. But says Mrs Eva, there was a lingering sense of vulnerability about the establishment; a sense that was sharpened with one particular incident. At one point, WAAFs were billeted close to an old convent.

'We were opposite it, and when we went on duty, a coach used to come up the Elstree Road and pick us up. One night, in a radio broadcast, Lord Haw Haw described in detail the comings and goings of this coach. And the Germans started to bomb. But they didn't bomb us – instead they got part of the convent.'

The tragedy of the nuns' deaths aside, says Mrs Eva, there was also a crucial security aspect. 'If they had hit one of our coaches, that would have been the Filter Room at that time – it would have been very, very difficult to carry on. But we didn't care. We didn't care about anything.

'We were only kids,' concludes Mrs Eva. 'We weren't fully grown. It was damn tiring. And off-duty you had nobody to do your washing and ironing and clean your room. We had all that to do as well on top of everything else. So you had to

217

have a break. You had to get away and have a laugh somewhere. You just had to – otherwise you couldn't do the work. We used to go up to London. Probably do a show or go and have a meal somewhere.'

Years later, John Willoughby de Broke, a duty controller in 11 Group Operations Room who later rose to be air commodore, told Dowding's biographer, Robert Wright:

> How lucky it was for those of us who were doing the controlling that we did not fully realise at the time what a desperately serious battle for existence this country was fighting. If we had, we might have felt an undue sense of personal responsibility in our actions. We regarded all that we did … as being part of our daily routine in life, and we carried out to the best of our ability our instructions … But none of us on my level quite realised the seriousness of the situation … we did not have access to the information that would have given us an overall picture.[2]

One might also see it as something of a mercy; understanding that the job is serious is one thing, but feeling personally responsible for the fate of each and every one of your fellow citizens is another.

But there were some in Fighter Command who were now foaming in their eagerness to bring the enemy down; and on the day that the Blitz began, Douglas Bader of 12 Squadron led a big wing formation into the skies above northeast London, once more disobeying instructions about the altitude to reach. In his biographer's account of the battle, Bader's squadron comrades struggled to keep up with him in the sky as they all took on 'a mess' of about seventy Dorniers and 110s. The scramble and the confusion worsened. 'It didn't come off – we were too slow,' Bader told

Leigh-Mallory on his return in his badly damaged plane. 'If only we could get off earlier, we could be on top and ready for them. Why can't we do that, sir?'[3]

It was on that same day, 7 September 1940, that an extraordinary demand was also made of Air Vice Marshal Keith Park by the Air Ministry. According to Park himself, his superiors ordered him to get ready to demolish every single aerodrome – and dismantle every single runway – in southeast England. If the invasion was to begin, the Germans would use these airfields. The only way to hold them off would be to make it impossible for them to land. Park was horrified by the idea, and he instantly refused. As his biography relates, he told his superiors that resistance to invasion would be utterly impossible without the airfields and 'he was determined to resist until the very end.' More than that, he argued, such a move would have a lethal effect upon morale; it would look like desperation, and giving up hope.

Also according to Orange, 'Churchill himself telephoned Park at Uxbridge that day to tell him of the invasion alert. He had not seemed particularly perturbed and neither was Park. Provided that his fighter force could still be controlled from the ground, he did not fear an invasion attempt because he believed the German fighters could be held off by part of his force, leaving the rest free to shoot down bombers and transport aircraft at will.'[4]

Throughout that summer, Air Vice Marshal Park had updated a careful and comprehensive (and, of course, highly classified) document for 11 Group, detailing closely what all personnel should do in the event of German invasion. Even as late as mid-September 1940, he was issuing new versions. 'Fighter role in the event of invasion,' he wrote. 'Fighter units will retain their full normal functions but some or all the units in 11 Group may be required to switch to other tasks ... An important role of our fighter defences in the event of an invasion will be the protection of our naval forces and their bases.' He went on to envisage the form that the German assault would take, and what his pilots could do to help repulse it. 'Fighter cover to be given to the bomber aircraft which will be attacking enemy's convoys and landing craft. Fighter cover for our Naval forces attacking the enemy's convoys ... fighter protection may have to be afforded to our own troops against the attacks of enemy dive bombers which may be operating in conjunction with a landing or covering a lodgement against our counter-offensive.'

And what if the invading Germans were to breach all forward defences? What if they were to start spreading like a contagion closer to the nerve centres of control and power? What if RAF Uxbridge itself were to be destroyed or overrun? What should the fighter pilots do then?

> Group control will be maintained as long as telephone communications and Sector Operations Rooms are intact. If Group control is not possible, Sector Commanders will immediately take control and operate their squadrons on the lines given above. If Sector control is not possible, the Senior Officer or Squadron Commander at forward aerodromes will act on his own initiative ... All squadron and flight commanders must impress upon their pilots that to defeat an attempted invasion will demand the utmost physical and mental effort from all flying personnel.

Park concluded on a note of implacable optimism: 'An attempted invasion will probably be defeated in 24, or at most 72 hours, and whilst an invasion is being attempted, all pilots must be prepared to do six patrols a day.'

In some ways it is quite easy to see how – at this ultimate moment of national emergency – Air Vice Marshal Park's position at the forefront of the expected invasion, with his seemingly natural and confident command of how to beat the enemy back, would have been a source of immense frustration to a man such as Trafford Leigh-Mallory, forced to look on from the distance of the Midlands. Park's defensive tactics did not address the central RAF schism: why not take the first available opportunity to take the fight to the Germans? To annihilate their air force before they got the chance to do exactly that to the British?

Park's pivotal position meant that he also attracted attention from elsewhere. Naturally Churchill was hugely interested in the workings of Fighter Command. And he was to visit Air Vice Marshal Park at Uxbridge the week after the Blitz began, turning up and then modestly announcing that if he was going to be in the way, then he could stay in his car and catch up with paperwork. Of course, Churchill was instantly welcomed in, and taken underground into the Operations Room, the mirror image of the set-up at Bentley Priory. The Prime Minister was advised that the air-conditioning – fine though it was – could not quite cope with the fumes from his cigar and so he had to let it go out. But as Churchill took his seat above the vast map, the German attack upon London began. Air Vice Marshal Park prowled around the table as the plots came in. Churchill commented on the vast number of enemy planes that appeared to be swooping in. Park quietly assured him that 'they would be met.' But then the Prime Minister watched as Park marshalled his very thin resources – the sparse numbers of fighters at his disposal, the backup in readiness from 12 Group. And it was brought home to Churchill what a slender thread this entire enterprise dangled from. What no one could quite know was that this day – 15 September – was also a turning point for the Luftwaffe.

In spite of the silent ill-will between 12 Group – Leigh-Mallory and Douglas Bader – and Air Chief Marshal Dowding, the flying on that Saturday from the point of view of all pilots was a breathtaking feat. Certainly the bombers got through, roaring angrily up the serpentine silver trail of the Thames Estuary to drop a massive weight of explosives on civilians below. But Bader and his big wing of five squadrons, all in formation, took them on with gusto; and those that evaded his fury met – on their way back towards the Channel – Park's 11 Group fighters, who had been waiting in ambush. Churchill had seen Park's acute anxiety that day, as the commander paced around the map table, listening for reports of losses and accounts of damage and devastation. But the Prime Minister had also seen confidence: the possibly irrational faith that despite being hugely outnumbered, the British would wear the Luftwaffe down to a point where they would consider invasion to be a most unattractive prospect.

Extraordinarily, Park was exactly right; the fury of the air fights that day, the losses sustained by the Germans, the exhaustion of the Luftwaffe pilots who limped back across the darkening Channel to their bases in France, in essence decided it for Hitler. Operation Sea Lion, the proposed plan for the Nazi invasion of Britain, remained on the table that autumn, and was mentioned in occasional messages decrypted by Bletchley Park. But Park and Dowding and Leigh-Mallory and the pilots of Fighter Command had made the case most decisively; after three months of sustained fighting, the Germans seemed no closer to gaining air supremacy over Britain. Without that, an invasion could not be counted on to succeed.

Yet the ferocity of the bombing campaign against cities now took the war to a whole new level. Where once the targets had been tactical – convoys, aerodromes – they were now civilians and their homes. The images are so familiar now that we unwittingly shut out the full weight and the horror. That first big night of the Blitz, the Luftwaffe might at least have claimed to be aiming to paralyse trade; the swoop on the mighty east London docks, the eighteenth-century warehouses filled with spices and timber. But the raids that were to follow – possibly the result of German pilots' failure to get a fix on their real targets – seemed cruelly random. Suburbs such as Kingston and Richmond and Purley were bombed, as were streets and terraces in the well-to-do district of Chelsea. And all the while, incendiaries and explosives continued to pour down upon the heads of poorer Londoners in areas such as Lambeth and Stepney.

The destruction was not just that of lives and homes; the Germans aimed for specific targets such as big railway stations, electricity stations and substations, telephone exchanges and large groups of gasholders. The aim was to render large areas completely uninhabitable. It was a continuation of the effort to wear down the morale of the working population, particularly by striking at the heavily working-class East End. Indeed, in the smarter political and artistic salons of the day – such as those frequented by Harold Nicolson and Virginia Woolf – there was some discussion of rumours that a socialist revolution was nigh, and that there was only so much the cockneys would take before attempting to seize control.

Weather made life even more difficult for the defenders; on some days in September, the cloud cover was so thick that the Germans might as well have been flying wrapped in invisibility cloaks. The radar stations, as ever, could only give limited warning of their approach – about ten minutes when they set off across the Channel – and there was little the Observer Corps could do in terms of reporting height and numbers when the attacking planes were enveloped deep in cloud. As a result, the intercepting forces often had to trust to blind luck.

On those black nights, the bombing would generally start at around eight o'clock. The uncanny wail of the air-raid sirens echoing through the streets sent families hurrying to shelters that – in many cases – were still makeshift. The bombing waves would go on until three or four in the morning. The disruption caused to infrastructure – the railways so expertly targeted, resulting in huge congestion and preventing goods from getting through in subsequent days – was one thing; the sleep deprivation was another. The psychology was acute: those forced into night after night of disturbed sleep, or indeed complete lack of rest, would find the subsequent days very difficult. They would be fatigued at work, their judgement sometimes as wobbly as that of a drunk.

Night fighting was still in the experimental stage; and the night-fighting squadrons were a force separate from the daytime Spitfire and Hurricane crews. They were obviously still needed for daylight attacks. In those early days of the Blitz, Dowding's options were limited; they involved a great deal of focus and indeed bravery from the anti-aircraft gunners, aided by those operating the vast searchlights that they would try to triangulate on circling bombers. In the shelters, this was a further disturbance; anti-aircraft gun strength was doubled, and as the guns were fired from their key positions all over the capital, from Nunhead to Primrose Hill, the report would send its shockwave of sound for miles.

In the meantime, working around the clock in the operations rooms were young women like Patricia Clark. In her case, promotion came quite swiftly, but the complexity and focus of the job did not let up. Obviously, the need for accuracy on the plotting table became even more demanding, she says, 'when there were an awful lot of aircraft'. The task was easy when it was one. 'But when you got a mass of counters, then you had to mentally get a picture of what was happening.' If a hundred planes were coming in, they were represented on the table with a box rather than with counters signifying a hundred aircraft. 'It became chaotic then and if you weren't watching what you were doing, it could lead to mistakes. Especially if there was a dogfight or something and you got a "friendly" plane near a "hostile" … but it became completely automatic after a while. You could visualise it. You didn't have to stop to work it out.'

The tension between Air Chief Marshal Dowding and Group Commander Leigh-Mallory was now boiling over. The question of taking on the enemy with all the might available – Douglas Bader's squadrons having flown like demons around the areas of North Weald and Hornchurch, looking for Luftwaffe targets to pick off – was now brought very much to the fore at the Air Ministry. Dowding was profoundly hurt by what was to follow – and remained so for decades afterwards. In essence, Leigh-Mallory went behind his back; and indeed, according to Park, he had long intended to do so, having declared after one meeting some weeks back that he wanted him removed.

Dowding mournfully told his biographer:

At the time I thought that this whole business of intense discussion about whether we should use three, four or five squadron wings was so simple and inconsequential that it really hardly deserved a long statement being made. But I must have been wrong there. Not about the principle of the thing or its importance. But about what people had in mind. It became obvious after a while that several people in responsible positions did hold opinions that were contrary to mine. And since in their eyes I seemed to be refusing to listen to what they had to say, I was sentenced without trial. There's no doubt at all in my mind now that it was on that subject – the big wings – that Park and I were judged and condemned.[5]

This internal battle was bruising to both sides; for instance, after Douglas Bader had made some spectacular claims about the high numbers of German planes successfully shot down in his big wing formations, Dowding had written to Leigh-Mallory with the rather tactless sentiment: 'I read a great many combat reports and I think I am beginning to pick out those which can be relied on and those which throw in claims at the end for good measure.' Keith Park, on hearing this, added his own question: were those German bombers shot down before – or after – they had reached and destroyed their targets?

There were also accusations and counter-accusations that Leigh-Mallory and the pilots of 12 Group were simply not obeying the orders passed on to them by Fighter Command; that there were instances where, for example, they had been told to patrol the air bases at North Weald and Hornchurch while 11 Group was down in Kent fighting off bombers – but that 12 Group had strayed into Kent themselves, leaving the bases undefended when the Germans came up the Thames and bombed them. There were, too, outbreaks of confusion caused by the vast formations favoured by Bader and his fellow pilot, leading to misunderstanding and misidentification in the skies over Canterbury, and on the ground too.

The technology was still in some cases rather primitive. Some planes, for instance, were now fitted with VHF radios, rather than the high frequency system still in use by other fighters; with differing frequencies in operation, however, it was impossible for pilots from different groups – in this case 11 and 12 – to communicate with each other directly. The result could be a carnival of confusion in the skies. But the real seeping poison was that Dowding and Park appeared not to have the confidence of Air Ministry figures such as Sir Charles Portal.

It might seem extraordinary now that meetings were being convened in the Air Ministry at a moment of such exquisite national emergency: surely the remorseless night-time bombing of London would focus priorities a little more clearly? And yet the Blitz was, in its own way, precisely the point. When, in October 1940, Park and Air Chief Marshal Dowding were summoned for a meeting at the Air Ministry, they found Leigh-Mallory and Squadron Leader Bader sitting there. It was unprecedented – not to say highly irregular – for an officer to be brought along to a conference. But Leigh-Mallory wanted William Sholto Douglas, then deputy chief of the Air Staff, to hear what the exceptionally forceful Bader had to say. Bader did not hold back. It was obvious even before he started where the sympathies of the senior personnel lay. This meeting cemented them. After having done so much to ensure that the Nazis never gained enough purchase to invade, both Park and Dowding sensed that they were regarded as hindrances rather than helps.

Neither of them could have foreseen just how abrupt and unjust their dismissals would be. But even as the scenario was unfolding, the Fighter Command structure that Dowding had constructed was growing further; there were operations rooms being established deep into the country. And working in them was an eager new generation of women and men who were about to step into a dazzling – and top secret – world.

Chapter Sixteen

'This Was War and We Were Fighting'

Having thrown herself with such gusto into life at Bentley Priory, Patricia Clark now found herself facing a new challenge within an expanding Fighter Command. 'I went to Rudloe Manor,' she says. This, as it turned out, was an extremely attractive proposition: a seventeenth-century house not far from the spa town of Bath, built with the same honeyed stone, and located amid green hills. It had an added dimension: a secret network of tunnels beneath. Moreover, Patricia Clark discovered that she was something of a pioneer. 'At that stage, the Rudloe station had never had women on it. They were not equipped for women. It was part of radar 10 Group, not long started.' She describes the first site of the Operations Room there: 'They had this converted cowshed. They hadn't built the underground block yet. It was very primitive. The hayloft had been turned into the balcony that looked down over the table. And the lights would go off; we had candlelight, we had to have greatcoats on in the winter because there was no heating. But it was all very exciting.'

Despite the low-tech surroundings, the work involved the newest technology; and in some quarters, there was still scepticism that delicate females would be able to cope. 'We were being tested to see whether we were able to do the work,' says Patricia Clark with a laugh. 'Which was ridiculous for anyone who was thinking about it.' The operations table, she says, was much better suited for women 'because clearly women's fingers are much narrower and smaller – so a conglomeration of great big men's hands are going to be less suitable for coping. And, of course, most women – not me – were good at embroidery. Or sewing, or things where they used their fingers.'

The early days of the Rudloe Manor establishment saw a great deal of cheerful extemporisation and mis-understandings. 'At first, there were six girls and I, all together, living in the same Nissen hut, and one day, a sign went up at the end of the hut with a notice: "You are to report for nit inspection at 2.30 on Friday afternoon." We looked at that and asked each other: "What's that supposed to be?" And then someone said, "It's a typing error of course, it's kit inspection." So we laid out all our kit. We had never heard of a nit at our schools.

'So along comes the sergeant,' she continues, laughing. 'He shouts, "What the bloody hell do you think you're doing? It's nit inspection! Don't you know what a nit is?" And of course, feeling very stupid and very ignorant, we trailed along for nit inspection – we were absolutely horrified at the idea that people had bugs in their hair. Inconceivable from the homes we came from! Even though it sounds awfully snobbish.'

The early days at Rudloe Manor also posed uniquely delicate problems; the notion of having women working in such a place was still highly novel, and not all the ideal arrangements had been made beforehand. 'Being a men's station, they were not equipped for women's monthly problems. Inevitably, within a very short while, the camp plumbing system broke down.'

The solution was very far from ideal. 'Eventually they decided that until they had got organised, we were to go to the incinerator which was across the camp,' continues Mrs Clark. 'In order to cross the camp, you had to cross the men's quarters. And, of course, whenever we were down there, the only reason we could be down there was for that. We all knew this and the men used to make noises as we went by.'

This exquisite embarrassment led to one more misunderstanding. 'Up goes another sign,' says Mrs Clark. '"Report to Hut such and such for VD lecture." We looked at that and thought, is this another typing error? We decided it was. We thought it was WD – Works Department. So down we went, a bit on the late side. We went in the back of the hut and the place was full, all seated. And at the platform at the end, there was a huge blackboard, and on it a diagram. And there were two yellow circles and then two mauve pipes that came down into another coloured pipe. Quite obviously, we thought it was a diagram of the camp plumbing system. We went out of that building as ignorant as we came in. Not only had we never heard of VD, we knew very little about anatomy! Let alone men's anatomy. We were totally innocent.

'Some of the girls had a clue – one of the girls had a brother and she was a font of information because she knew what men looked like. And we were nearly twenty. When I talk to my grandchildren, they think I'm making it up, but it's quite true. So our life at Rudloe Manor had its complications and its difficulties but we all settled down in the end. It was very easy going at first because there was no female administration there, it was the men who were responsible for us.'

After her time studying in pre-war Germany, Patricia Clark was used to being independent, and naturally welcomed the chance for more such freedom. Allied to this was the immense satisfaction of doing a job – a highly secret job – where she could see, right before her eyes, the difference that they were making, day after day. The kind of life she was now leading had its own appeal; wartime privations were a nuisance, but she found that she rather loved her new rural billet, nestled deep in the heart of Wiltshire. 'We were billeted out to Corsham village where we were in a little self-contained four-up two-down with one bathroom. Four girls in a room, about sixteen in total – and one bathroom. And we had been brought up to have a bath every day. So there would be queues for the bathroom and the water would run out. And the loo was in the bathroom as well, so – well, concessions were made by everybody. But it was all rather exciting. Here we were, this was war and we were fighting it.'

Eileen Younghusband also recalls the exhilaration not merely of working at Rudloe but being picked out as exceptionally good at what she did: 'There was a wing commander called Rudd, and he knew I was quite good at maths.' One day he launched a surprise on her. 'He sent me into a separate room and said, "I want you to convert the Filter Room table as if it is on a globe." Why he ever asked me to do that I don't know, because it wouldn't have been feasible to have it on a table made like that. It was just a test. I did it.'

Wing Commander Rudd was clearly impressed. 'He said, "I'm putting you forward as a filter officer."' However, the news was unwelcome – by that stage, Eileen Younghusband had her own ideas of what she wanted to do. 'I've already applied for Intelligence,' she told him.

He replied, 'I'm sorry, I've cancelled it.'

To which she responded, 'But I'm going up for an interview next week. He said, "Well you won't get it." And it was perfectly true.'

Determined to get her own way, Eileen Younghusband travelled to London for her Intelligence interview; it took her a while to realise that anything was wrong. On arriving at the central London address, 'I was told to go to room

fifty-two up the stairs ... there was no one in there. I sat down
– it was one of those rooms with glass in the door and a
corridor outside and people looking in. People kept on
looking in at me, but no one arrived. And then I went
downstairs – and I realised that it had been fixed, that I
wouldn't see anybody. So I came back to Bath. And Wing
Commander Rudd said: "I told you so."'

It hadn't been that Eileen Younghusband had wanted to
escape from Fighter Command; she simply had energy and
a thirst for excitement. 'I ticked all the boxes. And I suppose
I was a bit ambitious,' she says now, laughing. 'I didn't want
to just be a plotter all my life.

'But Wing Commander Rudd had this idea and that was
it. And to be quite honest, he was probably right, as there
were only a certain number of people who could do the job
– who had the right attitude. So I went straight away on the
filterer course.'

In the end, she was not too disappointed; the work was
intensely involving as well as a challenge to pick up. 'To be a
filterer was a really demanding job, more demanding than a
plotter obviously. The plotter was only putting on the table
what they had been told. They had to be correct, they had to
understand but they didn't have to make many great
decisions ... unless they couldn't get information. Then they
had to say to whoever was on the balcony, "Ma'am, I can't
get what I want to know from the radar station." But that
didn't happen very often because everyone worked so well.
And we got to know the radar operators. Because we were
there eight hours at a time, you knew all about the radar
operators – their background, whether they were married,
what they liked doing ... and that talking when you weren't
working was called binding.'

In the depths of the country, the nights were clearly a
great deal quieter than in London. But this sense of peace

presented its own difficulties when it came to shifts in the early hours of the morning. 'On quiet nights you had to keep alert in case anything happened. But when it was foggy for example, and you were underground, heating wasn't as good, you were either boiling hot or freezing cold, the air-conditioning was indifferent. There was no smoking, either.' In order to combat any longueurs and to help keep their eyes open, some women developed side interests during their shifts. 'Lots of them brought knitting to do,' says Mrs Younghusband. 'They dropped it immediately if anything started to happen. Then they were writing love letters. But you had to be ready.'

As she said, Eileen Younghusband did not stay long at Rudloe Manor – she was about to be given grander responsibilities – but some aspects of the place she found utterly intriguing. 'We were underground in the quarries,' she says with delight. 'Where all the stone was taken out to build Bath.' More importantly, she adds conspiratorially, 'that's where the Crown Jewels were rumoured to be kept.' Such apocryphal stories, or tales that entire collections of paintings from the National Gallery were stashed down there as well, gave tea breaks an almost surreal dimension of interest.

Back east, the assault on London was ineluctable; night after night of burst sewers, of hospital wards being hit, of buses flattened into roads. The German planes were once more ranging more widely across the country: to Coventry and Birmingham, to Manchester, Liverpool and up to Glasgow. The prospects of invasion were felt to be receding, and with the season of storms upon the Channel, any attempted crossings with large quantities of materiel would have been impractical. But the internal pressure upon Fighter Command was intense, and for senior War Office and Air Ministry figures to have to pick their way through the traffic chaos engendered by each night's Blitz can't have cast a tremendously positive light on Dowding's tactics for the defence of the city.

The differences between Keith Park's 11 Group and Leigh-Mallory's 12 Group widened and became ever more belligerent, Park firing off memos complaining about the length of time it took for 12 Group's squadrons to fly south to back up 11 Group. Air Vice Marshal Sholto Douglas seemed to be hearing a lot of the complaints from both Park and the Leigh-Mallory camp, and this fierce internal dispute was now exhausting his patience. Sholto Douglas commented in a confidential letter to Dowding at the time:

> I think that it is important that this difference of opinion should be resolved as quickly as possible, since it seems to be leading to a good deal of bitterness not only between the two A.O.C.s but between the squadrons. This obviously cannot be allowed to go on and I think it is for you to put the matter right by an authoritative statement of your views. This could be far more satisfactory than for the Air Ministry to try and act as the referee.[1]

Tellingly, though, Sholto Douglas also observed in the same letter: 'I have a feeling – which may not be justified – that Park has a subconscious aversion to another Group coming down and fighting in his area.' This was the insinuation that shocked Dowding. The entire point about his system was that it was based on careful calculations, and on knowing exactly who was where; this alternative laid open the possibility of anarchy in the skies, a shoot-out free-for-all that Fighter Command at Bentley Priory would not easily be able to follow, preventing them from issuing effective orders for battle.

The ebb and flow of power is ceaselessly fascinating; there comes a point at which one is simply going to lose the argument, even if all the logic is in one's favour. The Battle of Britain was a tremendous psychic shock to the nation, for all of the blithe insouciance relayed by the newspapers and the newsreels. The country was facing an enemy that had already forced it into a miserable and utterly humiliating retreat off the beaches of northern France; that same enemy was now soaring high above every night, dropping hundreds of tons of bombs on vulnerable civilians. The mass psychology of helpless anger was intense; which was why, even at the height of the Battle of Britain, the brave pilots were turned into something approaching a cult. And it was Douglas Bader who best expressed the outrage and the fury; it is wholly unsurprising that the Air Ministry was so receptive to his bellicosity. He was a hugely skilled, hugely courageous warrior; exactly what was needed to inspire the other pilots. Looking at the austere, unsmiling, late middle-aged figure of Dowding, perhaps his superiors in the Air Ministry subconsciously wondered if such a careful, fastidious figure was any use against an enemy so unprecedentedly ruthless. Even if all his arguments had been accepted, would Dowding really have survived?

There is, in the archives, a crisply written and deeply felt memo from Dowding to Winston Churchill, dated 24 October 1940 and headed simply 'Prime Minister'. It was an impassioned defence against a hostile briefing that Churchill had received from the Air Ministry:

The Secretary of State's minute contains a few inaccuracies. Only one of these is really important. This is the statement that it is an undoubted fact that time is saved in getting Squadrons into the air by filtering at Group Headquarters. If this were a fact, it would be a very valid argument in favour of decentralisation; but it is substantially untrue. Plots are 'told' to Group headquarters from my table without delay, and the average lag in the transmission of a plot is less than 15 seconds.

And who was the architect of this system? 'The fact is,' continued Dowding, 'that the metaphorical edifice which you have seen in my Operations and Filter Room has been built up, brick by brick, under my own eye, during the past 4 years.' After addressing several other points, in a tone that was unmistakably aggrieved, Dowding wrote: 'The system which I have devised may not be perfect; but it cannot be improved by disruptive involvement on the part of people who do not understand it as a whole.' He went on – via means of an appended diagram – to explain the positioning of 11 and 12 Groups, and the radio direction finding system, and how, if both groups spotted an enemy aeroplane on their systems, and if they both independently decided to act without telling each other, the result would be dangerous chaos. 'I mention these, perhaps trivial, points to show what a number of things one has to think about when coming to a decision in these matters.

'My main grievance, however,' Dowding added, 'is in the matter of the expenditure of my time in arguing with the Air Staff every intimate detail of my organisation. Surely a Commander-in-Chief should be left to manage his own affairs if the general result is satisfactory.'[2]

The protests were not enough; the foundations of Dowding's command were being corroded beyond saving. For months and years, he had been kept dangling on the subject of his retirement. At the height of the Battle of Britain, the Air Ministry had the goodness not to stipulate a specific date at which they wanted him gone. But after his Air Ministry meeting with Leigh-Mallory and unexpected guest Bader, Dowding once more felt that chill, seemed to understand that any authority he had had was fast draining away. Even more of that command flowed away when he received a copy of a report by Harold Balfour, Under-Secretary of State for Air, which was sent on to the Air Ministry. Balfour had visited Bader's station – Duxford – and had heard a series of complaints from the pilots there about Fighter Command: the way that they were never told in time about raids; the way that Air Vice Marshal Park's 11 Group wanted to keep them out of the action; and the way that their carefully practised wing formations were all in vain as they were never given the chance 'to shoot down Germans'. Worse yet was a suggestion that 11 Group pilots were suffering from damaged morale being forced day after day to take on incoming forces in such small numbers, knowing that their colleagues in 12 Group operated in much bigger packs.

There are times when one can argue with all the vigour in the world; but the people listening are firmly set, and are now only hearing the tone of one's voice. And so when Dowding was forced to respond, he was lethally also forced to voice criticism of Douglas Bader, as well as the author of the report, Harold Balfour. Balfour himself had been a pilot of great skill. He was no pin-striped politician. Nonetheless, Dowding complained of 'the question of an Under-Secretary of State listening to the accusations of a junior officer against the Air Officer Commanding Group, and putting them on paper in the pious hope that the officer will not get into trouble. Balfour has been in the service and ought to know better.' Then there was Douglas Bader, who 'whatever his other merits suffers from over-development of the critical faculties'.

Dowding added: 'This might give an opportunity of moving young Bader to another station where he would be kept in better control. His amazing gallantry will protect him from disciplinary action if it can be possibly avoided.'[3]

But that amazing gallantry stood in sharp contrast to what must have looked like grey desiccation. Since then, all sorts of 11 Group pilots have come forward to testify that Bader was wrong; that their morale throughout the Battle of Britain remained high. James 'Ginger' Lacey, a pilot with the second-highest 'score' of hits against the Luftwaffe, later said: 'If anyone's morale should have been affected, it should have been ours, but it was not. We were tired, and frightened, and under strength, but we were never lacking in morale, and certainly not over the fact that we weren't using big wings. Far from morale being affected by the lack of big wings, with the job we had to do in 11 Group, we preferred to be without them.'[4]

Further discussions took place to which Dowding was not invited; night after night, as the German bombing campaign over London echoed across to the hill on which Bentley Priory stood, he worked into the early hours, seeing off paperwork. It was in mid-November, against this backdrop of a city being ruthlessly smashed, that he received the telephone call from the Secretary of State for Air. As Dowding recalled years later:

He told me that I was to relinquish my command immediately. I asked what was meant by immediately, and I was told it would take effect within the next day or so. Since that was tantamount to my being given 24 hours notice, and verbally at that, I pointed out that it was perfectly absurd that I should be relieved of my command in this way unless it was thought that I had committed some major crime or something like that.

But all I could get in reply was that the decision had been reached, and that was that, with no explanation for such a precipitate step being taken.[5]

It is sometimes said that, the term 'fair' is for the playground; and though it still seems shocking that Dowding could have been treated so peremptorily, his wounded feelings have to be balanced against the day-to-day context. Over that weekend – 16 and 17 November – London and coastal towns in the southeast were once again pounded. 'Hospitals, churches, chapels, a rest centre for the homeless … were all selected as targets,' reported *The Times*. But over and above those cases was the now notorious bombing of Coventry on the night and early morning of 14/15 November. By the moonlit midnight, the night the fires were so intense that iron pipes melted and ran molten and orange along street gutters. There were hundreds of deaths, and hundreds of casualties: and because of the relatively small size of the city, the damage was much more focused. To this day, controversy about whether it was known in advance that the city was to be bombed continues to flicker. There was a theory – promulgated by an early book about the work of Bletchley Park – that the codebreakers had intercepted messages revealing that Coventry was to be the target. According to this theory, it might have been possible either to stage an evacuation or send in extra air reinforcements – but nothing could be done. For if the Luftwaffe saw that the town was prepared, then they would know that their codes had been cracked, and they would ramp up the security of Enigma to a point that would render it unbreakable in the future. The story has been dismissed consistently – Bletchley Park knew only that a town in the Midlands was to be targeted, and it became totally clear only when the bombers were approaching that it was Coventry, and not Derby or Birmingham, that had been selected.

Coventry was ringed with industry; but on that clear November night, the bombers reduced the historic town centre to a bloody inferno. By the Monday morning – when Air Chief Marshal Dowding knew that he was to be removed from his job – the thick smoke was still rising above the city. The King and Queen had been to visit. The broken bodies were still being accounted for.

And it was on that same Monday, 18 November, that – as often seemed to be the case with the beleaguered Air Chief Marshal – his new job was announced to the world via page four of that morning's edition of *The Times*. 'At the special request of the Minister for Aircraft Production,' the report ran, 'Air Chief Marshal Sir Hugh Dowding, who has held the post of Air Officer Commanding in Chief, Fighter Command, since July 1936, is being seconded to his department for special duty, in the United States of America.' His successor was announced as Air Vice Marshal Sholto Douglas.

Readers must have been a shade puzzled, especially given that America was not yet in the war; what would Sir Hugh Dowding be doing over there at this crucial point? And why at the behest of Lord Beaverbrook? There was one more turn of the screw for Dowding: Sholto Douglas was not quite ready to assume command. Still reeling from his sacking, Dowding got home in the early hours that Monday morning to receive this letter:

> The Secretary of State has asked me to consult you about the announcement and date of Douglas taking over from you. There has unfortunately been a slight leakage to the Press which we all much regret and therefore we want to announce a list of appointments ... Douglas cannot be made available to take over until Monday week the 25th, and what I am asking is whether

you would agree to carry on in command until the latter date.[6]

It was a resounding final insult: yet one more postponement after years of being told that his time was up. Yet it had a further shading of cruelty. The house in Stanmore was there at the disposal of the commander-in-chief. Dowding and his sister Hilda would have to move out – very quickly – to make way for Sholto Douglas.

What did the Prime Minister make of it all? Such internal upheavals and furious politicking were not unknown. Just months before, General Lord Gort had been replaced as commander-in-chief of the British forces evacuated from Dunkirk; he was sent off to oversee matters of training. A little later on in the war, Commander Alistair Denniston, director of the Bletchley Park codebreaking operation, would be bumped sideways to another department back in London while his younger, more aggressive deputy Edward Travis took over. Dowding met with Churchill not long afterwards, and the Prime Minister asked him how he had felt about being replaced. There was a curious sense – clearly fostered by Churchill – that he had known nothing of these behind-the-scenes conflicts, and that moreover he was powerless to interfere in such matters.

Yet it is inconceivable that he knew nothing of the distaste for Dowding in the Air Ministry. And psychologically, from what we know of Churchill the warrior – from the headstrong adventuring journalist onwards – it is fair to speculate that he would instinctively have sided with the gung-ho Trafford Leigh-Mallory and the roaring Douglas Bader. Dowding never made any secret of the deep hurt he felt. Later he said: 'That is what I have never been able to understand. Everything seemed to go by the board: courtesy, good manners, the customary practices, the drill or procedure or whatever you like to call it. The whole way in which it was done was so hole-in-the-corner, just as if … well … as if something had to be hushed up … So many times I have asked myself why this extraordinary situation was forced upon me.'[7]

Squadron Leader Douglas Bader later expressed his feelings on the way that events turned. He was, he let his biographer know, 'deeply upset'. But the sacking was reconfigured as a 'reshuffle'.[8]

The same fate was visited upon Air Vice Marshal Keith Park the following week; to his own horror, he found himself being replaced by Trafford Leigh-Mallory, the group commander who had in his own view done so little to support him. Park had been working on the technical issues surrounding night fighting, and any chance that there might have been of taking on the Luftwaffe under cover of perfect darkness. Different planes – Beaufighters – would take the place of Hurricanes and Spitfires with their all too visible exhausts. The tactics would have to be different too. Yet for Park, all of this came to a juddering halt; he was told that he was to be relieved of his command. He later wrote to the Commander of 13 Group, Rand Saul: 'As I was told that the only reason for my leaving 11 Group was because I had carried the baby long enough for one man and was due for a rest from the responsibility, I do not quite see why I should be stuffed into a very busy office job at the Air Ministry.'[9]

Given the place that he now occupies in history, the treatment of Keith Park is startling in its abruptness. He himself recalled that his successor Leigh-Mallory did not even 'attend to the usual formality' when it came to one man handing command to another. Just a week or so later, though, Park was swiftly honoured: he travelled to Buckingham Palace to be invested as a Companion of the Most Honourable Order of the Bath. Park's pilots appeared to be unified in their astonishment at the idea of him moving on. It was the Hornchurch station that provided the most heartfelt send-off, not least because of Park's friendship with Group Captain Cecil Bouchier, who wrote to tell him that Park first coming to 11 Group meant that 'we gained the one man above all others in our Service who by his own infinite efforts and personal example would not only ensure ultimate victory but inspire it.'

Group Captain Peter Townsend was astonished by events as well. Writing of Dowding and Park, he said: 'The two victors thus realised the sad truth: that men are seldom grateful for their saviours. But in this case, the British people, themselves under heavy fire from the enemy, could be forgiven for not knowing they owed their salvation to Dowding and Park, especially as both men had remained in the background throughout the battle.'[10]

He went on to quote Park's comments given a few years later: 'To my dying day I shall feel bitter at the base intrigue which was used to remove Dowding and myself as soon as we had won the Battle of Britain.'

Park had been thinking confidently ahead to a 'spring offensive'; all the warmest words and honours could not conceal the anger that he was to nurse for decades afterwards. The work at Bentley Priory and Uxbridge, and at the fast-multiplying stations across the country, would take on quite a different flavour. Douglas Bader was transferred to 11 Group and on top was awarded the Distinguished Flying Cross. It in part made up for his frustration that the RAF seemed unable to prevent the nightly onslaught, the bombing raids in the dark. Technology was evolving too; Bader's squadron was getting used to the new generation of Hurricane Mk 2s. Paul Brickhill wrote that these new planes brought out a kind of glee in Bader. They had 'more power, were faster, could climb higher and all had the new and better VHF radio. Now in the routine of unexciting readiness,

Bader sometimes swashbuckled about, jabbing his thumb nostalgically on an imaginary gun-button with an accompanying "raspberry" to signify the rattling guns.'[11]

It is greatly to Bader's credit that even after the events of the last few weeks and months, that essentially exuberant spirit could not be repressed. And with the Battle of Britain over, life for the pilots and for the hundreds of WAAFs working alongside them was to take on a range of different dimensions as well.

Chapter Seventeen

A Dog Called Heinkel

Even the most extraordinary lives can come to seem normal; and in the war, the women as well as the men adapted quickly to the demands being placed upon them. At seventeenth-century Rudloe Manor in Wiltshire, there were moments of high comedy and irrepressible spirits. Patricia Clark and her coterie of privately educated young women were especially amused at the way, in the early days, the command system worked. 'The men were very lax with us,' says Mrs Clark. 'Think about it – think about a forty-year-old man, a regular officer, in charge of the camp. He suddenly gets this English boarding school girl on a charge in front of him. What's he supposed to do?' There was an awkwardness; the officers didn't feel able to bark orders at genteel young ladies. But there were also wider questions of rules, and when they could be bent or broken.

'As an example,' says Mrs Clark, 'whilst I was at Rudloe, I had Heinkel. He was called Heinkel,' she explains, 'because all the other dogs on the camp were called Spitfire, Bow – all English planes. I was originally going to get a Dachshund. I had to wait for it because it was coming from a litter. And we decided if it was going to be a German sausage dog, it would have a German name. But the litter turned out to be all bitches, which you couldn't have on a camp. So the dog-breeding woman said to me, "I have a very nice corgi puppy, I'll send it down to Bath on the train."

'We went in to get it off the train,' continues Mrs Clark, 'and it looked like a drowned pig – dark wet fur, it had obviously wet itself in its cardboard box. It was the most miserable looking, unattractive object you have ever seen. I said to the girls, "No way, I can't have it, it's going back." The next train wasn't for an hour, and the weather was lovely. I had the roof down on the car. I left the dog in its cardboard box with the lid open, on the back seat. Off we went to do some shopping. When we came back, he had somehow managed to get out of the box and had got at a packet of Smiths potato crisps and he was sitting there surrounded by crumbs and looking up at me as if to say, "I've enjoyed myself. Had lunch." I fell in love with him.'

Mrs Clark, it seems, was not alone. When she took the adorable scrap back to camp, even senior figures such as Wing Commander Rudd were bowled over. Others, however, were sterner.

'This administrative woman officer arrived on the camp a bit later,' says Mrs Clark, 'and declared that we could not have dogs running about. I was told to get rid of him.'

She said, 'That's not fair, there are other dogs on the camp – the group captain has got a dog.'

The woman officer said, 'The group captain is entitled to have what he wants.'

This was unfair, thought Mrs Clark. She said, 'I'll go and see him.'

The group captain told her, 'I suppose there's a reason. Possibly,' he added, 'my dog is better behaved than your dog.'

She replied, 'No dog is better behaved than mine and I can prove it to you if you like.'

So they had a competition: which dog was more obedient? The trial involved a thrown ball to be fetched, and the requirement for each dog to hold back until told otherwise. The group captain's dog folded, however. Heinkel had had a secret advantage: he had been trained with a toy rabbit. The group captain conceded defeat and had a word with the strict female regulation officer. Heinkel stayed put.

As a postscript, Mrs Clark adds, 'Years after, on Victoria station, people would come up and say, "That's Heinkel isn't it?" They didn't remember me – but they did remember the dog!'

Among the Fighter Command stations up and down the country, RAF Watnall, which became the operational headquarters of No. 12 Group in Nottinghamshire, was less popular among some WAAFs; the Midlands countryside was flatter, the nightlife less exotic. Some women made their own entertainment, as Gladys Eva, later promoted to flight corporal, discovered one day: 'You had to see that all the girls had made their beds properly and were dressed properly. Get them into line to march them on. But one day when I came on duty, two women were missing. I said: "Where's so and so and so and so?"'

'Oh,' she was told, 'They're not here. They were caught in bed together last night.'

'Whatever for?' she said.

'The whole place erupted. The girls were absolutely hysterical. I had no idea at all what a lesbian was. But most of them had worked in an office and had seen … things that I hadn't. Soon I knew EVERYTHING. Oh dear!'

Working with the WAAFs also brought moments of intense professional pride; this was especially true for Eileen Younghusband, who found herself being promoted and becoming a commissioned officer. At a time when young women had practically no voice at all in any sort of workplace, this was a remarkable development, and initially there were a few awkward matters to negotiate.

'There was one brilliant moment,' she recalls of the time when her commission came through. 'It was on the train. Because as a commissioned officer, you were entitled to go and sit in first class.' There was a sense of initial discomfort too. Wearing the very smart new blue officer's uniform, she felt a spasm of what might be termed imposter anxiety: would male officers remonstrate with her for having the brass neck and audacity to claim privileges that she perceived not to be rightfully hers? But they did not.

Then there were other things to get used to. 'Like when a male sergeant saluted me one day when I was going on duty, about a week after I had been commissioned – well, he saluted me and I had to salute him,' says Mrs Younghusband. 'I had to acknowledge it. But I did think for a moment, what do I … I was twenty. Neither my brother nor my father nor (later) my son ever knew about the work that I was doing.' She had, of course, signed the Official Secrets Act. 'But my parents knew I had been commissioned. They were proud.'

Patricia Clark also found herself being elevated to the level of officer; like Eileen Younghusband, she was tremendously young. 'I was commissioned very quickly. I was lucky. We were more or less the first girls in there. So when the men left – and they needed people quickly – they had to promote quickly. I don't think I should have been promoted at all. I suppose I did the job adequately because otherwise I wouldn't have been promoted again – I must have been able to do it. But there I was, twenty years old, giving people orders who were perhaps thirty or forty, it didn't seem right. Didn't do it round the camp, only on duty. But when some middle-aged man would go by and salute me, I would feel slightly odd … and I never got to grips with what stripes meant what. The war made an enormous difference to the whole class system. You realised that there was an acceptable other half.'

But Mrs Clark was to find that some aspects of the officer – and class – system were very rigid. One night in Bath, on leave from Rudloe, she had met a young man called Mel.

'Not long after I had arrived at Rudloe, and I had the car, there was a dance at the NAAFI on the camp. All the men were at the bar and all the women were down the far end of the room. When the music started, the men came down, picked a girl, took them on to the dance floor.

'I thought, whatever have I come to? When I'd been out with my mother's friends' sons, they would call with a camellia or whatever, and you were then escorted there and back. So I was standing in the NAAFI hut talking to this girl – one of my friends, very pretty, blonde, lovely long legs. And this chap comes down and his intention is to ask her to dance. But a second chap appears at the side of her and beats him to it. So the first chap, rather than having to look stupid and walk back up to the bar, taps me on the shoulder and says: "Would *you* like to dance?"

'I didn't know what I was going to do. I didn't want to be left standing there, so I said yes. He took me on the floor – he was a super dancer, and great fun. He was,' Mrs Clark adds, sotto voce, 'lower class.

'But it was such fun, I thoroughly enjoyed myself.'

It was very hot in the NAAFI, and her companion asked if she would like to come outside for some fresh air. Once they were outside, he said, 'Do you smoke?'

'No,' she replied.

So he said: 'Would you mind if I smoke?' He lit a Woodbine, held out the match and said, 'Blow it out.'

'Can't you?' she answered.

'No, no,' he said, 'I want you to do it.'

So she blew out the match, and was thus ensnared in his cunning trap. 'Well, you know that's a forfeit,' he said.

'What do you mean?' she asked.

He answered, 'If you blow out a match like that, you have to give a person a kiss.'

'Innocently, I thought, oh, I didn't know that. So ... I kissed him. Dear oh dear.' At this, Mrs Clark dissolves into loud laughter. 'But of course,' she continues, 'he realised after a few minutes what he had got: something out of his normal ... ken. So there we were, discovering how the other half worked.' By which she means the British class system.

'Anyway, Audrey, another girl, had also got picked up by one of these airmen, whom she had had great fun with. Well, that night when we got back to our billet, we were up till about two in the morning discussing it. Did we dare see them again? We knew our parents would never allow it.'

This was an age in which – for the smarter sort of girl – the considerations of family weighed heavily. Balanced against this was a certain ignorance about what men – especially 'lower class' men – might get up to. 'And in the end,' she says, 'we decided that provided we stayed together, and provided we had my car, if anything untoward happened, we could make a dash for the car and drive to safety. When I told Mel all of this later on, he had hysterics. "What in God's name did you think we were going to do to you?" he said. We didn't know! We only knew that we weren't supposed to be mixing with them. Well, if you weren't supposed to be mixing, why not? It was something ominous, obviously, or we would have been allowed to.'

It now sounds less like class, and more like caste. Mrs Clark finds it extraordinary that this was only seventy-five years ago. 'Anyway, that following evening, we stuck as a foursome. We agreed: that way it would be safe. We went to a dance, had a lovely time, thoroughly enjoyed ourselves. And Mel said, "Before we go back, what about some fish and chips?" So we thought, sounds quite nice. We stop outside a caravan-looking thing where they're serving fish and chips in newspaper. Handed us this paper. I said: "Don't they give you a knife and fork?" "No – you just eat it." It was a complete eye-opener. I think then men were seeing how much further they would go, in the sense of getting a giggle out of it.'

In a sense, this was *Pygmalion* in reverse: the elegant ladies gradually being indoctrinated into the ways of the lower orders. 'The men took us to a pub,' says Mrs Clark, laughing, 'and they said: "What would you like to drink?" Well, neither myself nor Audrey had really drunk, other than wine at dinners. They were drinking beers. One of them said, "What about a lager and lime? That's not too alcoholic." So we had lager and lime.'

A little later, when Patricia went on leave, her father asked what she had been doing. 'I told him I went to the pub and had a lager and lime and it was absolutely lovely. My father said: "You had WHAT?" He was absolutely appalled.'

Quite apart from the horror of parents, there was another fearsome obstacle in the way of this wartime romance: Patricia Clark was a commissioned officer and Mel was not. Such things not only mattered enormously, but were also strictly policed.

'Although in general terms nobody supervised our off time at all, the only thing I was never allowed to do was go out with Mel,' says Mrs Clark, shaking her head. 'Officers may not mix with other ranks. We weren't allowed out together. So what I used to do was this: I used to get into my civilian clothes, put my greatcoat and my hat on, go through the Guard Room, take my salute, then go down into Bath, into the ladies' room, off with the coat and hat and once more a civilian for the rest of the evening. And then put it all back on again to go back into camp. I wouldn't have been allowed to go out with him. But it made it more exciting, more dangerous. If spotted, you would have been on a charge. You could have been decommissioned.'

As was so frequently the way with wartime love, the two of them were wrenched apart by duty; Mel was posted elsewhere in the world. Patricia Clark continued to write him letters. But in time, both she and he found other people. They were not to be reunited until the 1970s, and even then there was an element of chance: a bunch of mixed family holidays in Switzerland. It was only after all those years that they realised just how deeply they loved one another. The extraordinary upshot was that, after some thirty-five years, Patricia and Mel left their spouses and finally got together. And they stayed together until the end. Mel died in 2012.

Elsewhere, crews were being refreshed and replenished. At RAF Hornchurch, an American pilot – flying for the RAF, since the USA was not to enter the war until December 1941 – gained his first glimpse of intense Englishness as soon as he arrived. Arthur Donahue went straight to the officers' mess and managed to put his name down for a room with a fireplace. That misty November of 1940, he recalled his first day flying with a Spitfire squadron.

> The day begins with my elderly batman waking me up by coming into my room at about 6.30am to get my uniform, shoes and flying boots, I sink back to sleep again to be wakened by his voice saying 'it's 7.30am now sir.' I wash, shave and dress. Dressed, I walk down the hallway to the large dining hall where other pilots of the squadrons are drifting in, clomping with their big boots, and rubbing their eyes sleepily.
> Copies of all the morning London papers are laid out on a table in one corner of the hall: some of us pick up copies to read while we're eating breakfast. Breakfast consists as usual of cereal, bacon and eggs, toast, marmalade and tea …

Then it was time for the 'roar of the Spitfire's Rolls Royce engine at full throttle'.[1]

In other words, the measured insouciance of the English pilots was more than matched by those who joined them; this was true both of the Americans and of the courageous Poles and Canadians whose squadrons were proving equally invaluable.

Meanwhile, on another day that same month at RAF Hornchurch, pilot Edward Wells was taken aback, while on patrol in the skies, to come face to face with a formation of biplanes that were flying over Southend-on-Sea. They were Corpo Aereo Italiano – planes belonging to Mussolini's Italian air force. Italy had entered the war in June and Mussolini had provided some fighters more as a gesture of goodwill towards Hitler than as the essential components of some diabolical plan. 'I could not recognise them, but I assumed them to be a friendly training flight, which seemed to have lost its way, and strayed into a highly operational area,' recalled Wells. 'Almost at once, two or three of them opened fire on me, at what seemed extreme range. I found this behaviour to be unacceptable, irritating and even slightly dangerous.'

Wells makes it sound as though he was a motorist being cut up by an exasperating road-hog. 'I turned on the nearest biplane and gave him a good burst of 3-4 seconds,' he continues. 'He immediately disappeared into cloud and was not seen again. I repeated this performance with three more different aircraft, by which time I had exhausted all my ammunition.' Even after that, Wells had not been able to make a positive identification of his attackers. It was only when he got back to base and was able to consult an identification chart that he was sure who he had been up against. 'I claimed only one damaged, as I had seen some parts fly off one of the targets, before he disappeared into cloud. I now believe that all four of them must have fallen into the sea ... as far as I know, the Italian Air Force never came to England again!'[2]

The Battle of Britain itself had already become – in one sense – a cult that attracted celebrity attention. Pilots at the Biggin Hill station in Kent found that film stars were seeking them out. There was David Niven, who had already tried to enlist to fly but was turned down; there was Laurence Olivier, then at the height of his Hollywood powers having starred in *Wuthering Heights* (1939) and Hitchcock's *Rebecca* (1940). Olivier paid a visit, together with his even more famous wife Vivien Leigh (*Gone with the Wind*, in which she starred, had opened in 1939 and was still running in many cinemas). On top of this came attention from fine theatrical stalwarts like Ralph Richardson and Roger Livesey. Such attention was borne of fascination, and also appeared to have a distinctly social dimension, the upper-middle-class pilots mingling quite easily with the sophisticated actors. And unusually, the pilots having the greater glamour.

As 1940 drew towards its close, still the skies were filled with threat. There had been daytime raids, which the squadrons of 11, 12 and 10 Group had attempted to fight off; bombs had been dropped on Norfolk coastal towns, causing Anderson shelters to be lifted into the air, twisting as they did so; then heavy raids on towns in the southwest, again resulting in death and damage, and rendering hundreds of people homeless. The cold determination of the Luftwaffe was unabated. At 11 Group, where Leigh-Mallory and Squadron Leader Douglas Bader had been drilling pilots, finessing big wing formations, there was a sense at one point that, as Bader's biographer puts it, 'the RAF was nearly helpless. The fighters went up and roamed and now and then they caught a bomber but not often, and the news reports spoke more confidently than the men behind them.'[3]

The size of wings made no difference at night; but nor was the ability of the bombers to get through in any way the responsibility of those working in the Operations and Filter Rooms at Bentley Priory. Even by December 1940, the available technology was still primitive; they knew that the bombers were coming in – they would have known that without radar – but night bombers were sleek against the sky and even if multiple squadrons of fighter pilots had been patrolling the Kent and Essex coast for as many hours as their fuel would allow, the early RDF would still not have been able to give them an exact fix. Very few German planes, therefore, were brought down at night; Fighter Command managed just four throughout the month of December 1940.

'A glance at the map of England, Scotland and Northern Ireland must show that we cannot be expected to cope with the numbers of night-bombers that the enemy can put up against us with only six squadrons,' wrote Air Chief Marshal Sholto Douglas in a secret and anguished memo to Air Chief Marshal Sir Charles Portal on 9 December 1940. 'The initiative lies with the enemy. He chooses his target and the direction of the attack and he can and does vary the latter in the same night. We may have to take on a concentration of three hundred bombers on Newcastle one night and on Plymouth the next, or 150 on both on the same night. We must, of course, be as flexible as possible and be prepared to move night fighters from one sector to another. I have already in fact issued orders to this effect, but there are definite limits to the extent to which this can be done if the fighters are going to arrive on the scene in time.

'You said yesterday that I would have a stronger case in asking for additional night fighter squadrons if we were in fact shooting down enemy bombers at night,' he continued, underscoring a certain sense of impotence in the face of the demoniac blitzkrieg. 'I admit this, but I am convinced that in a reasonable period, we shall begin to get a modicum of success at night ... prolonged training and experience is required to make successful night fighter pilots ... Let us therefore take time by the forelock, and get the squadrons formed now.' He pleaded that day fighting and night fighting were two entirely different techniques; that squadrons could not be expected to be on readiness throughout the day and then again in the blackness of night; and that Spitfires and Hurricanes could only be effective at night when weather conditions were perfect. 'I do feel most strongly about this,' he concluded. 'It is vital to defeat the enemy night bomber – we may even lose the war if we don't. Actually I think my demand is really a modest one.'[4]

Christmas brought respite, though the Londoners were not to know it beforehand. 'There was so little air activity anywhere that this may be fairly described as a raid-free Christmas,' reported *The Times* on 27 December 1940. 'A blessed relief not merely for the obvious reasons but also because it granted to our airmen the rest and seasonable pleasure they deserved.'

The Christmas silence was shattered on the night of Sunday 29 December, when fighter squadrons were sent up into the darkness to deal with formations that were dropping incendiary bombs on London. 'The warning came at an early hour,' read the report in the *Manchester Guardian*. 'A bomb started a blaze on the roof of a Wren church and commissionaires and messenger boys ran in from the street to save the furnishings, which included a heavy brass lectern, vestments and pews.' They all got out just in time: the roof collapsed shortly afterwards. But this was just the start: the bombers were relentless and the incendiaries fell across the city: 'The sky over the capital was lit up by flames with the brilliance almost of daytime, and the sky was filled with dense volumes of smoke.' And still the flames blossomed further; the intention of the Luftwaffe, in an eerie prefiguring of what was to come to German cities later in the war, was to create a firestorm. About 1,500 fires were set off that night, in the heart of the city and out towards the docks. It was an extraordinary feat on the part of so many hundreds of volunteers to ensure that the conflagration was in any way contained.

Even if they could not stop all the bombers getting through – such a thing would not have been possible – the call for extra night fighters would have gone a little way towards helping the morale of the citizens below who were being bombed in the freezing darkness of the blackout. December had seen raids on south coast towns and a heavy attack upon the steel-making industry of Sheffield, and similar raids continued as the new year began. In the news reports that followed each attack, plus the nightly pounding of London, the night fighters were acknowledged. 'British night fighters were believed to have engaged German raiders over the London area late last night,' *The Times* reported on 16 January 1941. 'Roof-watchers heard the roar of engines as though a dog-fight was on. Our fighters were also heard over an east England town after Anti-Aircraft guns had blazed away at enemy machines.'

The following night brought even more heartening and reassuring news. The newspaper reported on 17 January:

Enemy raiders over this country on Wednesday night were intercepted by RAF night-fighters and two were destroyed. One of these, a Dornier 17, was brought down in flames on the outskirts of London. One of the crew baled out. The others were killed. Early yesterday morning, Mrs Hollick, who lives in the district, heard someone calling 'German, German'. Opening the door, she saw a young German who could not speak English. He was wounded and Mrs Hollick took him into her house and sent for the police. The German, who is 22, wore the ribbon of the Iron Cross and he was later removed to hospital.

In other words, the night fighters had succeeded in bringing down a decorated pilot.

And the Royal Air Force was determined to keep its nocturnal successes in the news, so that the public at least had a sense that some fierce resistance was being offered to the exhausting onslaught. A few days later, on 28 January, the King and Queen made a tour of five RAF aerodromes. As the newspaper reported:

When they were in a pilots' rest-room, they had a long talk … about night-fighters and the difficulties of intercepting enemy bombers at night. A young Squadron leader, when asked by the King about his experiences, said: 'I think we may be going to be much more successful in the future, sir.' The King and Queen discussed with the night-fighter pilots the difficulties of their work and the new secret equipment with which our fighters are being fitted.

This 'secret equipment' was Mark IV Air Intercept radar, looked after by a separate operator on board. Moreover, Air Chief Marshal Sholto Douglas's request had been granted. As 1941 went on, increasing numbers of Beaufighters came into service; by May, there were some 200 flying nightly intercept missions. Later in the war, Beaufighters were sent to Malta and to the Far East.

——

The issue of aeroplane production also caused flurries of internal Air Ministry ill-will in the early weeks of 1941. Air Chief Marshal Sir Charles Portal was moved to compose an icy letter to Sholto Douglas concerning the influence of the buccaneering Lord Beaverbrook, who was still champing about plane manufacturing in his ministerial role. Clearly his full-on approach was not loved by all. Sir Charles's letter began:

My dear Sholto,

You asked me the other day if I had any objection to you writing direct to Lord Beaverbrook, and I told you I had none. At the time, I had supposed this correspondence would only concern such matters as shortage of spares, faults in aircraft and engines, successes and failures of equipment in the field and so forth. It now appears from copies of letters that have passed between you and the Minister that I have seen, that you are advising him on the allocation of Merlin engines, and since this subject concerns all three Commands (Fighter, Bomber, Coastal), it can only be satisfactorily dealt with by the Air Ministry. I am very anxious that collaboration between the RAF and the Ministry of Production should be of the closest, but you should avoid as far as possible communicating about matters of policy which have not been fully discussed at the Air Ministry.

Sholto Douglas was very swift to realise his error, and equally swift to write back with a note of contrition. 'I am sorry if I have transgressed,' he wrote (a half-apology, really, casting doubt on whether he had in fact transgressed at all). He went on to explain that he and Lord Beaverbrook had fallen into conversation while watching a display at RAF

Northolt, and that subsequent letters had been copied to Sir Charles's department. 'I hope therefore that you will agree that I have at least retrieved my transgression,' Sholto Douglas concluded. He had; a few days later, Sir Charles wrote to him with the news that Lord Beaverbrook had presented him with the figures for the numbers of new Hurricanes and Spitfires being constructed. 'These are very much higher than previous expectations,' wrote Sir Charles, 'and I think they will rejoice your heart.'[5]

But at Fighter Command in that bitter bombing winter of 1940, when the Germans had left gaping, burning holes where houses and families had been, there was not only anxiety about whether enough planes were being made; there had also been an ongoing struggle to make radar fulfil its potential. As a result of the technology's shortcomings, the co-ordinates provided by Bentley Priory were not a great deal of use to the anti-aircraft gun emplacements on the hills around London. Very often they fired shots into the impenetrable sky as much to keep up the morale of the people sheltering around as aiming for an enemy plane.

And, even with Dowding deposed, the question of the effectiveness of 'big wing' formations itched; for Leigh-Mallory and Sholto Douglas, there was a deeper point about the purpose of the RAF to be made. A few days into the new year, Leigh-Mallory arranged for a bombing simulation exercise, to demonstrate beyond doubt that his conduct at 12 Group – and the apparent ungovernability of his pilots – was much more effective than Dowding's perceived havering. The exercise, on 29 January, was carried out over Kenley airfield in Kent; a 'big wing' formation was put together to defend it from enemy 'bombing'. Catastrophically, it failed completely. If the exercise had been real, then the airfield would have been utterly destroyed. But the nature of belief is such that even the baldest of facts cannot sway it. When it was pointed out by his superiors that the exercise had been a travesty, Leigh-Mallory's response was simply that he and his men would do better next time. His view, moreover, was that it was almost immaterial whether or not the enemy bomber hit its target. The important thing, the one thing that Dowding never seemed to acknowledge, was the need to pursue these enemies as they turned to fly back.

The exercise demonstrates, moreover, the determination of Dowding's opponents – even in 1941, just months after the Battle of Britain – to prove that he had been wrong. There was a scramble within the higher commands of the RAF to write the definitive history of that 1940 victory; accordingly, the early official histories in 1941 were astonishingly brutal in minimising the influence and impact of Dowding and Keith Park. It was not until much later, and after some anguish on his part, that Dowding's own version was to receive properly sanctioned publication.

As much as Hugh Dowding and Trafford Leigh-Mallory were bitterly opposed when it came to the methodology of aerial combat, they had in common one rather haunting interest. Both men, during their RAF careers, grew increasingly convinced about the truth of spiritualism. Dowding was to write books on the subject and indeed was to cause some controversy when he suggested to a newspaper that he was sensitive to the presence of dead pilots. Leigh-Mallory came to hold similar beliefs; and you cannot help thinking of how, for fighter pilots, violent death and the wild beauty of the skies were so intimately entwined; and how, when one is soaring high in the firmament, it must surely have been natural for thoughts to ascend higher, to the illimitable skies to come. Fighter pilot Roald Dahl later went on to write one particularly ghostly story about a pilot who, at 20,000 feet, suddenly became aware of planes either side of him, both flown by colleagues long since killed. During the Battle of Britain, one in six pilots met swift, terrible deaths. Back at their stations, what chance was there for friends to mourn their passing? And we see that the same was true for their commanders, the men who were sending them up to their fates on a daily basis.

The passion and belief involved in spiritualism tells us that both Dowding and Leigh-Mallory, in their own ways, felt each loss with dagger keenness. But more than that (otherwise every general and admiral would have subscribed to the same beliefs), there was something essentially metaphysical about the act of flying itself.

Yet there was also that grim purpose; and among many pilots, a sharpening sense of vengefulness and anger. For every house demolished, every inferno sparked, every city dweller killed by lethal shrapnel, arteries severed by molten glass shards, there was a surge of the sort of furious bloodlust that squadron leader Peter Townsend described feeling when, above the clouds, he found himself closing on his prey. In the New Year, the pilots of Fighter Command were to go on the offensive, and over a much broader theatre of war.

Chapter Eighteen

Rhubarbs

As well as the visceral carnage, and the scale of destruction, there was the dull clang of futility; for so many nights and days, weeks and months, German pilots had been targeting shipping, naval bases, aerodromes and then, in frustrated fury, ordinary streets and houses. For the Luftwaffe bomber, so high up – a famous photograph of an enemy plane above London's docks shows the buildings and streets below simply as map-like abstractions – the mission was cold: drop the bombs as close to the targets as possible, then turn and fly. The blood only warmed for the chase back: the efforts in the dark to evade the white glare of the searchlights, the unknowable trajectory of the missiles, the odd night fighter who might materialise in front of the moon.

But even for these pilots, there must also have been a sense of nihilistic uselessness. The invasion was off, Operation Sea Lion cancelled. The Germans were not going to cross the Channel and occupy England. And all this bombing: what was the end result? The factories kept working, and the working-class revolution that some Nazis had hoped for never happened; the commuters kept struggling into their offices on trains diverted past wrecked rails, their morale apparently buoyant. The mass psychosis confidently predicted by government experts – and therefore also by German government experts – stubbornly refused to break out.

Britain could take it; and the Luftwaffe were exhausted delivering it. By 1941, the attentions of the Luftwaffe were being diverted towards the Mediterranean and to north Africa. And it was now time for Fighter Command to link with Bomber Command in order to strike back beyond Britain's shores. Just as the Germans had soared over the Channel with bombers protected by fighters, so the RAF was now to launch its own raids, first against specific targets in France. The plan was called 'Circus'; and in its first phase, six Blenheim bombers, escorted by Hurricanes and Spitfires, set course for an ammunition and weapons dumps in Calais.

Of this new offensive, Air Chief Marshal Sholto Douglas later wrote:

> After the first three Circus operations, an inevitable difference of view between Bomber and Fighter Commands as to the primary objects of these attacks became apparent. The principal aim of my command was to shoot down enemy aircraft, while Bomber Command, naturally enough, attached more importance to the bombing … we agreed that the object of Operation Circus was to force the enemy to give battle in conditions tactically favourable to our fighters. To compel the Germans to do so, the bombers must do enough damage to make it impossible for them to refuse to fight.[1]

And so from January 1941, these speculative raids across the Channel were stepped up. For pilots such as Douglas Bader, the promise of activity after the seething impotence of the Blitz was extremely welcome. Indeed, his biographer Paul Brickhill recalls the morning when Air Vice Marshal

Leigh-Mallory, now installed at 11 Group Headquarters at Uxbridge, called the veteran in and said: 'I suppose life seems pretty dull lately?' As Bader gruffly responded in the affirmative, Leigh-Mallory, with that absurd bluff jocularity ascribed to him by Brickhill, said: 'What do you think about going over to France and giving them a smarten up? We thought we might send a few bombers over with a pack of fighters?'[2]

There was also a pleasing matter-of-fact curtness about the typed orders that preceded each such mission; documents which now speak of growling confidence, brimming with certainty that a vital contribution is being made. 'Circus – Twenty-Nine – to take place Wednesday 2nd of July 1941', one such itinerary was headlined. The objective was immediately stated below: 'Target: City of Lille Electric Power Station on Western Outskirts of Lille. Target no. Z 246.' And how was it to be carried out? 'Rendezvous: Clacton 12.00 hours. At 8,000 feet, crossing French coast at 12,000 feet.' The bombers were assembled, their fighter escorts primed. '1 Hurricane squadron to be detailed by station commander, North Weald; Nos 303 and 308 squadrons, Northolt. Height 13,000 feet to 15,000 feet.' Refuelling was to take place at Martlesham. And in the event of the bomber squadrons having to turn back shy of hitting the target, the fighter escorts were required to give a codeword to their controllers. On that mission, the word was 'Parsnip'.

There was an extra dimension of psychological satisfaction. As well as giving the fighter pilots something concrete to do – anything in the world was better than the limbo of waiting – it allowed them to feel the confidence of the aggressor. Whereas constant, months-long defence could prove, for some, corrosive – no matter what one did, it seemed, the implacable enemy just kept on coming, while there was no apparent means for the pilot to follow them back and annihilate them – these missions had an element of audacity and ruthlessness. Even though the pilots of Fighter Command were quick to realise that their actions in 1940 had ensured the survival of the nation and the cancellation of Nazi invasion plans, the autumn and winter of the Blitz were nonetheless a draining test of morale. Now, in this high summer, it was their turn to cross the Channel.

Alongside the Circus, Leigh-Mallory had conceived of another way to keep his pilots in a state of battle-ready alertness: a series of attacks he termed 'Rhubarbs'. The idea was that any day when the layer cloud hung low or clung to the land, the fighter pilots could roar across the Channel under natural cover and take aim at any sort of German target. And if the Luftwaffe were to respond a little too heavily, the pilots could then use that same cloud as a means of covering their escape. Sholto Douglas had approved the idea; as he later wrote, the raids

> provided valuable experience alike for pilots, operational commanders and the staff of the formations concerned … It was obvious from the start that in many cases pilots engaged on these patrols would not succeed in meeting any German aircraft and they were authorised in this event to attack suitable objectives on the ground. Nevertheless, I considered it important that the primary object of the operation – namely, the destruction of enemy aircraft – should not be forgotten and discouraged any tendency to give undue emphasis to the attacks on ground objectives.[3]

'Everyone wanted to jump into the Hurricanes and try the same lark,' reported Douglas Bader's biographer.[4]

Bader was appointed wing commander of 242 Squadron in Tangmere, West Sussex – just across the coast from France, as he noted with a little satisfaction. But he was also swift to spot that even this many weeks after the Battle of Britain, the young pilots were still under some nervous strain; the after-effects of those daily flights, those nightmarishly regular brushes with death, were clearly showing. It would have been extraordinary if they had not; but in an age where the phrase 'lack of moral fibre' still loomed horribly large, such things were not discussed to any great degree. Instead, as happened with other squadrons, it was arranged for the pilots to be transferred elsewhere in the country, to quieter postings where there was no pre-dawn wakefulness about the possibility of German incursion. And in their place came fresher pilots from those quieter postings, eager and apprehensive, and open to the new flying techniques that commanders and tutors such as Bader could impart.

In the aftermath of the winter Blitz, the Ministry of Information needed some form of morale-raising news, and they found it in the form of a night fighter. Pilot John Cunningham – among many others – had been soaring into the deep darkness in a Bristol Beaufighter. He had the advantage of a technological breakthrough not yet available to Spitfire or Hurricane pilots: a simplified form of radar (or direction finding) hidden in the nose of the plane. Beaufighters were two-seaters; and with John Cunningham was radar operator Jimmy Rawnsley. The amount that they and their fellow crews could do against multiple incursions was limited; nonetheless, these planes came to be feared, and not just by the Germans. Later on, as the war moved far east, these black-painted aircraft would come to be nicknamed 'whispering death', a tribute to their stealth and speed. Cunningham himself, however, was not entirely happy to find himself suddenly a nationally known figure.

Like so many of his colleagues, Cunningham seemed destined for the RAF from a very early age; even as a very small boy, in middle-class South Croydon in the 1920s, he had been fascinated both by the new technology of aircraft and by the aerodynamics of birds. As soon as he could leave school, Cunningham joined the aeroplane manufacturer de Havilland and enrolled in the Royal Auxiliary Air Force. By the late 1930s, de Havilland's company was still making luxurious passenger aircraft, as well as fulfilling ever more urgent orders from the War Office and the Ministry of Supply. The poetry of flying was scored on Cunningham's heart. He was to become a test pilot for the firm, and he worked alongside the owner's son, Geoffrey – an equally obsessive and (one might say) addicted flyer. Call-up came swiftly in 1939.

After an initial period of night flying in the less nimble Blenheims, Cunningham made the switch to the fleeter Beaufighters in the deep autumn of 1940; soon he was making a name – in an otherwise atrocious period of destruction – for downing the enemy, including three Heinkels in the space of one night. And so it was that the Ministry of Information pounced.

They had just one problem: how to avoid alerting the Germans to the nature of the extraordinary new radar technology that was giving Cunningham such a steady and true aim. So instead, in publicity, his successes were ascribed to carrots. Carrots, it was said, imbued him with almost uncanny levels of night vision, which enabled him to pursue bombers through the thickest night. The Ministry, when referring to his skill in downing German bombers, gave him the nickname 'Cat's Eyes'; Cunningham didn't care for it, but he was lumbered with it for the rest of his blessedly long life.

The myth about carrots and their super-powers persists today. John Cunningham found that his 'Cat's Eyes' status was also being used as a means of encouraging urchins to develop a taste for fresh vegetables, and to wean them off heavily rationed sweets. The story is also instructive in the government's keenly developed sense of how the achievements of pilots and the RAF were to be projected to the public.

Interviewed a few years after the war by *The Times*, an amused yet exasperated Cunningham explained the truth of the matter. 'As a matter of fact, my night-sight is only about average,' he said. 'That nick-name was absolute baloney. I've always disliked it but I have had to learn how to live with it.' However, there was one grain of truth: despite the radar innovation, Cunningham's RAF superiors were convinced that Cunningham had a kind of preternatural ability. So much so that they sent him for repeated tests at the opticians. 'They didn't seem to realise that whether a chap could see 400 or 500 yards in the dark was irrelevant. The point was, could he and his navigator fly an aircraft under instructions from radar close enough in to get their targets at short range?' Even by 1941, it seems, there were still a few in the RAF who persisted in thinking of radar as an uncertain miracle. Not Air Chief Marshal Sholto Douglas, though. In an article some years later, Sir Robert Watson-Watt, who had brought the technology into being, cited him as – of all the senior officers – the one who did the most to fashion this new science into an effective weapon.

And, of course, the secrecy applied on the ground as well, as WAAF filterer Gladys Eva now recalls. 'You didn't talk about anything – you didn't go off duty and chat about anything. No way,' she says. 'Nobody but us knew about the Filter Room. One day, not all that many years ago, there was a Fighter reunion outing. We were having tea afterwards and the people we were with had worked on the screens on the coast, in the coastal stations. Not one of them knew where their information was going to. I asked them, "Where did you send the information?" No idea. I said: "Well, you sent it to me." They had absolutely no idea. That's how deadly secret it was.'

Even though things were quieter now on the home front, the underground operations rooms could still be a source of immense claustrophobia and resulting friction. Patricia Clark, who had been based in the West Country, recalls an encounter on the balcony with Wing Commander Rudd, the man who had outwitted Eileen Younghusband over her desire to join Intelligence. 'When we were on the table, if one of these men did something wrong, from his balcony he would bawl down at them and shout and tell them off – what the bloody hell, that sort of thing. I thought this was awful.'

After a while came an unexpected development. 'Rudd – who I think may have taken a fancy to me – comes through on my earphones.' Would she like to come up on the balcony and watch proceedings from above? Not particularly liking him, she said: 'Thank you for asking me but no thank you.'

A few minutes later, he said: 'I thought I asked you to come up on the balcony.'

She said: 'You asked me if I'd like to, and I don't want to.'

'Why don't you want to?'

'Quite honestly, I would just rather not.'

'Right, it's now an order, you will now come up on the balcony.'

Knowing she had to obey orders, up Patricia went on the balcony. Rudd sat her down on a chair beside him and said: 'Right, why don't you want to come up here?'

She replied: 'You shout at these officers on the table, my father was in the army and he was taught that you were never rude to your servants because they couldn't answer you back. And it seems to me that the men can't answer you back and it's not fair.'

Mrs Clark concludes: 'I think Rudd was absolutely shattered. But do you know he never did it again? I was there three years and towards the end, we became quite friendly.'

And so the pilots of Fighter Command flew out over the grey Channel, accompanying bombers just as the Germans were doing over Britain. For some, the burst of action was welcome. For a few others, there was a faint hint of scepticism, at least when the 'Rhubarbs' began. Young Geoffrey Wellum and his mate Tommy Maitland-Thompson had some difficulty keeping straight faces when their commanding officer outlined the plan for the first raid on France with a portentousness that suggested these bombs would turn the war. They were reprimanded for their schoolboyish tittering. When Wellum at last was in the sky among a formation of fighters escorting Blenheim bombers, he justified his gut reaction.

'If one is at all cynical, it is difficult not to poke fun, to a certain extent, at the importance attached to this "offensive" of one and a quarter hours,' he wrote. 'Anyone would think the target was Berlin, not Boulogne. However, at least we are going over there and taking the war to the enemy, which makes a change.' Yet this first-mission blitheness was not to last; as Wellum and his fellow pilots reached the French coastline, he understood both the danger they faced and the danger that they posed. It was a curious moment:

A black inky-looking thing like a chunk of dirty cotton wool brings me back to the reality of the present. What on earth is that? Another one appears and, as if by magic, a whole lot more. They are pretty close as well, not far away at all. How interesting. Two more puffs happen to be nearer than the others and a batch is right among the rear of the Blenheims. Finally, it dawns on me. It's flak, that's what it is, anti-aircraft fire. I'm being shot at and there's not an awful lot I can do about it.

For a pilot used to fighting above home territory, the change of emphasis must have come as a salutary fright (even though, on many occasions when in combat over the Channel, pilots found themselves having to dodge friendly fire from naval vessels):

Dreaming as I was, it's with something of shocked surprise that I see the French coast almost under our noses. The Blenheims have their bomb doors open, their course straight and steady as they complete their run in. Down there someone is going to get hurt, and presumably it doesn't matter who. What a funny war. Don't like the idea of bombing much. At least the role of fighter pilot seems cleaner somehow. Makes you wonder what life is all about. It must be a lousy way to get yourself killed, to have a bloody great bomb dropped on you.[5]

Wing Commander Douglas Bader entertained no such doubts or philosophical speculations. He was a totem of pure confidence. Bader's biographer related how, on missions, the veteran pilot would cheer younger pilots by making jokes about the landscape beneath them – commenting, for example, when flying over the golf course at Le Touquet that 'those greens could do with a trim.'

This image of the airman as a figure of light-hearted wit was cemented firmly in the months after the Battle of Britain, when the Ministry of Information understood just how powerful such stories were in terms of boosting morale. The

RAF fighter pilot became an emblem for the national character itself: unflappable, cheerful, touched with a shade of whimsy yet unbreakably stoic. Indeed, the tone had been set in the aftermath of Dunkirk with the publication in *The Times* of a letter written by a bomber pilot to his mother. It was anonymous; the writer had stipulated that it should be sent in the event of his death or disappearance. In fact, it was from Flying Officer Vivien Rosewarne, who had been based at RAF Marham in Norfolk. His commanding officer, having forwarded the letter to the pilot's mother, asked for her permission for it to be reproduced in the newspaper's letters column; she assented. The text evoked that exact mix of courage and swooping romanticism with a certain lyrical intelligence.

'Dearest Mother, though I feel no kind of premonition at all, events are moving rapidly and I have instructed that this letter be forwarded to you should I fail to return,' he began. He went on to tell her of the importance of the missions he had flown; the convoys saved, the lighthouse crews rescued. He asked her to accept news of his death dispassionately, for 'I shall have done my duty to the utmost of my ability. No man can do more, and no-one calling himself a man could do less.' He went on to declare:

> For all that can be said against it, I still maintain that this war is a very good thing: every individual is having the chance to give and dare all for his principle like the martyrs of old. However long the time may be, one thing can never be altered – I shall have lived and died an Englishman … I have no fear of death; only a queer elation … I would have it no other way. The universe is so vast and so ageless that the life of one man can only be justified by the measure of his sacrifice.

The letter ended with references to biblical adversity, and with the airman's one regret: that he would not be there to make his mother's declining years more comfortable.

The letter caused an instant sensation: *The Times* was besieged with readers wanting specially printed copies. A run of 10,000 pamphlets containing the text was printed. But the airman's letter resonated further in 1941 when it became the subject of a short film directed by Michael Powell. The letter was read out, in character, by John Gielgud, over a montage of shots in crisp black and white: the exterior of a pretty country cottage, which a postman approaches on a bicycle; the interior of the cottage, where a collie dog can be seen. And as Gielgud's narration fills the soundtrack, the camera glides across the young airman's mementos, including (strikingly) a portrait of T.E. Lawrence, the most romantic of individualists. The camera then swings out back to the window and to the rural landscape beyond, and thence up to the sky and the clouds. It is as if the airman is neither dead nor alive, but is a presence still skimming those clouds, a spirit infusing an archetypal English landscape where there were, even then, wheelwrights and blacksmiths.

Gielgud's crisp Received Pronunciation locates the airman firmly in the upper middle classes (this was also the case in the later Michael Powell/Emeric Pressburger epic *A Matter of Life and Death* (1946) where airman Peter Carter – played by David Niven – is a well-spoken poet whose mother lives in Hampstead). Powell's message in this short film was quite clear: the immortal souls of the airmen are the essence of the spirit of England itself, a spirit that will always prove indomitable. So we can see that in 1941, pilots served not only a vital strategic military purpose but also an almost metaphysical one. Their planes might fall out of the sky, but the sense was that their immortal souls would continue swooping through the empyrean.

———

If the departed airmen had a kind of beautiful evanescence about them, there was still an air of Captain W.E. Johns about the RAF recruitment advertising at the time. One such advertisement, in *The Times*, featured an image of the view from a Spitfire cockpit, a German fighter in its crosshairs. The copy ran:

> Look at the war THIS way ... reserve your place in the cockpit of one of the world's best war-planes ... do your part amongst the airmen who are holding and increasing Britain's mastery of the skies ... This is the role for the man who can relish a first-class scrap above the clouds – who knows that in air war, individual daring, tenacity and self-reliance count above all. You who have these qualities – volunteer today!

The advertisement's small print stated: 'If you are 17 and a half and not yet 31, go to the RAF section of the nearest Combined Recruiting Centre and say you wish to volunteer as a pilot.'

Another advert from 1941 featured an image of a handsome pilot in traditional fleece-lined flying jacket; he was an 'RAF instructor' addressing the reader. 'You're physically fit and take a pride in keeping so,' ran the copy. 'You're the sort who knows by instinct just how much he can ask from his machine ... You're in your element in a scrap, all the more so when it is against odds ... in short, you are the man the RAF is looking for.'

The language in both cases was deliberately that of Biggles; first-class scraps, individual daring, against all odds. The gap between the schoolboy terminology and the lethal reality was massive. Yet there was no dishonesty here; the advertising accurately reflected the spirit of the more youthful pilots at stations from Hornchurch to Tangmere.

Women were being enticed in different ways. Eileen Younghusband and Patricia Clark had their commissions, taking on responsibilities never previously granted young women. Now the possibility of such advancement was used as a means of drawing more women into the service. An advertisement in *The Times* in the middle of 1941, designed to look like a garden party invitation, put it elegantly:

> From the ranks come the efficient and capable officers who lead their fellow women … yet many of them were not long in the ranks, for keen eyes at the Recruits Depot are ever quick to note the potential officer. More and more commissions are being granted as the WAAF expands and the woman who joins today will be earmarked for promotion as soon as possible if she has suitable qualifications. The ability to lead … to use initiative … to take responsibility … to see things through … These qualifications, added to a good education, are the requirements for a good WAAF officer. You who have these qualifications are needed in the WAAF now.

Indeed, a new era was opening up. Just as women generally were flooding into factories and steel smelting works to replace the men who had been called up, so the Women's Auxiliary Air Force was offering all sorts of different jobs that had previously been all-male closed shops. For those keen neither on cooking nor running messages, in fact, the options were quite wide and satisfying, from the evolving and quick-witted art of wireless telegraphy (many were drawn into noting down Enigma-encoded Nazi messages intercepted from all theatres of war), to sparking plug testers, to radio and teleprinter operators. Women were needed for highly complex map work; they were drawn from pools of commercial artists.

And at Bentley Priory, Rudloe Manor, Watnall in the Midlands and Bawdsey Manor in Suffolk, women had a commanding presence that went far beyond the patronising term found in Douglas Bader's biography: that of 'The Beauty Chorus'. In the case of Eve Lockington, a young woman from Essex who was inducted into the mysteries of 'Clerk – Special Duties' in 1942, this ever-changing war landscape opened her eyes not merely to the inner secrets of vectors and plotting, but also to subtleties of class and sex. She was posted, to her delight, to RAF Debden, and was billeted in the pretty town of Saffron Walden. 'I subsequently learnt,' she recalled, 'that in the early days of the war, Clerks Special Duties had been recruited mainly from girls who had been to public or private schools. However, there had not been enough of these to man the Operations Room during the Battle of Britain so the field had been widened to include grammar school girls. However, among the WAAFs on the fighter stations, the clerks SD were considered rather snobbish. By the time I joined up, this was not so, but it was certainly true that I did find myself among girls from county families, as well as from families similar to mine.

'Occasionally I was conscious of the difference,' added Mrs Lockington, 'and felt embarrassed when my friend Anne invited me to her home as I knew I could not invite her back. Consequently I did not accept the invitation.' Mrs Lockington was also to witness – in microcosmic form – the shifting tectonic plates of the 'special relationship' between the UK and the USA. 'Debden was a station which was in the process of being taken over by the Americans,' she recalled. 'And these Yanks definitely added a new dimension to our lives. My friend Anne Sidebotham and I went out with a couple on one occasion. I remember their names were Buzz and Duck! I also remember how annoyed I was when my "partner" – I think he was Buzz – casually said how the Americans would leave an army of occupation here after the war. I also remember wondering how easy it would be to get an American interested in me so I went out of my way to flirt with one. I wish I hadn't! I had a very difficult time trying to get rid of him. That taught me a lesson.'[6]

For other women, British airmen still had as much allure as Americans. Mary Wesley, later a hugely successful novelist, had an illicit tryst in a London hotel with a squadron leader, though she noted some years later that any erotic charge was dissipated by his 'stockbroker' technique. Elsewhere, many dreamy preconceptions of Fighter Command life were swiftly dissolved, whatever the social background of the WAAF. Joan Wyndham, who came from a wealthy though dissipated family – classics of the Chelsea Bohemian genre – joined up in 1941 with a range of frankly amorous intentions, having done everything in her power to be 'de-virginised' in London during the Blitz. First, there was the ice-water shock of the WAAF induction at West Drayton; all this out of the way, Joan Wyndham's quest for lively physical romance was on. Posted to Scotland, she conceived a fierce, if short-lived, lust for a pilot called Lovat; it was only when she had the chance to inspect him at closer quarters off-duty – he favoured aristocratic tweed, pin-stripe trousers, orange suede waistcoat and a chin that had the potential to double – that she dropped the matter.

She was also posted, like Eileen Younghusband, to RAF Watnall. There she met a Spitfire pilot whose face had been badly burned when he was forced to make a crash-landing. Unlike the pilot in Scotland, though, here there was a powerful charge. She told her diary that he 'was very good-looking in spite of it'. They went out on dates; Wyndham, unusually for the time, took the initiative in the first kiss – the pilot was too intensely self-conscious about what he saw as his disfigurements. Joan told him that his face was beautiful; then she persuaded him, under cover of dark, to come with her to the perimeter of the airfield, where they proceeded to have sex. The atmosphere was certainly much more conducive than her posting to Fighter Command itself in Stanmore. She immediately noted that the drawback of being in such a place was paradoxically the absence of fighter pilots, all based elsewhere. Instead, there were either older, former pilots – crusty commanding officers – or administrators ('wingless wonders' as she crossly put it).[7]

Romantic entanglements aside, thousands of women like her, in bases up and down the country, were quietly and skilfully upholding the infrastructure of a vast and complex enterprise. Indeed, the huge importance – and concomitant anxieties, tensions, and moments of euphoric release – would prove so central to the lives of these women that what came after the war was often shatteringly disappointing, to the extent that among a few, very serious depression set in. But for the moment, in that high summer of 1941, with Germany launching its surprise attack on Russia, opening up an eastern front that took a great deal of the Luftwaffe with it, and with the RAF striving for more permanent mastery over its own and neighbouring skies, there was for men and women alike a giddying sense of possibility, a feeling like a thermal current carrying them aloft.

Chapter Nineteen

Knitting, Smoking and Great Literature

The *Daily Mirror* columnist Cassandra – the vinegary, pithy, witty William Connor – had warned earlier in 1941 that the great man Douglas Bader had already done quite enough; that the double amputee had shown fantastic valour but now should be held back a little, simply for fear of losing such a vital asset. Bader – not the most natural of *Daily Mirror* readers – was apparently incensed by the sentiment. The thrill and exhilaration of Rhubarbs and Circuses was not something to be ducked from. Moreover, we see in Bader's almost pathological restlessness some essential fear of stillness. Certainly he wanted to fly out there and win the war, but there was more to it than that; almost a deliberate refusal to sink into any kind of reflectiveness.

He knew – as did every pilot – that the end could come at any moment. Yet, as his biographer Paul Brickhill wrote, 'everyone felt he [Bader] was invincible, and that this power shielded those who flew with him.' The feeling was to disintegrate in the late summer of 1941. As he had done so many times previously, Bader flew out to France, near Le Touquet, in order to lure German fighters up into the sky. The more of them he managed to shoot down, the more stretched the Luftwaffe would find itself between the two fronts. Below him the Messerschmitts materialised. Somehow

Bader was pulled away from the rest of his wing and climbed to 7,315 metres (24,000 feet) – 'deadly to be alone in this dangerous sky'. What had started as a mission to entrap German fighters was now turned on Bader; unable to resist the chance to chase more Messerschmitts that had appeared, he had failed to realise the nature of what was on his tail. 'Something hit him,' wrote Brickhill. Bader was bewildered to suddenly find himself plummeting in a spiral; looking back, he realised that the rear half of his Spitfire had simply disappeared.

First there was oxygen-starved befuddlement; a sense that he could just stay in the warm cockpit. Then, with horror, he realised what was happening and fought to free the parachute. By now what was left of the plane was spinning wildly; utterly disorientated, Bader struggled to see as he whirled. Then, after a metallic snap, he was suddenly aware of floating free; a moment of extraordinary and illusory tranquillity, a sense of stillness, and an overwhelming desire to sleep. He remembered to pull the parachute cord just in time.

In the crisis to get out of the cockpit, he had lost one of his prosthetic legs. Now, with his parachute open, he was floating down to earth over France. His trousers were in ribbons. A couple of agricultural labourers watched him incuriously. The landing brought unconsciousness and when he surfaced, he had been captured by the Germans.

'Legless air pilot a prisoner', reported the *Manchester Guardian*. The 'destroyer of over fifteen Nazi planes' had been confirmed as a prisoner of war, being eventually held at Colditz Castle in Germany. A little later after the crash, Bader's wife divulged the contents of a letter that he had sent her, explaining how the disaster had happened. In fact, Bader was rather gracious about his early treatment, and rightly so; his German captors had managed to find both the wreckage of his plane and his missing leg. They were even able to fix him up so that both legs were restored to their pre-crash condition. (A little later on, his endless harrying of his captors caused them at one point to confiscate those legs). But tellingly, he received curious visits from aristocratic Luftwaffe pilots – 'Count von Someone-or-other', as he put it. They wanted to talk aeroplanes; not by way of interrogation but simply as fascinated pilots. They were gripped by Spitfires. They were also understandably gripped by Bader's amputated limbs; it is conceivable that they had known about this before their illustrious prisoner arrived. They were intrigued to know how this changed his flying techniques. Again, we see here almost a brotherhood of the air, and indeed of knights, openly admiring the skills of their rivals.

In the lengthening days of spring and summer 1941, the remorseless Luftwaffe onslaughts on London and the major industrial cities diminished in intensity; in a matter of weeks, many of those German pilots would be needed on quite another front. But for the women of Fighter Command, there was no let-up; vigilance at Bentley Priory – now under the control of Air Chief Marshal Sholto Douglas – was still absolute.

There came a point where, as a filter officer, Eileen Younghusband was transferred to the station where so many of the original leaps in radar development had taken place: Bawdsey Manor, on the Norfolk coast. If Rudloe in the West Country seemed a little remote, Bawdsey seemed to many young women working there to be the very edge of the world.

'Once they had got in there, they were captive virtually,' says Mrs Younghusband. 'We had to learn to shoot while we were there.' This was no idle whim, a means of beguiling the time: it was about the ever-present fear of invasion, and the particular vulnerability of this frequently foggy patch of the country.

'Bawdsey was very much cut off. One day we were taken down to the coast and I think there was a sort of cliff and down below was the beach and it was all mines and barbed wire – no one was using that beach. We were taught to shoot – Bren or sten – from the hip. And we got complaints from the fishermen out at sea, saying they were being peppered!

'The point was,' she continues, 'that that was one of the places where they thought the Germans would land. The Highland Regiment was in charge there – they were protecting us because it was very vulnerable. And it was very strictly controlled going in and out. If the Germans had known what was being done there, then it would definitely have been a target. And if they had landed, they would have come in and shot us all whether we were men or women, because we were in battle dress.'

Both at Rudloe and at Bawdsey Manor, the need for pressure valves was terrific. But then it is easy to forget that the young, when they laugh, tend to do so very intensely. 'One thing I can particularly remember: if you came off duty and you had had a hectic night – you would almost be hysterical when you were having breakfast. The slightest thing would make you laugh. We all went out when we could, we went dancing when we could, we had dances at the mess. That's how I met Peter, he brought his band there from Northolt.'

Peter was Eileen's husband-to-be. Now, of course, the abiding image of wartime romance is that perhaps of David Niven and Kim Hunter in *A Matter of Life and Death,* in which Hunter's radio operator falls for RAF pilot Niven just at the point when he is transmitting what he thinks is his final message from a plane that is diving into the sea; in other words, swooning romance touched with a profound note of mortality. This being said, a great many courtships were obviously much more light-hearted. Eileen

Younghusband could see it going on all around her during her time as an officer.

'A lot of them had affairs,' she says. 'Especially the air crew. Now that was much more with the ops girls – we filterers didn't see many pilots. The time I met more pilots was when I was at 10 Group, Rudloe Manor. And at 10 Group, there was a mixed officers' mess when I was there. So you actually had the men with you, that's when Rex Harrison was there.' The actor Rex Harrison – he had hoped to be a pilot but poor eyesight had debarred him, so instead he became a flight officer, guiding crews via radar – and Eileen Younghusband did not see eye to eye. She recalled that every time they sat opposite each other taking breakfast in the mess, he would never deign to say a single word to her. As a result, she considered him to be one of the rudest men she had ever met.

More agreeable company was 'Cat's Eyes' Cunningham. 'If the pilots had had several sessions they'd been flying, they were often sent back to group during their relaxation period and given some sort of job. But this also gave them the chance to see how the Ops and Filter Room worked. Because lots of pilots never knew anything about it.'

For Patricia Clark, the quieter night shifts at Rudloe Manor opened the door for a spectacular literary career. It all started with the circumstances by which she came – very rare for a young woman this, especially in wartime – to be the owner of a car. Splendid though it was, she wondered how she would be able to afford the petrol for it. She needed more money.

'I started writing for the magazine that I had been working on before. As a junior there, one of my jobs was to read unsolicited material to see if it was suitable to be considered by someone higher up than me. And there were criteria – the hero mustn't be divorced, no sex past the bedroom door, no illegitimacy, proper behaviour. So I knew exactly what was acceptable for short stories and what was turned down.

'I wrote one story, sent it in, and they paid me £10, which was an absolute fortune. It was about a month's pay. So I continued every time I could, which really began my writing career.

'You never knew what would happen from day to day. We were very young. The people I met were all new to me. Everything was an experience. From a writing point of view – well, I wasn't aware then that I would be absorbing people's stories, what was going on. I think it helped me a lot.'

For Gladys Eva, the lull in Luftwaffe activity led to some surprising recreational opportunities throughout the night shifts. 'Generally, there was knitting and sewing. But we had one very bad spell of weather. No one flying. And guess what I was doing? Well, there was a voice from the balcony: "Anybody down there play bridge?" I said: "I do, sir." So I was up on the balcony playing bridge.'

By summer 1941, as increasing numbers of troops set sail for Alexandria and Cairo, and engagements in the desert between Germans and Italians and the British intensified, the broad focus of the conflict for the British was moving to the sands of the Middle East and away from the RAF squadrons based at home. There were other developments too; later in the year – in what proved another fine propaganda coup for the Air Ministry – half a dozen Fighter Command pilots were attached to units of the United States Army Air Corps, morale-boosting evidence of the concrete existence of the 'special relationship'. Among the pilots was the greatly admired Wing Commander Malan of 74 Squadron. The news of his transfer gave two signals to the public: first that the German bombing threat had abated sufficiently for British expertise to be redeployed, and second that the Americans greatly admired the work that these pilots had done throughout the Battle of Britain and the Blitz.

Throughout the sorties over France, the Air Ministry were careful to let it be known that old alliances and friendships had not been forgotten, in spite of the military situation. A couple of Hurricane pilots sweeping over northern France 'passed low over a church from which the congregation was just filing out', it was reported. 'The British pilots pushed back their hoods and waved. The French people waved back.'

In later years, senior figures became aware that these adventures across the Channel were being criticised as a waste of time and men, vainglorious gestures that made little or no difference to the conflict. Air Chief Marshal Sholto Douglas addressed these accusations fiercely in a secret memo not long after the war ended:

> Let me say one word about the sweeps carried out by Fighter Command in 1941. It was said at the time and after that these were a waste of effort. I cannot agree with this view ... I would make the following points in their favour. First, the question of morale. I hold that no air force can achieve air superiority by remaining continually on the defensive and confining their efforts to the defence of their own country. The sweeps, therefore, were an essential preliminary to a switchover to the offensive, and in this sense, they were the fore-runners of the invasion of the continent.

Secondly, he added, such missions taught Fighter Command many tactical lessons; and thirdly, Fighter Command's activity forced a high proportion of the German fighter force to stay in Europe rather than being sent to the Eastern Front. 'Therefore,' he concluded, 'those sweeps were well worth while.'[1]

Fighter Command was still engaged in night fighting in 1941; Max Aitken, the son of Lord Beaverbrook, developed this style of flying and fighting into a distinctive art. Thinking back on it, he recalled:

Night fighting is a fascinating game. It is rather like a game of rather noisy hide and seek or better still, it is like a game my brother and I used to play some years ago. We used to climb down into a large maze of stone quarries near our home and start stalking each other. Our ammunition was sharp stones and the loser was the first to be hit. We used to play for hours, wriggling on our stomachs, slowly gaining a good position and then a hard throw.[2]

The metaphor was made clear: the game of stalking through the dark was exactly what he now faced as the operational phone rang at midnight, and the noise of sirens wailing in a distant town echoed across the landscape. On a black and muffled night, when he ascended into the cloud, there would be a chance moment when the searchlights from below would converge and starkly illuminate the silhouette of the enemy. Then it was a matter of ruthless pursuit; focusing sharply on the orange and red of the exhaust flame, then the burst of gun-power, then the sight of a deeper glow from within the enemy plane, and the darkness flooding through once more as the enemy plane went down over the sea. Such accounts, of course, deliberately ignore the fact that the stalking game worked the other way around as well. But Aitken's courage was unquestioned; as well as the Distinguished Flying Cross and Distinguished Service Order, he received a telegram from Winston Churchill: 'Renewed congratulations to your squadron and personally to you.'

———

Perhaps it was the burnished memory of the summer of 1940 – enhanced by a certain level of almost boyish impatience, alongside the desire for morale-boosting action – that led Churchill and his most senior commanders to yearn for a full-scale version of 'Rhubarbs' and 'Circuses' in early 1942. The idea, in which Fighter Command played its role, was that an assault should be carried out on a French port. The Soviets, deep in the blood and ice of the Eastern Front, were putting pressure on the Allies to open another front to help divert and dilute the Nazi forces. There was also a school of thought within senior military circles that with thousands of troops – English and Canadian – stationed but stationary in Britain, it was necessary to carry out an operation that would introduce battle virgins to enemy fire. And so it was decided that the port of Dieppe would be the target. The operation would involve all services.

As spring gave way to summer, there were cracks in the planning; internal War Office disputes and searing hostility directed towards Churchill's Chief of Combined Operations Lord Louis Mountbatten, whose aristocratic swagger and refusal ever to accept that he might be wrong about anything were fiercely loathed by other, more experienced commanders around him. The planned raid – codenamed 'Rutter' – was tossed about and then discarded. Somehow, in the late summer of 1942, when Churchill was out of the country, the plan was resurrected. Now codenamed 'Jubilee' (and subsequently better known as the 'Dieppe Raid'), it would involve around 5,000 Canadian troops, about 1,000 British troops, a team of marine commandos and a small naval presence, with a contribution from Fighter Command.

Air Vice Marshal Leigh-Mallory was in charge of this wing of the operation, and he could not have been more enthusiastic. Despite all the sorties over France, despite the bombing raids that had been carried out over Germany, the

288

Luftwaffe could not apparently be deflected from its larger battles. The idea of Dieppe was an encapsulation of Leigh-Mallory's air-warfare philosophy: that of taking the fight to the enemy, and attacking hard in order to reduce the enemy's forces. German fighters would not be able to ignore an Allied raid on a French port; the targets alone in terms of shipping and troops would be too great not to take on. Leigh-Mallory's hope was that there would be sufficient numbers, for 11 Group and its (by now) superbly equipped and skilled pilots.

It is not remotely the fault of Leigh-Mallory that the raid itself – ill-starred from the pre-dawn start when the Allies were spotted at sea by the Germans, and ultimately resulting in thousands of casualties and deaths – was in many senses a catastrophe. By the end of the day, almost 1,000 men had been killed, and around 2,000 Canadian soldiers were captured by the Germans. Over 100 Fighter Command aircraft were lost. Leigh-Mallory wrote a report on the role of Fighter Command just a few days afterwards; bearing in mind the terrible, tragic number of pilots lost – for the Luftwaffe certainly did respond after a slow, lumbering start and of course, because it was fighting over its own territory, eventually had speed and rapid refuelling on its side – Leigh-Mallory tried to find ways to treat the day as a series of lessons, and to suggest how future attacks could be reordered. Rightly defending the pilots who had fought bravely throughout the day, he tried to focus on aspects that might be counted upon to work in the future. The operation demonstrated, he said, that smoke dropped from aircraft was effective; that his planes provided good cover for the men below; that his pilots, though flying as many as five sorties, showed 'no undue sign of fatigue'; and that, as ever, 'much valuable information' had been gleaned with regard to tactics and organisation.[3]

Even though he had an adverse effect upon many who met him, Leigh-Mallory's philosophy and attitude certainly never held him back, in the way perhaps that Hugh Dowding's approach did. Nor – quite rightly – was he stained in any way by the Dieppe debacle. In November 1942, Leigh-Mallory succeeded Sholto Douglas as Air Chief Marshal of Fighter Command. By this point in the war the balance had decisively tipped; this was the time for Bomber Command, and for Desert Command. Britain and her new ally the USA were strongly on the offensive. And while the Germans were still executing bombing raids over England – notably the 'Baedeker raids', so termed after the influential tourist guides, which inspired the Luftwaffe to aim for cathedral cities like Exeter and Canterbury and much-cherished historic towns such as Bath and Norwich (the death tolls were high) – there was no sense in which an invasion was expected.

Further promotion swiftly followed as the Allied offensive sharpened; Leigh-Mallory was made air marshal, and then commander of a prospective Allied Expeditionary Air Force – the aim of which was to support the forthcoming Operation Overlord. Unfortunately for Leigh-Mallory, he was sharply elbowed into the darkened wings by the return from the Mediterranean of more battle-grizzled British and American airmen, none of whom it seemed would accept his superior knowledge or authority on anything. As 1944 came, others simply stole his command from underneath him; Eisenhower's deputy Arthur Tedder became overall Air Commander, with of course Eisenhower as supreme Allied Commander. Other roles, such as Tactical Air Forces, and indeed Fighter Command, fell to a mix of Americans and Britons. Leigh-Mallory's lack of charm was one thing; but in the jostling and the manoeuvring for position, he could not compete with the much more active service that his competitors had seen. He failed to impress the returning heroes and as such, it is almost as if they could not be bothered to give him a second thought; Eisenhower and his men had been blooded and now they were roaring to finish the job. Leigh-Mallory opted to move out of their way.

In the wake of D-Day and the Allied invasion of Europe, Leigh-Mallory was offered a new post by Lord Mountbatten; that of Air Commander of India. Leigh-Mallory accepted very quickly. His haste to get there brought him face to face with fate. He and his wife were flying out from Northolt, west London, in an Avro York in November 1944. There had been warnings that the weather over France was very bad that day, suggestions that it would be better to delay the flight until conditions became more congenial. Leigh-Mallory was determined; he was not going to be held up for anything. And so it was that he demanded that the plane take off. Just a few miles outside the southeastern French town of Grenoble, the plane swooped and smashed into a mountain ridge and all passengers were killed. It was the Chief of the Air Staff, Sir Charles Portal, who sadly observed afterwards that there really had been no need for Leigh-Mallory to hurry.

The direction of the war had changed but the Germans, pushed harder and further, were fighting back with extraordinary tenacity; and the weapons about which they had been theorising for many years before the conflict had even started, were at last about to be unleashed upon the people of London.

Chapter Twenty

Death Will Send No Warning

For such a narrow stretch of water, the English Channel – roiling, ill-tempered – has always proved formidable. In 1940, it was partly the prospect of sending landing craft across and making a sure and consistent landing that cast clouds of doubt over Operation Sea Lion, and its chances of success. Part of the miracle of Dunkirk – to some veterans, a literal miracle – was that the sea stayed uncannily calm largely throughout the evacuation. The technological achievement of D-Day – and that is without mentioning the courage and fortitude of the Allied troops – was tempered by the nausea that the angry waves conjured before the beach landings were made on 6 June 1944. Then, days later, Hitler deployed mechanical agents of vengeance that shot over the sea, and over the White Cliffs. It was to be Fighter Command's last extraordinary mission of the war to find a way of stopping the flying bombs.

As a proposition, it would have seemed, at first glance, many times more difficult and complex than intercepting a few enemy fighters. The V-1 missiles – the 'V' standing for *Vergeltungswaffe*, vengeance weapon – were fast; the novelty of a pilotless craft – which, in essence, is what they were – led some to describe them as 'robots'. Human pilots are fallible; how do you stop a pre-programmed robot, screaming at colossal speed at low altitudes across the meadows and plains of England, reaching London in a matter of minutes? How much time would any intercepting pilots have between the first warning being given and reaching not only the height but also the speed of these lethal machines?

Even by 21 June 1944, Bentley Priory and aerodromes in the southeast were claiming some success against the new weapons. 'Judging by the results achieved to date,' wrote a correspondent from *The Times*, 'the best answer to Hitler's flying bomb is the latest British fighter, the Hawker Tempest. During a stay of a night and a day at a fighter airfield in southern England, I have had a chance of seeing two Tempest squadrons – and ground defences – in action – and in that time, both added to their score.'

The best combination, it seemed, was that of fighters and anti-aircraft guns. What the reports could not mention was the added element of the plotting work being done at Bentley Priory. 'Fighters were on patrol when, from the direction of the Channel, came a sound like that of an angry bee,' continued the reporter, relaying the novelty of the terror. 'A tiny speck of light appeared over the horizon, growing bigger every second, and the buzz and the light soon synchronised themselves into what appeared to be a meteor with a flaming orange-red tail …'

A pilot described what it was like to attack one of these flying projectiles. 'As you close up on it,' he said, 'it looks like a large flame with wings sticking out on either side. Because it is so small it is not easy to hit but the flying bomb is very vulnerable.' Such a sentiment, it might be added, was very necessary; all those in London whose lives were soon to be punctuated by this innovative form of death falling from the sky needed reassurance that their defenders knew what they were doing. The fighter pilot continued:

If your bullets strike home on the jet unit, the whole thing catches fire and it goes down with a crash. If you hit the bomb, the robot blows up. When we started attacking these things, we trod warily, shooting from long range but as we have got experience of this new form of attack, we find that we can close in, sometimes to 100 yards [90 metres]. If you are close when the bomb goes up, you sometimes fly through the debris and some of our Tempests have come back with their paint scorched. Some have been turned over on their backs by the force of the explosion but the pilot feels no effect except an upwards jolt.

The pilot optimistically concluded: 'Often it is not necessary to hit your target badly. A few bullets sometimes upset the gyro [automatic pilot] and then the robot does some queer manoeuvres and crashes straight in. We can catch them without undue difficulty and making these attacks is helping to make our shooting very accurate.'[1]

The secret operation to intercept and thwart the new threat is recalled vividly by Eileen Younghusband, who was now back at Bentley Priory as an officer: 'D-Day was June 6 – and I think it was four or five days later that the very first V-1 landed. Now we hadn't been warned, I don't think. Probably Bletchley Park knew about it. We had been warned that there might be something, though – and it came. And we were told that if anyone heard it … there was a code-word, "Big Ben". I was at Stanmore and we were over-ground. I remember the day when we were told we would get this "Big Ben" signal from a radar operator who could pick it up because of the trajectory. Which meant the filter officer literally shouting out the codewords "Big Ben".

'I had to stand on the chair and shout out "Big Ben, Big Ben, Big Ben" … With the first one there were three people killed, lots injured. I used to see the results of it after they came. As you travelled around London, you would see quite a lot of damage. And you would see them sometimes hanging on the telegraph lines, caught.'

For a population who were now counting the days until the end of the war, these renewed attacks were corrosive to the spirit. Despite the airy colloquialism, 'doodlebug', by which they became known, there were many who hated the idea of nights spent anticipating these bombs falling from the sky. Moreover, there was the added stress of suspense – the buzzing noise of the approaching missile in the sky, followed by an abrupt silence when the missile's guidance system calculated that the target had been reached, and the missile went into a steep dive before the moment of impact. It was like a form of Russian roulette from the heavens. When you heard the buzz, then the silence, you had to brace yourself for the prospect that it might be you. 'I can ... remember a funny eerie feeling,' recalled social worker Judith Hamilton, a north London girl during the doodlebug attacks. 'Suddenly you could hear a bomb coming across and – it stopped. The noise of the bomb suddenly stopped and everybody bent down, covering their heads, hoping it wasn't going to be their house or our shelter that was blown up ... and then ... when you heard the All Clear, opening the door and going out, and the relief that it wasn't your house and seeing in the distance fires and things and feeling sorry for whoever it was.'[2]

The V-1 was launched from sites both in France and along the Dutch coast. In its own way, it was a curiously elegant and economic weapon – a simple gyrometer guidance system, a pulse-jet form of propulsion – and swift: the time between launch and impact was a little over twenty minutes. A total of 9,521 were fired, resulting in 22,892 casualties. Against this horror, however, is the extraordinary leap made by RAF

Fighter Command; of nearly ten thousand missiles launched, only around a quarter got anywhere near their targets. Around 2,000 were knocked out by the efforts of anti-aircraft gunners from the ground; another 2,000 or so were knocked out by pilots, either by firing upon them or – bravely – by getting close enough to tip their wings and cause them to crash over unpopulated areas.

One such fighter pilot was Peter Middleton, who was with 605 Squadron at Manston in Kent. He, together with his fellow V-1 'nudgers', was highly skilled – having previously trained other pilots in Hurricanes and Spitfires, he flew throughout this frenetic period in the summer of 1944 a de Havilland Mosquito fighter bomber to deflect the missiles. He might be better known today for a family connection: he was the grandfather of Catherine, Duchess of Cambridge.

Patricia Clark recalls that even though there was a chance to intercept the V-1 flying bombs, the nature and speed of the work – the mathematical effort involved in trying to anticipate route and trajectory and distance and velocity – was harrowing: there was no ambiguity about the nature of the threat, and of how many lives depended on its successful interception. Radar could pick up a V-1 coming in on a particular arc, and the Observer Corps could see where they landed. 'So they had all that – but what they didn't have was the launch site. We would calculate on a piece of paper where the arc went down and finished. And then when they had enough plots showing the point in France, they would send a squadron over to bomb it.'

For WAAF radar operator Marie Ebbeson, this new phase of the war brought some hair-raising moments in 1944. 'Because we were a somewhat seasoned group of radar operators, two of us were chosen to go to London for a special briefing,' she recalled. 'Once there, we were sworn to secrecy and we were asked to try and operate a very strange and different screen. We were then told that Intelligence had discovered that the Germans were going to launch a rocket that would reach London and that in its warhead there was over a ton of explosives ... it seemed unreal that a rocket could go that far. The strange screen was to be able to plot the rocket and at our side we, the operator, could press a button that would set off the sirens in London, giving people a chance to take shelter. However there was only a three minute time gap before the rocket would have landed ... so finally that plan was ditched.'

Back at her base at Bawdsey Manor in Suffolk, the doodlebugs also brought Marie Ebbeson moments of personal jeopardy: 'We were opposite the coastline of the Continent – in the direct line of the doodlebugs, we were able to plot them on our screens. We could always tell them as their signal moved much faster than a plane. We worked in an underground bunker, but we could hear them as they flew over making a sound not unlike a rattly motor-bike. We had an Ack Ack site nearby and their job was to try and shoot them down before they crossed the coast; not that easy, a small target and very often flying low down. Now as long as the Ack Ack guns were firing away with their frightful noise we felt secure. It was when they suddenly went quiet that we would listen with bated breath in the bunker or for that matter anywhere on the station because it meant the doodlebug was heading for us at a low level! Oh the relief when it chugged on past us to fall somewhere in a field!'[3]

Elsewhere, historian E.S. Turner looked back with some personal pride on this short chapter of the war; he had played his own part in downing the doodlebugs as an anti-aircraft gunner under the control of Fighter Command. He wrote in 1985:

For most of the war, we who served behind barbed wire in public parks and on lonely headlands, surrounded by jolly ATS girls, were well aware that the public thought very little of our marksmanship. Since every shoot depended on dozens of people doing the right thing at the right time, the capacity for error was enormous. Then came the unmanned V-1, or 'Doodlebug' ... the rate of execution was gratifying and the sky of southern England glowed with orange blobs as Hitler's cut-price weapon met its come-uppance. Anti-Aircraft Command seemed to have justified itself at last ... Regrettably, in the last months of the war came the V-2 supersonic rocket, against which the anti-aircraft defences were seen to be starkly impotent.'[4]

Indeed they were; yet conversely, amid the destruction they caused, it was a matter of good fortune that there had been so many delays in the manufacture of these weapons. Had different decisions been taken in 1939 and 1940, the rockets might have started hitting London in 1942, when the effect upon morale could have been catastrophic. Intriguingly, the very idea of these revolutionary rockets long pre-dated Hitler and the Nazi party; in the Germany of 1928, there were early experiments with rocket aircraft, and explorations of new liquid fuel systems. But in 1932, as the Nazis achieved power for the first time, and just months before Hitler became Chancellor, the party lured the brilliant young engineer Werner von Braun away from his own amateur rocket group and installed him at the University of Berlin. By 1937, with the air armaments race gathering ever more frenetic pace, the Germans built a top secret weapons centre at Peenemünde on the Baltic coast. It was only thanks to Hitler's capricious ebbs and flows of enthusiasm that research on rocket technology wasn't given higher priority.

'Then there was the V-2 – I gather the first time they sent them, they sent three. One on Paris, one on Ghent, one on London,' recalls Eileen Younghusband. The first V-2s were launched on 8 September 1944; hundreds more were to follow. 'Churchill apparently wouldn't tell anyone about them, and Hitler didn't announce it until November. And it wasn't until after he announced it that Churchill announced it.' In fact, censorship around the explosions that started hitting London in those closing months of the war acquired a blackly comic edge amid the carnage and the tragedy. The authorities passed off the house-destroying, limb-mangling detonations as the result of arsenals exploding, or of gas mains blowing; saloon bar wags were soon making jokes about 'flying gas mains'. But this was a form of death that you really could not see coming; unlike the doodlebugs, which buzzed, 'coughed' and then fell silent, the V-2 rockets – much more sophisticated and lethal in terms of design and purpose – simply whispered at enormous speed towards their targets.

'You didn't know till it was too late because the sound came after the fall,' says Mrs Younghusband. 'Of course more landed on Antwerp than on London – 300 more. And a lot didn't land; they didn't reach their targets. Some just went up and came straight down.' Initially taking off from a static ramp in the Pas de Calais area, the missiles later had to be launched from lorries with a trailer. The missiles were never launched from the base; they and the lorries were moved out – 'so that people didn't know where the big supply was, I assume.'

Nor was Fighter Command entirely passive in the face of this technologically advanced threat; for its own technology had been evolving throughout the course of the war. At

Bawdsey Manor in Suffolk, WAAF radar operator Gwen Reading recalled vividly this stage of the war. 'When the V-2s came along, we could plot them on special equipment,' she wrote. 'This set, known as "Oswald", recorded the rocket for a few seconds … We could only watch Oswald's screen for fifteen minutes before changing operator because the trace showed so briefly that if you blinked, it could be missed. A camera operating within "Oswald" was recording all that we had seen. As we espied our rocket, we yelled "Big Ben at Bawdsey" down the line to [Bentley] who, a few minutes later, instructed us to "change Oswald". This was our cue to take out the film, insert a fresh one, and then send someone to our dark-room to develop the used film. From the information gained from our film, and those of other Chain Home stations, the launching site could be traced and hopefully our bombers sent to destroy them.'[5]

There was also a macabre foreshadowing of the nuclear era, and the possibility of giving warning of an impending atomic attack against any major city. With the V-2s, according to Gwen Reading, 'Londoners could have been given a four-minute warning of the approaching rocket, but I suppose the disruption over the entire area would have been too great to warrant this.'

The fact that the authorities tried – and so signally failed – to create a news blackout around the strikes also demonstrates a sort of furious futility. The best that could be hoped for was not merely the destruction of launching sites – others would be found soon enough – but of the entire regime. That victory was a matter of weeks away.

Obviously it would be a source of jubilation; yet mixed with it must have been a shiver of foreboding about the world to come. For despite the unimaginable jeopardy and – for men and women operatives on the ground alike – extraordinary intensity and focus, there must have been a few who looked back over the last few years and thought to themselves: 'I am going to miss this.' Certainly, when we look at the post-war lives of the team at Bentley Priory, and all the stations and aerodromes around the country, the dull iron clang of the quotidian – the chilled grey landscape of a bankrupt Britain – somehow rings louder than it does for the other services. To the very end, there was something incandescent, even other-worldly, about the war that had been fought in the air.

Chapter Twenty-One

Grounded

The aftershock, for many, was intense; the weeks, months and years of flying to the defence of the country, and now the prospect settling down back on earth. For the men who had fought by the light of the moon, or in the thick billows of impenetrable cloud, or over clear-viewed domestic landscapes – the green rectangles, the lines of lanes, with which they were intimately familiar – this would mean in the most basic physical sense the shrinking of their lives. Despite the extraordinary danger, they had swooped high above the world and gazed at the firmament. To go from that to ordinary careers in ordinary offices, the hemmed-in cities, the flat views from train windows, was a sharp psychological jab. Some found that they could not stay away.

Air ace Douglas Bader was one such. Finally released from Colditz in April 1945, he returned to Fighter Command – in charge of the North Weald station – and was there to lead victory flyovers some months later in September. He had the chance to fly his beloved Spitfire once more, and also to become acquainted with the new generation of planes coming through, such as the Meteor. But the post-war atmosphere was something that he could not quite find a taste for. Naturally, there was now no urgency, no drive; no enemy to shoot out of the sky. The rest was training – but

Bader was also witnessing the dissolution of a mighty war machine, plane by plane, pilot by pilot. The epic efforts of the conflict were now being scaled back for peace. The other crucial missing factor was adrenaline: while routine flying had a beauty all its own, Bader had thrived on the knife-edge uncertainties of conflict. He knew that the future offered by this new air force would only make him melancholic and angry.

He returned to work for the Shell Company, which, in fairness, gave him the opportunity for travel; in fact, a great deal more than most others of his generation. Bader and his wife were to start flying right across the world on business. He was clearly a terrific asset to the oil company too; who could resist doing business with one of the greatest heroes of the war? He became managing director of Shell Aircraft. In the late 1940s and early 1950s, senior figures in the Conservative Party began to badger him; they could find him an agreeably safe seat somewhere, anywhere: would he please consider joining them? But Bader always refused rather curtly. Politics was emphatically not the line for him.

Then, in the mid-1950s, came *Reach for the Sky*, the biography of Bader that made him even more of a household name; followed swiftly in 1956 by the film, starring Kenneth More and proving one of Britain's biggest box-office draws. 'How magnificently everyone who takes part conspires to produce a really memorable and moving record of human courage and endurance!' rhapsodised one newspaper critic. 'Kenneth More takes the part of Bader and in his easy charm and dauntless single-mindedness, Bader could not have been better served.'

The same year came the award of the CBE. The recognition was clearly pleasing and gratifying; but even this could not have been enough for him. Bader's energetic bullishness never left him, even in the years after the war. He successfully sued a tabloid newspaper in 1961 for suggesting that he had terrorised a party of schoolchildren by deliberately flying low over them. Even if the story had been true, this would have been a risky way of writing about such a widely admired hero.

As well as flying to all regions of the world on business (managing, on one occasion, a round of golf in Los Angeles with David Niven, Errol Flynn and James Stewart), Bader also quietly involved himself in a number of disabled charitable concerns. He was particularly attentive to children who had lost limbs; to this day, the Douglas Bader Foundation, based in west London, raises funds and organises scores of special events for young amputees. There is a consistent tone of cheerfulness and optimism; the website is headed with pictures of the ace in his flying heyday. Bader himself lived until 1982; even in his final weeks, he was giving speeches and having lunches with journalists at grand London clubs – happily encouraging hacks to drink while, of course, remaining teetotal himself.

What of the younger pilots? The story of Geoffrey Wellum – just nineteen years old as he fought in the Battle of Britain – spoke not only of the immense stresses imposed by such combat, but also of the body's miraculous powers of regeneration. He had continued with Fighter Command, flying on various 'Rhubarb' and 'Circus' missions over France until the summer of 1942, when he was posted to Malta. But while he was overseas, the stabbing headaches that he had been experiencing for some time in the cockpit suddenly became very much worse; the subsequent collapse hospitalised him. Harrowingly, he was aware of his head being held as doctors probed up through his nose – a sensation of excruciating pain followed by a cascade of 'strawberry-coloured fluid' through his nostrils. One of the doctors proclaimed that it must have been a cyst. The wider effect was that it left the young man, even now only twenty-two, feeling and looking very much older. Wellum was wracked with guilt, with an overwhelming sense that somehow he was letting his fellow pilots down. But he was flown back to England for a lengthy period of recuperation, during which he experienced profound depression and physical exhaustion.

The physical trauma had built up as a reaction to the intense pressures of combat flying; what Wellum had refused to acknowledge to himself consciously had nonetheless left him physically devastated. But when one so young is addicted – and it is clear that Wellum was passionately devoted to flying – there is then the additional difficulty of getting them to quietly recover while denying them the solace of flight. Wellum went home and forced himself to re-learn relaxation and tranquillity – the pleasure of fishing by a quiet river.

Eventually he was able to return to active duty in the RAF, though now he was not involved in direct combat, but in training. He was introduced to the new generation of Typhoons. And so he took to the air once more and it became clear that this was all that he had ever really craved; not the fighting, but the beauty of gliding along on top of the clouds. He stayed with the RAF until 1961.

There were, of course, many who didn't make it. During the Battle of Britain, 544 pilots were killed. Another 814 pilots died before the war ended. Many of them were men from other parts of the world who had signed up for the honour of fighting for Britain. Brendan 'Paddy' Finucane, an Irishman who had defied his own government to fight for the British, became the RAF's youngest wing commander aged twenty-one in 1942; shortly afterwards, he was hit while flying over France, and perished in the Channel. The American pilot Vernon Keough, who had specialised in aerobatics, was on convoy protection missions in 1941; his plane was last seen spinning off in ferocious weather over the North Sea.

After the war, some found that their battles in the air had given them an extraordinary social magnetism. For instance, the frisson of glamour experienced by Douglas Bader in Hollywood was as nothing compared to the post-war activities of 92 Squadron's Anthony Bartley: already familiar with troupes of admiring film stars turning up to the Biggin Hill station, he too had been guest of honour at Los Angeles parties – invited by notable British actors such as Laurence Olivier and feted by American ones like Clark Gable. Others, such as Basil Rathbone (most famous as the big-screen Sherlock Holmes), sought out Bartley – as he had done Bader – to make them the centrepieces of smart Hollywood dinners. On one glittering social occasion, Bartley met the young British actress Deborah Kerr. The pair of them found an instant connection; their wedding took place swiftly afterwards back in England at St George's, Hanover Square. This, if anything, was the apotheosis of RAF elegance, confirming all the popular images of the dashing brave young men and their deserved place at the pinnacle of society. Moreover, they were turning their faces towards a future that many British people dreamed of: a life in the United States. They moved to California, had two children, and Deborah Kerr's career grew and developed; the image of her and Burt Lancaster embracing on the sand as a wave hits in *From Here to Eternity* (1952) is as famous now as it was then.

And initially, it looked as though Bartley would be moving into film production; he studied the profession with Metro-Goldwyn-Mayer and then formed his own production company, writing and producing dramas for various television anthology series. For a time, Bartley worked for the television station CBS as its European representative. By the late 1950s, it became clear that he and Kerr had drifted apart. They agreed to an amicable separation. Bartley continued with his television career, joining the hugely successful Associated Rediffusion in the 1960s and remarrying. It was doubtless exciting to be involved in a new popular medium that was beginning to explore its own power and potential. And Bartley was well acquainted with the crossover between real life and screen dramas. Having fought so hard and so harrowingly in the Battle of Britain, he had gone on to perform aerobatic stunts in 1941 for the British film dramatisation *The First of the Few*. A pilot would accept any reason to take to the air – even to play-act what, months previously, had been lethally real. There must have been days in Bartley's later television executive career that felt thin compared to all that had gone before. Given the innumerable stresses of his earlier years, though, he lived to a commendable age, dying in 2001 at the age of eighty-two.

The sense of the air as another realm had seeped deep into the bones of Hugh Dowding. Although elevated to the House of Lords in 1943, he was denied the kind of honours and tributes – such as promotion to marshal – that routinely went to other senior air personnel. Unlike William Sholto Douglas, there was something about Lord Dowding that made him fundamentally – to use that most Establishment of expressions – un-clubbable. He remained adrift from the usual networks of colleagues and friends. Perhaps the other senior airmen were put off by more than his dry and abstemious manner. In the latter years of the war, Lord Dowding began writing books about his intense belief in, and passion for, spiritualism. He wrote, without inhibition, of suburban séances that he had attended, of the spirits of the deceased that had come through, and of his theories about the sort of landscape they inhabited. He also became deeply interested in Theosophy – the movement that suggested that all world religions had some deep common root. In this age, these beliefs would perhaps meet with a polite interest; in 1940s and 1950s Britain – a nation of spectacular social restrictions – they could be a source of huge awkwardness. Even Lord Dowding himself wryly remarked that there was something 'non-U' – not quite the thing, as another phrase from the time went – about the new faith that he had acquired.

But it was more than just social awkwardness; for he also came to believe that he was in communication with the spirits of dead fighter pilots. This was possibly territory too raw and fraught for many of Dowding's RAF colleagues, who themselves would have been working hard to keep old griefs and traumas far from the surface. Such unease was manifested in the form of a temporary publishing ban: Dowding's monograph *Twelve Legions of Angels* was suppressed on the orders of Churchill, ostensibly because it spoke of matters still covered by the Official Secrets Act, but also presumably on the grounds of taste, since it detailed long conversations with dead pilots – and it saw the light of day only in 1946. Coincidentally, speculation concerning airmen and the new heavenly dimension of light also found cinematic expression that year in Powell and Pressburger's *A Matter of Life and Death,* in which David Niven's pilot somehow cheats death – and attracts the subsequent attention of heavenly messengers – when his plane is brought down.

Later, as the Cold War UFO craze took off in the late 1940s (the first was seen in 1947) Lord Dowding confessed that he also believed utterly in the prospect of aliens in flying saucers. He went on early BBC television discussion shows in the 1950s to discuss the phenomenon with sceptics. Again, what might in some seem quirky or eccentric had a powerful internal logic for a man whose life was spent above the clouds; if there were spirits in this airy realm, then why should there not be powerful beings from other worlds too? They were united as souls who had defied the pull of the material earth below.

The spiritualist beliefs of Dowding's bitter enemy, Trafford Leigh-Mallory, had apparently developed following the illness – and subsequent recovery – of one of his children. As well as faith healing, Leigh-Mallory was said to be adamant about the existence of ghosts, and claimed to have seen one in Lincolnshire. Of course, sailors are well known for various atavistic beliefs; in the intense world of Fighter Command, perhaps it is not so surprising that experienced aviators, who had witnessed so much death, would come to believe that that simply could not be the end, that there was a world elsewhere.

And is there a possibility that Leigh-Mallory's spiritual convictions had also been influenced by the death of his brother George – famously, the Mallory who climbed and perished on Mount Everest? The cult of mountaineering – of which George Mallory was a totemic figure – is in some poetic way quite similar to the love for flying. Mountaineering, especially in an age before technology made it accessible to all, was a mental as well as a physical ordeal. It was not merely a question of reaching unthinkable heights, or of conquering the most bitter wildernesses to do so, or indeed of facing the jeopardy of not having quite enough air to breathe. It was also about venturing into a different world, being a pioneer on a fresh new planet never before seen by human eyes. To look at photographs of George Mallory now is to see a man staring determinedly out into a hinterland that few others can guess at. Mallory froze to death near the summit of the mighty mountain; his corpse, a bathetic sight, discovered only in 1999. It's hard not to wonder whether something similar in his brother's soul craved the solitude of great heights, no matter the risk.

———

For the women of Fighter Command, there was an equal struggle after the war to depressurise; to return to the roles that were expected of women without crying out in anguish at the flavourless blandness of this austere, bankrupt country. In that sense, Patricia Clark was swift to see the possibilities and equally swift to circumvent them. Just before the war ended, she suddenly found herself back in Stanmore at Fighter Command HQ, this time in the position of helping fellow women to negotiate their way back into a normal life. 'The V-2s stopped. And then to give me something to do, they attached me of all things to the Education Officer,' Mrs Clark says now. 'The Education Officer had to go around Stanmore giving lectures on what was available educationally in order to help people back into Civvy Street.'

The tuition was not confined to women. There were pilots badly in need of advice too. 'These officers – one in particular, Charles Crusoe – were teasing me. Now, I had a flat in London and he thought it would be a good idea if we all met and had a night out in London – and that's how I met my husband-to-be Donald, who was the other chap there at the lecture. A very serious Scotsman. I found him extraordinarily interesting. Nothing you talked about he wouldn't know the answer to, from politics to a remote river in China. He intrigued me up here and I decided it was time I got married because I very much wanted to have children.'

But Patricia Clark was also unusually independent; her writing career was beginning to take off, partly thanks to those long nights in the Filter Room when the Germans decreased the scale of their attacks. What life at Fighter Command also offered this budding novelist was material. She had been given a unique chance to see, close up, people under the most serious duress – had experienced it for herself – and she now had a much sharper understanding of the wilder shores of human nature. All the pilots and officers she had worked with, all the romances that she had seen flowering in the most unlikely circumstances, gave her an insight at a very young age. Her own mother, Denise Robins, was still the country's outstandingly successful romantic novelist (a crown that Barbara Cartland was yet to appropriate); Mrs Clark now says that this could not help but rub off on her.

As a result, when the war came to an end, Mrs Clark felt that she had a purpose other than simply having a family and making a home; the choice that was expected of women of all classes then as men returned from theatres of war. 'It was a slow transition,' she says. 'But I was lucky.' It was more than luck: short stories led to children's books, and these in turn led to romantic novels which were to become huge transatlantic bestsellers. As an author, Mrs Clark is still writing and also giving talks today.

For Eileen Younghusband, the end of the war was in some ways just as dramatic as the start; instead of gradually winding down the shifts, she and a handful of other female WAAF officers were chosen in 1945 for a very specific mission when the Low Countries had been liberated. Even though the Germans were in retreat, the fighting continued. And RAF units on the continent needed more immediate support. 'Only eight of us were chosen to go over to Belgium,' says Mrs Younghusband. 'And again, we had to be the best at the level of mathematics they needed – probably trigonometry. It was that that we used. We were told what formulas to use. We went governed by the Filter Room initially. It was 33 Wing we were in. It wasn't just RAF people. We had the serving regiments. We once had a mixed hockey match – several of the army bods were in the hockey team with us. And we played the Belgians who were made up of Belgium's international ice hockey team. All male!'

The popular image of liberation now is of Allied soldiers surrounded by adoring crowds, of young women bearing flowers. The unvarnished reality of life just before that, recalls Mrs Younghusband, was rather different, and sometimes intimidating. 'I was billeted with a very strange family – they weren't very nice to me at all. They were terribly jealous because I was having proper food. And the other thing that I remember: coming off duty at midnight and having to walk across the town centre, with no one else around, to get to my billet. It was a big sort of market square with a big cover over it. The ground was either tessellated or bricked and as I walked in this silence – I had black strong shoes – you could hear me, clip clip clip. When we were first over there, there were still German snipers about. And that was the only time I was really frightened. I wasn't frightened so much about the bombing but I was quite frightened of walking through that town centre alone.

'After a very short time, the stray German soldiers and snipers were all captured. But in general, people weren't supposed to be out at night. So if you ever heard footsteps in the dark – well yes, that is rather a memorable thing.'

While, over the Channel, her WAAF colleagues celebrated the end of the war in Europe, it was all a little more involved for Eileen Younghusband and her colleagues in Belgium: 'Actually, I came off duty at eight o'clock in the morning of VE Day. We didn't know then but we knew that the Germans were in retreat and we had a feeling that the end was very, very near. I walked out into the street and this little car came to a jerk. Two British pilots got out – who had been prisoners of war – and hugged me and said, "You're the first English woman we've seen since 1940." Those words ring in my ears!'

Mrs Younghusband had been on duty all night; and she and the two RAF pilots saw in VE Day almost delirious with tiredness and disorientation. 'When I brought these men back into the mess, I'd been up thirty-six hours by then,' says Mrs Younghusband. 'The MO came and he probably thought I looked tired and he gave me sleeping tablets. He said: "You're so hyped up because it's VE Day, you had better have one of these." I didn't have a room in the mess – all the senior officers had taken those. So I had to walk quite a way to get to my billet. So I took this pill, went up to my room, got into bed, and then I thought, this is bloody stupid! This is VE Day! What am I doing? So I got up again, went back to the mess, and that's when the MO said, "Oh God," and then gave me an upper, after I had had the downer! And then we went in a little tiny car – three of us – and we drove through the streets of Brussels in this sort of victory parade. They gave us flowers and cakes and all sorts of things. Then I came back and went to sleep.'

Post-war life was – in some ways – a disappointment for some of Fighter Command's senior figures. Right the way across the world, on 12 September 1945, Sir Keith Park – alongside Lord Mountbatten – accepted the surrender of the Japanese in southeast Asia. Back in 1940, in the aftermath of his dismissal from 11 Group, he had gone on, first to supervise flying training in Gloucestershire, and then back out on active service when he was posted to Malta. There, on an island that took particularly heavy bombardment in the Mediterranean war, Park's skill in handling the tactics of fighter pilots won admiration from the Americans, as well as his British colleagues. By then Park was fifty; his experience was vast, his manner ever more calm and assured. He received a knighthood in November 1942. A year later, he was promoted and moved; appointed an air marshal, he found himself Commander-in-Chief of Middle East Command in Cairo. Again, experience counted for a lot; but his innate good manners were invaluable in keeping peace among the Allies at a time when any notion of the 'special relationship' being completely harmonious would have been greeted on all sides with satirical laughter.

From there to South-east Asia Command, backing up General Slim's army, and a period which once more brought forth golden opinions, Park found that his talents were being recognised on a wider stage. He was gracious about it too, and his immediate post-war months were spent carefully winding down the vast and effective fighter operation that he had led. After that, he left the RAF and turned, like so many other pilots, to the burgeoning world of commercial flight. Moving back to his native New Zealand, he took a job with Hawker Siddeley as its Pacific representative; this was a new age of mass flight, no longer the domain of the very wealthy. Now ordinary tourists were going to be able to feel the wonder that he himself had yearned for when he had joined the Royal Flying Corps during the First World War and trained at the Netheravon station in Wiltshire.

In those post-war years, Sir Keith Park was quite forthright on the subject of those who had done him down in the autumn of 1940; his anger (as opposed to Lord Dowding's tone of hurt) was palpable. But at the same time, the invaluable role that he had played was openly acknowledged by a variety of RAF establishment figures. His retirement in New Zealand was peaceful; he died in 1975, aged eighty-three. Movingly, Sir Douglas Bader spoke at his memorial service at St Clement Danes in London. There was no further band-standing about 'big wings'. Instead, his tribute was plain and gracious: 'The Battle of Britain was controlled, directed and brought to a successful conclusion by the man whose memory we honour today.' In the years following 1940, history had been adjusted, and Sir Keith Park was acknowledged as a hero.

And just as Sir Douglas Bader had had the honour of a film based around his wartime exploits, so Sir Keith and Lord Dowding had had the satisfaction of the 1969 epic production *The Battle of Britain*, starring Sir Laurence Olivier as Dowding and Trevor Howard as Park. Even more satisfying for Dowding was the opportunity to meet and talk to the producer (Harry Saltzman, well known for his partnership with Albert R. Broccoli and the Bond films) and the actors. Here was a vast production that would reach worldwide audiences; and here was a film that substantively stood by Lord Dowding and his system. Dowding was to die a year later. It must have been gratifying for him to know that not only had he been vindicated by historians and RAF colleagues alike; but his achievements were also woven into the tapestry of national culture. Unfortunately, the film, fantastically expensive to make, itself proved something of a turkey – by 1969, the cinematic war genre was very much past its peak, and younger audiences were after cooler, gaudier entertainment. Happily, its reputation has grown in the intervening years as a perennial television favourite.

Immediately after the war, as fighter pilots posted around the world were gradually returned home, one particular contingent of men were understandably reluctant. The Polish pilots, who had fought with such exceptional determination, now looked across at a country behind a dark Iron Curtain; Poland had been annexed by the Soviet Union. And these men knew that far from being received as heroes, the new Communist regime would view them in a very different light: as lackeys of the western powers, corrupted and infected by those alongside whom they had fought. For these pilots, any sense of victory was fleeting. They had been fighting the fascists, and now their country was controlled by a no less lethal form of totalitarianism. So it was that an Act of Parliament was passed, allowing any Poles who wished to stay in Britain to do so.

For others who had served, there were other difficulties to face. Eileen Younghusband had one last terrible job to do before she could leave the WAAFs; she was still based in Belgium in 1945, so it fell on her to guide fellow RAF officers around the prison of Breendonk, in which the Nazis had carried out an extraordinary number of atrocities. Mrs Younghusband had to hear accounts of torture – burnings, drownings – and she found the atmosphere of the place extremely unsettling. Having seen the nobler side of the conflict, she now had to descend into its unutterable squalor; the reality of what ordinary people were capable of doing to one another, the limitless suffering that they could inflict. 'The army worked with town mayors in Belgium and elsewhere,' says Mrs Younghusband, 'and because I spoke fluent French, they sent me down to Breendonk. They thought that the RAF personnel that were stationed anywhere around that area should see what the Germans had done so they would begin to see the truth.' They saw it.

Then, on her return to Britain, and as part of her very last WAAF duties, Mrs Younghusband returned to Bentley Priory – and immediately began working with Polish airmen, helping to improve their English. 'I was living bang opposite the Filter Room aerial in Hill House where we had been moved to.' Because she stayed in the air force until January 1946, she took on the job of teaching English to the Polish officers at Stanmore. 'They gave me a book called *Poland's Progress*, and they all signed it. One of them was Group Captain Bayeun, a First World War Polish pilot. Because I was only over the road, and the pilots were all enjoying their English lessons, they asked if I could continue.' She continued giving lessons as long as she remained a WAAF.

So what sort of impact did their Filter Room experiences have on the postwar lives of Eileen Younghusband and the other women who had worked there in secrecy? For Mrs Younghusband, life acquired a different rhythm but nonetheless a very hard-working one. She married Peter, the bandleader she had met at RAF Northolt. And as he tried to establish a new civilian working life, as a salesman, she found her mathematical and accounting skills in demand from her father-in-law, who ran stables in Stanmore, leasing out horses for film productions. Thereafter she and her husband went into the hotel business, working ferocious hours in a less than congenial economic climate; but as austerity gave way to the new Elizabethan age, trade grew brisker and again, Mrs Younghusband found herself thoroughly occupied. The war – and her contribution – was a never-to-be-spoken secret in ever-lengthening shadows.

Some other WAAF women found happiness elusive and everyday life grimly unendurable after having been at the nerve centre of the war effort. Eileen Younghusand sadly recalls that one of her colleagues went into a disastrous decline afterwards: 'One girl had been on the balcony of the Filter Room. She was one of the first, she had been in very early. She married a bomber pilot, and after the war ended, they went up to Scotland. They had a croft up there. Well, can you imagine? After being on the balcony, in contact with the controllers and the radar stations – a very vital job – and then to have it all cut off and go and live in a croft. The girl took to drink – she always drank quite a bit – and she drank herself to death. The end of the war was like taking the rug from under her feet. Having given orders – and then to go from that to end up probably milking cows – if that – in that lonely landscape. When before, you had had all that life going on.'

Some fighter pilots went on to cultivate unexpected fame. A young man called Ian Smith, for instance, who had flown fighter planes in the Mediterranean towards the end of the war, returned afterwards to his farming life in southern Africa. About twenty years later, as Prime Minister of Rhodesia, he made a Unilateral Declaration of Independence from Britain, amid worldwide condemnation of racism (though the condemnation did not go so far as tightly controlled economic sanctions, and the country thrived), and he remained a hugely controversial leader until 1979. The country is now, of course, Zimbabwe. It is tempting to wonder if there is a streak of implacable recaltricance in the fighter pilot, or even a maverick disdain for the rules that everyone else must abide by.

Another fighter pilot, Roald Dahl, was curiously ungovernable as well. A fighter ace, having scored five victories in the Mediterranean, Dahl was later posted to Washington as part of Air Intelligence; sent back to Britain by senior British embassy officials for insubordination, he was swiftly recalled by intelligence supremo Sir William Stephenson. His sardonic approach to both authority and social norms informed his later best-selling fiction. His children's stories – among them *Charlie and the Chocolate Factory* and *James and the Giant Peach* – have an edge of anarchy and a near disgust with grown-ups; and his adult short stories and novels are frequently both macabre and cynically sour.

Other fighter pilots retained a quintessential boyishness in their later careers. One such was Raymond Baxter: he had flown Spitfires and taken part in sorties over Sicily (for which he was mentioned in dispatches) and in missions against V-2 launching sites, and his post-war career took him swiftly to the BBC. He started as a commentator but specialised in broadcasting from annual events such as the Farnborough Air Show. He became best known as one of the presenters of the BBC science show *Tomorrow's World*, for which he became one of the pioneer passengers on Concorde, as well as trying out outlandish devices such as outboard motors designed to be strapped to the body.

This sense of a boyish rebel spirit was also captured brilliantly by one of only three German-born men to have flown for the RAF during the war. Klaus Hugo Adam, who had emigrated with his family from Berlin in 1934, sent countless badgering letters in his eagerness to be accepted in the RAF. In 1941, he joined, and by the end of the war, he was flying Typhoons over France, escorting American bombers towards their targets (at this point, his younger brother Dennis managed to join up too). He came under enemy fire many times; and friendly fire too, from American fighters who had never before seen Typhoons. Adam was in a unique situation for another reason too: had he been shot down and captured by the Germans, he recalled, he would not have been a prisoner of war; instead, as a German-born male, he would have been instantly executed for treason.

Klaus Hugo Adam had also changed his name to Kenneth; he had an abiding fascination with engineering and design. After the war, he moved into British film production. It was he, Adam, who as production designer, created the unforgettable look of the James Bond films starting in 1962; from Dr No's modernist lair to the cathedral of gold in Fort Knox to the extraordinary extinct volcano base (with added monorail) of Ernst Stavro Blofeld. Not long ago, Adam received a long overdue knighthood. Sir Ken is an interesting synecdoche for his generation of fighter pilots: that combination of lightly worn bravery, unorthodox creativity and a certain cussed individuality.

The end of the war did not bring the decommissioning of Fighter Command HQ in Stanmore. But it did bring an altogether new phase, with a different flavour, different priorities and perhaps just the smallest spark – quite quickly ignited – of melancholic nostalgia.

Chapter Twenty-Two

Afterlife

In the 1960s, the popular television comedy thriller *The Avengers* featured a couple of episodes whose action was centred around abandoned fighter stations in Britain. In one, 'The Town of No Return' (1965), bowler-hatted protagonist Steed, investigating a series of disappearances in a remote Norfolk coastal village, spends some time absorbing the atmosphere of the old airfield, with its roofless Nissen huts and scraps of topless pin-ups still attached to mildewed walls. The landlord of the local pub, the extravagantly moustachioed former fighter pilot 'Piggy' Warren, tells Steed that he was stationed there himself: one of 'The Fighting 33'. 'Grand days, bang on days,' he sighs. Although 'Piggy' later turns out to be an imposter, part of a bizarre invasion plan involving replacing one by one the populations of local villages, smallest first; and despite the menacing atmosphere of the pub and village, there is also a twang of genuine sadness about the old airfield, filmed on location: the crumbling shelters, the weeds growing through the concrete.

This sense of eerie abandonment was amplified in a later episode, 'The Hour that Never Was' (1966), in which Steed and Mrs Peel are due to attend the closing down of another fighter base, RAF Hamelin. Once again, there is a sinister atmosphere, verging on the hallucinatory; and once again what comes through most clearly is a sense that in the real world, so many bases and stations which had once launched some of the finest heroic actions were now being abandoned, as if a new generation – in a new, technocratic era – was turning its back on the wars of the old. This was now a post-atomic world; the Spitfire already looked charmingly anachronistic.

Yet the functions of Fighter Command – in the chilly new conditions of the Cold War – remained philosophically the same, and the RAF held on to Bentley Priory as an administrative headquarters. Though the technology was changing fast, and being outsourced to different corners of the kingdom, its basic functions remained the detection of incoming aircraft and the ability to strike back at any enemy incursions. From the 1940s, the Royal Air Force became more and more involved in the realm of signals intelligence, and though this was not Fighter Command's area of expertise, there was enough international tension during the period to keep all personnel alert to unauthorised incursions into British airspace. At a distance of some seventy years, it grows increasingly strange to think of the sheer monolithic size of the Soviet Union, from the Baltic states to the border of China, from the Adriatic to the Berlin Wall. The RAF and her allies were now facing an air force of ever-increasing scale and ingenuity. From 1949, Soviet Russia had the Bomb. Any fighter from behind the Iron Curtain flying over NATO waters had to be monitored, intercepted, repulsed.

The early 1950s brought a variety of skirmishes – American planes flying over Soviet territory were fired upon – and potentially lethal mistakes, such as the 1953 incident when a British European Airways passenger flight was targeted near the border of Germany by Soviet fighters who mistook it for an RAF plane. There was an urgent sense that agreement over air routes had to be reached and throughout this period, RAF fighters were in no doubt that if they were fired upon, then they were to fire back.

There were other menaces to consider too, as time and technology moved on. It fell to Fighter Command during the Cold War to monitor the skies for incoming ballistic missiles – an echo of the V-2 rocket campaign. But the speed of this new generation of weapons was far greater; and the precise and specialised task of providing early warning was no longer the province of fast, sharp women calculating vectors at speed. The computer era was dawning; the first satellites had been launched into the heavens. Intelligence in all senses was still essential, but this was a new world where there might conceivably have been a chance either to deflect such missiles, or at least warn personnel and civilians in potential targets to take shelter.

Yet Bentley Priory itself kept a certain old-fashioned feel. From the 1950s to the 1970s, new recruits to the Royal Air Force were taught to look on it almost as a shrine, or at the very least as a source of inspiration: by now, it was widely understood what Air Chief Marshal Dowding and Air Vice Marshal Park had achieved, and the fresh generation was keen to remain true to that. The house was still used for squadron reunions, and for royal visits too. The young Queen Elizabeth II attended a dinner there in 1958 to celebrate the fortieth anniversary of the RAF. As in the war, the estate was still strictly fenced and patrolled, with sentries on permanent duty at the main gate. Nor was the Royal Observer Corps forgotten: in February 1966, it was presented with a special banner at Bentley Priory by the Queen.

The 1960s and 1970s brought all sorts of familiar difficulties; funding was squeezed, priorities had to be decided. Nonetheless, the RAF as a whole was, in terms of morale, very healthy. In terms of recruitment, it did not have to go to the sometimes strenuous lengths of the army.

So even many years after the war, 'the romance of flying coupled with the security and respectability of the job and the prospect of a reasonable second career outside have made up an attractive package,' reported *The Times* defence specialist. At Bentley Priory, the terminology was changed slightly, as the technical nature of defending airspace evolved: in 1968, there was a transmogrification to Strike Command. By 1970, the Priory oversaw an array of the newest weapons, as well as planes: among the missiles were 'Phantom', 'Lightning' and 'Bloodhound'. It remained the spiritual home of the still-extant 11 Group; now, in this new era of SALT (Strategic Arms Limitation Talks) and détente, whoever commanded the group also sat in on vital NATO conferences.

The site became a source of fascination for those who opposed both nuclear power and weaponry; the security services were teased by the *Guardian* newspaper in 1984 by its then diarist, a young Alan Rusbridger, who reported that he had been sent, in an unmarked brown envelope, 'the drawings for the bunker and communications centre at Bentley Priory'. These, he added, featured a droll note of comedy: the carpet colour for the bunker was described as 'Warlord Burnt Orange'.

And despite the secrecy surrounding the site, members of the Campaign for Nuclear Disarmament went there the same year to protest against nuclear proliferation. The demonstration was slightly in vain, not least because control of nuclear weaponry had almost two decades beforehand been transferred to the Royal Navy. Nonetheless, they argued that the site would be a target for enemy nuclear missiles should war ever break out, and that in turn spelled doom for the entire population of north London.

As soon as the Berlin Wall collapsed in the autumn of 1989, the Cold War assumptions and fears of the last forty years dissolved into the air; whatever the many threats that hung over Britain, they would no longer centrally involve fighter aircraft and ballistic missiles conquering the country's airspace – though obviously there were many other regions of instability in the world, and many reasons to remain as vigilant as ever. The terrible events of 11 September 2001 brought new possibilities for death from the skies; and it was clear that London would be a target for potential terrorists. The skies by then were being comprehensively monitored by a huge range of satellites and sources; there was not a wisp of cloud that could not be accounted for. In recent years, Israel seems to have led the way in establishing the sort of air defence that other countries have long yearned for: the so-called 'Iron Dome' system, working at unfathomable speed, using missiles to intercept and bring down missiles. From a pilot 'tipping the wing' of a V-1 flying bomb in 1944 to fully automated computerised intervention seventy years later in 2014; though the technology is astounding, the principles remain the same.

RAF Bentley Priory came to the end of its working life in 2008. In its latter years, a little of that modest veil of secrecy was lifted, on group open days where the public at last had a chance to look around the old house, walk in the grounds and gaze across, as Lord Dowding had done, at the distant prospect of Harrow on the Hill. But what was to happen to the property once it had been relinquished by the Royal Air Force?

There was a precedent about thirty miles to the north in Buckinghamshire; another fine country house that had found extraordinary new life during the war, and which had entered a twilight period of official secrecy. Bletchley Park, discarded by the government in the early 1990s, was rescued by a group of energetic volunteers, who tackled the decaying house, started raising funds, and made it their mission to let the world know that it was there that some of the greatest feats of the war – the cracking of the German Enigma codes – had taken place. Recently it became clear that the house and grounds of Bentley Priory offered up a similarly excellent educational opportunity: the site at which the defence of the realm was masterminded at a point in history where the country could quite easily have fallen. As all subsequent RAF pilots looked to the house as a sort of spiritual base, so now the general public should have a chance to visit and to understand why it generated that sort of emotion.

And like Bletchley, after some years of enthusiastic lobbying and eager fund-raising, Bentley Priory is now a brilliant and engaging museum. As well as the Spitfire in the driveway before the house's front door, there are the countless moving exhibits – flying logbooks, photos, a beautiful Battle of Britain stained glass window, not to mention a startling recreation of Lord Dowding's office, in which his words and orders are brought back to animatronic life via special recordings and clever film tricks. The centrepiece is a meticulous and fascinating recreation of the Filter Room; the museum was officially opened in 2013 by HRH the Prince of Wales and the Duchess of Cornwall. On the day, Battle of Britain veteran Wing Commander Bob Foster DFC AE declared: 'Along with my fellow veterans, I felt it was so important to preserve Bentley Priory because of its enormous symbolic and strategic significance. To see it so beautifully restored as a museum that tells the story of Dowding, as well as of the Battle of Britain air crew and the huge network that supported us, is fantastic.'

It is rare for era-defining events to be recognised as such while they are occurring; amid the chaos and cacophony of history, it takes time for the prevailing narrative, the widely understood and deeply felt version of events to emerge. Not so with the work of Fighter Command; those who flew, those who supported them on the ground, and those who so carefully monitored the movements of that celestial ballet, knew that they were involved in something extraordinary. What lingers now is a sense of purity, both of purpose and of action. The teenage boys receiving their orders, running for their planes, to defend the blue skies above; and the young girls down below ensuring that the enemy does not elude them.

Today, many walking on the chalky ridges of the South Downs, or through the rich orchards of Kent, look up at the pale sky and feel the proximity of history; they imagine with ease the white trails, the flashes of silver, the arcs and the curves. There is still, to this day, shrapnel to be found embedded in the green meadows and beneath the roots of little apple trees. Those who stand on the tops of hills, gazing down over Kentish villages or looking at Canterbury in the distance, momentarily superimpose on the horizon barrage balloons and distant black formations of incoming bombers. It is still so close that it doesn't even quite feel like history. Those battles resonate loudly in the present – because the impossibly young pilots who sacrificed themselves to ensure that generations to come would be free of tyranny embody an ideal that goes far beyond national or temporal boundaries. They represented not just the best of British, but more pertinently the best of everyone: acting bravely in conditions of unimaginable stress and fear; putting their lives on the line every day while at the same time behaving with grace and good humour and intelligence. They hardly seem like ghosts now; their memories are too robust and substantial. The man who commanded these pilots, and who yearned to communicate with them after their deaths, deserves that place among their jostling, lively presences.

There is debate, and will be for decades to come, about how ready the Nazis were to invade Britain, and about whether any such invasion could have been a success. Lord Dowding – who contrived to be both stuffy and visionary – had no doubt of the peril. The system that bears his name is one sort of memorial; the fact that he felt so piercingly for the lives and immortal souls of his brave young pilots is another.

Endnotes

1 The Celestial Ballet

1 *Angels 22: A Self Portrait of a Fighter Pilot* (Arrow Books, 1977)

2 The Vision of Wings

1 'The Use of Balloons In War': talk delivered by Eric H. Stuart Bruce, printed in *Journal of the Society of Arts*, February 1902

2 Michael Paris, 'Air Power and Imperial Defence 1880–1919', *Journal of Contemporary History*, April 1989

3 Basil Collier, *Leader of the Few: the Authorised Biography of Air Chief Marshal the Lord Dowding of Bentley Priory* (Jarrolds, 1957)

4 Ibid.

5 As quoted on raf.mod.uk, 'The Early Years of Military Flight'

6 John Ferris, 'Fighter Defence Before Fighter Command – The Rise in Strategic Air Defence in Great Britain 1917–1934', *The Journal of Military History*, October 1999

7 From Giulio Douhet, 'The Command of the Air' (pub. 1921), cited in Paul K. Saint-Amour, 'Air War Prophecy and Inter-War Modernism', *Comparative Literature Studies* (Penn State University Press, 2005)

8 As quoted in Philip S. Meilinger, 'Trenchard and "Morale Bombing": The Evolution of Royal Air Force Doctrine Before World War II', *The Journal of Military History*, June 1996

9 As quoted in Malcolm Smith, 'A Matter of Faith – British Strategic Air Doctrine Before 1939', *Journal of Contemporary History*, July 1980

10 Philip S. Meilinger, 'Trenchard and "Morale Bombing"'

11 Philip S. Meilinger, 'A History of Effects-Based Air Operations', *The Journal of Military History*, January 2007
12 Philip S. Meilinger, 'Trenchard and "Morale Bombing"'
13 National Archives, AIR 1/2692
14 T.E. Lawrence, cited in Priya Satia, 'The Defence of Inhumanity: Air Control and the British Idea of Arabia', *The American Historical Review*, February 2006
15 RAF Archives, AC71/17/17

3 The Seduction of Flight
1   Paul Brickhill, *Reach for the Sky – The Story of Douglas Bader* (Collins, 1954)
2   R.J. Overy, 'The German Pre-War Aircraft Production Plans 1936–39', *English Historical Review*, October 1975
3   Peter Fritzche, 'Machine Dreams – Air Mindedness and the Reinvention of Germany', *American Historical Review*, June 1993
4   Martin Francis, *The Flyer: British Culture and the Royal Air Force 1939–45* (Oxford University Press, 2008)
5   Peter Townsend, *Duel of Eagles* (Weidenfeld and Nicolson, 1970)
6   Jane Oliver, cited in Martin Francis, *The Flyer*
7   Vincent Orange, 'The German Air Force Is Already the Most Powerful in Europe': Two RAF Officers Report on a Visit to Germany Oct 1936', *Journal of Military History*, October 2006

4 The Lines in the Heavens
1   Gordon Mitchell, *R.J. Mitchell, Schooldays to Spitfire* (Stroud Publishing, 2002)
2   Ibid.
3   Ibid.
4   Ibid.
5   Peter Townsend, *Duel of Eagles*
6   Geoffrey Wellum, *First Light* (Viking, 2002)
7   Quoted in Martin Harris, *The Flyer*
8   Foreword to Gordon Mitchell, *R.J. Mitchell, Schooldays to Spitfire*
9   E.G. Bowen, *Radar Days* (Hilger, 1987)
10 Robert Watson-Watt 'Radar Defence Today – and Tomorrow', *Foreign Affairs*, January 1954
11 E.G. Bowen, *Radar Days*

5 The Secret Under the Hill

1 National Archives AIR 16/408
2 Ibid.
3 National Archives AIR 16/677
4 National Archives AIR 2/4400
5 Ibid.
6 As quoted in Peter Flint, *Dowding and Headquarters Fighter Command* (Airlife, 1996)
7 W.E. Johns, *Popular Flying*, November 1937
8 National Archives AIR 2/1774
9 National Archives AIR 2/4261
10 Vera Charlton, as contributed to the BBC's 'People's War' website

6 We Are At War

1 Richard Hillary, *The Last Enemy* (Macmillan, 1950)
2 Ibid.
3 Ibid.
4 Vincent Orange, *A Biography of Sir Keith Park* (Methuen, 1984)

7 Dress Rehearsals

1 Richard C. Smith, *Hornchurch Scramble* (Grub Street, 2000)
2 Ibid.
3 Ibid.
4 Vincent Orange, *A Biography of Sir Keith Park*
5 Basil Collier, *Leader of the Few*
6 T.C.G. James, *Royal Air Force Official Histories: The Battle of Britain* (Frank Cass, 2000)
7 Peter Townsend, *Duel of Eagles*

8 'Interesting Work of a Confidential Nature'

1 Vincent Orange, *A Biography of Sir Keith Park*
2 Geoffrey Wellum, *First Light*
3 Lord David Cecil, 'The RAF', in William Rothenstein's collection of drawings and sketches, *Men of the RAF: Forty Portraits With Some Account of Life in the RAF* (Oxford University Press, 1942)
4 Roald Dahl, 'Death of an Old Man', first published in *Ladies' Home Journal*, 1945

5   Athol Forbes and Hubert Allen (eds), *Ten Fighter Boys* (Collins, 1942)

9 Blood Runs Hotly
1   Dowding correspondence held in RAF Archives AC 71/17/24
2   RAF Archives AC 71/17/28
3   RAF Archives AC 71/17/29
4   RAF Archives AC 71/17/30
5   Paul Brickhill, *Reach for the Sky*
6   Ibid.

10 Alert
1   As cited on the RAF's official website, raf.mod.uk

11 The Sky was Black with Planes
1   Robert Wright, *Dowding and the Battle of Britain* (Macdonald, 1969)
2   As quoted in Basil Collier, *Leader of the Few*
3   The captain in question quoted in *The Times*, 11 July 1940
4   Geoffrey Wellum, *First Light* (Viking, 2002)
5   As quoted in Jeffrey W. Legro, 'Military Culture And Inadvertent Escalation In WW2', *International Security*, Spring 1994
6   RAF Archives AC 71/17/24
7   Ibid.
8   Ibid.
9   Wright, *Dowding and the Battle of Britain*

12 Nerve Endings
1   Basil Collier, *Leader of the Few*
2   Francis Wilkinson interviewed by Robert Wright in *Dowding and the Battle of Britain*

13 Big Wing
1   Basil Collier, *Leader of the Few*
2   Ibid.
3   Iris Cockle, as contributed to the BBC's 'People's War'
4   Paul Brickhill, *Reach for the Sky*

14 'We Will All Be Here Soon'

1 Geoffrey Wellum, *First Light*
2 Vincent Orange, *A Biography of Sir Keith Park*
3 Ibid.
4 Ibid.
5 Paul Brickhill, *Reach for the Sky*
6 Mollie Mellish, as contributed to the BBC's 'People's War'
7 Dennis Robinson, as contributed to the BBC's 'People's War'
8 Robert Wright, *Dowding and the Battle of Britain*
9 T.C.G James, *Royal Air Force Official Histories: The Battle of Britain* (Frank Cass, 2000)
10 Richard Hillary, *The Last Enemy*

15 'Resist Until the Very End'

1 Robert Wright, *Dowding and the Battle of Britain*
2 John Willoughby de Broke, interviewed for Robert Wright, *Dowding and the Battle of Britain*
3 Paul Brickhill, *Reach for the Sky*
4 Vincent Orange, *A Biography of Sir Keith Park*
5 Robert Wright, *Dowding and the Battle of Britain*

16 'This Was War and We Were Fighting'

1 National Archives AIR 40/307
2 National Archives AIR 16/677
3 National Archives AIR 20/435
4 Recorded for the BBC in 1978
5 Robert Wright, *Dowding and the Battle of Britain*
6 RAF Archives AC 71/17/8
7 Robert Wright, *Dowding and the Battle of Britain*
8 Paul Brickhill, *Reach for the Sky*
9 Vincent Orange, *A Biography of Sir Keith Park*
10 Peter Townsend, *Duel of Eagles*
11 Paul Brickhill, *Reach for the Sky*

17 A Dog Called Heinkel

1 Richard C. Smith, *Hornchurch Scramble*
2 Ibid.

3   Paul Brickhill, *Reach for the Sky*
4   National Archives AIR 2/9904
5   National Archives AIR 16/622

18 Rhubarbs
1   National Archives AIR 16/212
2   Paul Brickhill, *Reach for the Sky*
3   National Archives AIR 16/212
4   Paul Brickhill, *Reach for the Sky*
5   Geoffrey Wellum, *First Light*
6   Contributed by Loughton Library to the BBC's 'People's War'
7   Joan Wyndham, *Love Is Blue – A Wartime Diary* (Heinemann, 1986)

19 Knitting, Smoking and Great Literature
1   National Archives AIR 40/307
2   Richard C. Smith, *Hornchurch Scramble*
3   This account can be found in full at www.scholars.wlu.ca/cmh/vol12/iss4/6/

20 Death Will Send No Warning
1   Norman Longmate, *The Doodlebugs: The Story of the Flying Bombs* (Hutchinson, 1981)
2   Judith Hamilton, as contributed to the BBC's 'People's War'
3   Marie Ebbeson, as contributed to the BBC's 'People's War'
4   E.S. Turner, 'A Potent Joy', *London Review of Books*, 4 July 1985
5   Gwen Reading, as contributed to the BBC's 'People's War'

Further Reading

Radar Days by EG Bowen (Hilger, 1987)

Reach For the Sky: The Story of Douglas Bader by Paul Brickhill (Collins, 1954)

Leader of the Few: the authorised biography of the Air Chief Marshal the Lord Dowding of Bentley Priory by Basil Collier (Jarrolds, 1957)

1940: The Story of no 11 Group by Peter G Cooksley (Robert Hale, 1983)

Going Solo by Roald Dahl (Jonathan Cape, 1986)

Fighter: The True Story of the battle of Britain by Len Deighton (Cape, 1977)

Twelve Legions of Angels by Air Chief Marshal Lord Dowding (Jarrolds, 1946)

Lychgate by Air Chief Marshal Dowding (Rider and Co, 1948)

The Fatal Englishman: Three Short Lives by Sebastian Faulks (Hutchinson 1996)

The Flyer: British Culture and the Royal Air Force by Martin Francis (OUP, 2008)

The Last Enemy by Richard Hillary (Macmillan, 1950)

The Battle of Britain by TC James (Cass, 2000)

The Growth of Fighter Command 1936–1940 by TCG James (Whitehall History/Cass, 2002)

The First Biggles Omnibus by Captain WE Johns (Hodder and Stoughton, 1953)

You Never Know: A Memoir by Claire Lorrimer (Pen Press Publishers, 2006)

RJ Mitchell, Schooldays to Spitfire by Gordon Mitchell (Tempus/Imperial War Museums 2002)

Fighter Command: 1939–1945 by David Oliver (Harper Collins, 2000)
Dowding of Fighter Command: Victor of the Battle of Britain by Vincent
    Orange (Grub Street, 2011)
A Biography of Sir Keith Park by Vincent Orange (Methuen 1984)
Pilots of Fighter Command: 64 Portraits by Captain Cuthbert Orde
    (Harrap, 1942)
German Atrocities: a Record Of Shameless Deeds by William le Queux
    (George Newnes, 1914)
Richard Hillary: The Definitive Biography of a Battle of Britain Fighter Pilot by
    David Ross (Grub Street, 2000)
Hornchurch Scramble by Richard C Smith (Grub Street, 2000)
Duel of Eagles by Peter Townsend (Weidenfeld and Nicolson, 1970)
The War in the Air by HG Wells (Penguin reissue, 2005)
First Light by Geoffrey Wellum (Penguin, 2000)
Dowding and the Battle of Britain by Robert Wright (Macdonald, 1969)
Love Is Blue: A Wartime Diary by Joan Wyndham (Heinemann, 1986)
One Woman's War by Eileen Younghusband (Candy Jar, 2010)

Index

1 Group 33
1 Squadron 88, 265
10 Group 75, 254, 284
11 Group 75, 126, 149, 157, 158,
    162, 182, 183, 195–6, 197,
    198–9, 207, 209, 210,
    219–20, 222, 226, 234, 236,
    237, 238, 243, 254, 289, 323
12 Group 137, 183, 190, 201–2,
    207, 209, 210, 222, 226, 234,
    236, 237, 247, 254
12 Squadron 210, 218–19
32 Squadron 155
65 Squadron 177
74 Squadron 105
87 Squadron 187
213 Squadron 167, 187
242 Squadron 266
249 Squadron 9
303 Squadron 148–9, 265
308 Squadron 265
501 Squadron 197
601 Squadron 91
602 Squadron 112
603 Squadron 112
605 Squadron 296
609 Squadron 130
610 Squadron 177

Adam, Kenneth (Klaus) Hugo 319

air shows 36–8
air-raid warnings 205, 224
aircraft design and production 18,
    26, 52, 53–61, 90, 113, 168,
    187, 196, 259–60, 268
airfield raids 177, 186, 187, 197–8,
    205, 208–10, 211, 215
airships 17, 22–3, 23, 24, 77
Aitken, Max 91, 205, 287
Allied Expeditionary Air Force
    290
American pilots 149, 252–3,
    277–8, 305–6
Anson, Mrs 72–5
anti-aircraft guns 23, 77, 83–6, 90,
    161, 210, 224, 260, 293,
    297–8
Atcherley, Flt Lt Richard 48–50
Attlee, Clement 74–5
Australian pilots 149
The Avengers (TV series) 320–1

Bader, Sqn Ldr Douglas 37, 46–7,
    87, 126, 137–9, 158, 174,
    183–4, 185, 190, 191, 196,
    201–2, 207, 209, 210, 214,
    218–19, 222, 225, 226, 227,
    235, 237–8, 241, 242, 243–4,
    254–5, 264–5, 266–7, 272,
    277, 280–2, 302–4, 314

Baedeker raids 290
Baldwin, Stanley 41
Balfour, Harold 59, 237
Ball, Albert 26
balloonists 16–17
barrage balloons 9, 77, 161, 174
Bartley, Anthony 92, 306–7
Battle of Barking Creek 104–7
Battle of Britain 1–2, 12, 152–227,
    235, 244, 254
pilot fatalities 262, 305
The Battle of Britain (film) 315
Battle of France 134–7, 139–40
Bawdsey Manor 65–6, 67–8, 147,
    282–3, 297, 300
Baxter, Raymond 318–19
Bayeun, Gp Capt 316
Beaufighter 242, 258, 267
Beaverbrook, Lord 168, 196, 206,
    240, 259–60
Bentley Priory 4–6, 9, 14–15,
    69–77, 88–9, 144–7
    and Battle of Britain 156–7,
        171, 215
    and the Blitz 216–17, 224–5,
        255
    Filter Room 5, 7, 69, 72, 75,
        97–9, 124, 146, 156, 163,
        175, 216–17, 255, 269
    museum status 325
    Operations Room 5, 6, 11,
        71–2, 97, 98, 99, 100, 146,
        156, 211, 224–5, 255
    post-war 321, 322, 323,
        324
    royal visits 108, 215
    and the V-1 missiles 294–5
Benzedrine 180–1
Berlin, bombing of 3, 200
big wing formations 184, 185, 195,
    209, 210, 222, 226, 238, 254,
    260–1

Biggin Hill 130, 155, 162, 209, 254
Biggles 35, 36, 275
blackout 113–14, 116
Blenheim 88, 268
Blériot, Louis 17
Bletchley Park 143, 239, 241,
    324–5
Blitz 7–10, 169, 216–17, 218,
    223–5, 227, 233–4, 239,
    254–7, 266
Blitzkrieg 80, 133–4, 136–7
Bomber Command 13, 61, 125–6,
    175–6, 200, 264, 290
Bouchier, Gp Capt Cecil 243
Bowen, E.G. 63–4, 67
Braun, Werner von 298
Breendonk 316
British Expeditionary Force
    11–12, 133, 137
Brooke, Maj Gen Alan 83
Bushell, Roger 90–2, 106
Byrne, Paddy 106

Cambridge, Duchess of 296
Campaign for Nuclear
    Disarmament 323
Canadian pilots 149, 253
Cecil, Lord David 127
Chain Home System 66–7, 68, 75,
    107, 109, 300
    see also RDF stations
Chamberlain, Neville 47, 67, 79,
    87
Charlton, Vera 82
Charteris, Brig Gen John 170–1
Churchill, Winston 12, 20, 21, 22,
    29, 32, 48, 50, 67–8, 133,
    134, 141, 160, 162, 167–8,
    205–7, 219, 221, 222, 235,
    241, 287, 299, 308
'Circus' missions 264–6, 286, 288,
    304

civilian bombing 30, 222–3,
    239–40
    see also Blitz
civilian morale 205, 223, 257, 260,
    263
Clark, Patricia 7, 45–6, 50–1, 95–6,
    121–3, 147, 224–5, 228–31,
    245–7, 248–52, 270–1, 276,
    284–5, 296, 310–11
class system 122, 248, 249–51, 277
Clostermann, Pierre 58
Coastal Command 88, 186
Cockle, Iris 188
Cold War 308, 321–2, 323–4
Connor, William (Cassandra)
    280
Coope, W.E. 158–9
Corpo Aereo Italiano 253–4
Cotton, Sidney 60
Coventry 208, 239–40
Cranwell 31–2, 44
Croydon 162, 186
Cunningham, Gp Capt John
    267–9, 284

D-Day 292, 294
Dahl, Roald 128, 261, 318
de Havilland 26, 268
de Havilland, Geoffrey 18, 268
Debden 183, 277
decoy flights 157, 189, 198, 209
Deere, Alan 92
Defiant 163, 167, 198
Denniston, Commander Alistair
    241
Detling 186
DH.2 26
Dieppe Raid 288–9
direct assault technique 200–1
dislocation bombing 205
Donahue, Arthur 252–3
doodlebugs *see* V-1 missiles

Douglas, Air Chief Marshal
    William Sholto 25–6, 81–2,
    227, 234, 240, 241, 255–6,
    259–60, 264, 266, 269, 282,
    286, 290
Douhet, Giulio 29
Dover 161, 174, 176–7, 197
Dowding, ACM Sir Hugh 5, 11,
    12, 20–1, 33, 54, 59, 64, 67,
    76–7, 108, 109, 113, 171, 315
    and air support for France
    131–2, 134–6, 165, 166
    and the Battle of Britain 161,
    163, 167–8, 169, 171–2,
    182–3, 191, 195, 201, 209,
    215
    and the Blitz 216, 224
    death of 315
    First World War 26
    interest in spiritualism,
    Theosophy and UFOs 261,
    262, 307–9
    on defence of shipping 155
    on German invasion, threat of
    153–4
    on the Luftwaffe 153
    opposition to 11, 161–2, 163–6,
    172, 174, 183, 202, 209,
    225–6, 227, 235–6, 237–8,
    261
    postwar life 307–9
    relieved of command 227,
    238–9, 240–2
    see also Bentley Priory
Dowding system 62, 69, 71, 77, 78,
    108, 147, 202, 210, 234, 236
Dowling, Plt Off 207–8
downed pilots 116, 159, 175, 189,
    208, 212–13, 258
Dunkirk evacuation 11–12, 91–2,
    137–9, 140, 142, 241, 292
Duxford 183, 237

E-boats 157, 159
Eagle Day 185–9
early history of aviation 16–21
   see also Royal Flying Corps
Eastchurch 186, 187
Ebbesen, Marie 296–7
Edwardes-Jones, Humphrey 55–6
Eisenhower, Gen Dwight D. 290
Elizabeth II, HM Queen 322
Elizabeth, The Queen Mother
   215, 240, 258
Ellesmere Port 208
Ellington, ACM Sir Edward 40
Enigma codes 143, 239, 325
Eva, Gladys 6, 9, 88, 89, 96–7, 120,
   123–4, 145–6, 156, 215,
   216–18, 247, 269–70, 285

Fairey Battle 60
fighter pilots
   anti-authority behaviour 204,
     214, 218, 318
   Arthurian imagery 12, 141
   average age (Battle of Britain)
     14
   cult status 24, 235, 254, 273,
     274
   drinking 46, 128–9
   drugs 180–1
   fatalism 93–4, 214
   fear, experience of 125–8, 180,
     204
   flying stress 125–6, 267
   glamour and style 14, 44, 254,
     306
   grief, dealing with 129, 262
   hunter-killers 115–16, 194, 262
   individualism 94, 274, 318, 319
   insouciance 11, 14, 26, 127–8,
     158, 253, 272–3
   novice pilots 47, 142–3, 211
   pilot shortages 196, 211, 214

pilot's wings 20
post-war lives 302–7, 315–19
respect for the enemy 208, 282
training 31–2, 142, 173, 211
films 10, 17, 25, 26, 91, 274, 283,
   303, 307, 308, 315
Filton 192, 193
Finucane, Wing Cdr Brendan
   'Paddy' 305
First World War 21, 22–8, 35–6,
   77–8, 184
Fiske, William 174
flying suits 60
Fokker 26
Forbes, Wg Cdr Athol 129
Foster, Wg Cdr Bob 325
France, British air support for
   131–2, 133, 134–6, 166
Freeborn, Wg Cdr John Connell
   105–6

Gable, Clark 306
gas masks 79–80, 108
George VI 84, 108, 118, 215, 240,
   258
German Air Defence League 41
German Air Mission 47–8
German invasion, threat of 140–1,
   142, 153–4, 170–1, 173, 192,
   197, 200, 211, 216, 219–21,
   222, 233, 263, 292, 327
   defensive scenario 219–20
Gielgud, John 274
Gillan, Sqn Ldr John 60–1
gliding 42–3
Goering, Hermann 6–7, 25,
   39–40, 103–4, 153
goggles 23
Gort, General Lord 241
Graham-White, Claude 18
Great Depression 33–4, 38–9
Great Yarmouth 197–8

Griffiths, Jim 76
ground staff 143, 211
Guernica 80, 90

Halton-Harrap, Plt Off 106
Hamilton, Judith 295
Harrison, Rex 92, 284
Hastings, Sir Patrick 106, 107
Haw Haw, Lord 217
Hawkinge 139, 162, 187
Heinkel (dog) 245–7
'Hellfire Corner' 170, 214
Herivel, John 143
Hillary, Richard 93–4, 212–14
Hitler, Adolf 3, 40, 42, 48, 153,
    159–60, 298–9
Hoare, Samuel 105
Hood, H.R.L. 158
Hornchurch 76, 91–2, 105, 106,
    107, 118, 162, 181, 197–8,
    204, 207–8, 212, 225, 226,
    243, 252–3
Howard, Trevor 315
Hurricane 59, 60–1, 106, 256
Hurricane Mk 2 243

incendiary bombs 256–7
industrial targets 8, 30–1, 113,
    151, 187, 192–3, 205, 208,
    257, 265
Inskip, Sir Thomas 52
interwar neurosis 38–42, 43
'Iron Dome' defence system 324
Isle of Wight 67, 68, 178, 189
Italian aviation 19–20, 253–4

Johns, W.E. 35–6, 80, 110, 275
Jones, Plt Off Robert 201
Junkers Ju 87 (Stuka) 49

Kellet, Sqn Ldr Ronald 148
Kenley 188, 260–1

Kent, Flt Lt John 148–9
Keough, Vernon 305–6
Kerr, Deborah 306, 307
'knock-out blow' 30

Lacey, James 238
'lack of moral fibre' 124–5, 128,
    267
Lawrence, T.E. 32, 93, 274
Leigh, Vivien 254
Leigh-Mallory, ACM Trafford 119,
    183, 202, 209, 210, 221, 222,
    225, 226, 227, 241, 242, 254,
    260–1, 262, 264–5, 266,
    288–91, 309
literary heroics 35–6
Liverpool 205, 208
Livesey, Roger 254
Local Defence Volunteers 142
Lockington, Eve 277–8, 279
log-books 158–9
London Air Defence Area 28
Luftstreitkrafte 25
Luftwaffe 7, 14, 39–40, 48, 50–1,
    104, 151
    Baedeker raids 290
    see also Battle of Britain; Blitz;
        specific engagements

McCudden, James 23, 26
McIndoe, A.H. 213–14
MacLean, Sir Robert 54
Macpherson, Fg Off A. 88
magneto phones 79
Maitland-Thompson, Tommy
    271
Malan, Wg Cdr Adolph 'Sailor'
    57–8, 105, 106, 285
Mallory, George 309
Mannock, Mick 26
Manston 197
Marham 273

Martlesham Heath 55, 187, 190, 265
mascots 130
melancholic nostalgia 319, 320–1
Mellish, Molly 202–3
Meteor 302
'Mickelthwait' 79
Middle East operations 27, 31, 32, 33, 285
Middleton, Peter 296
Milch, Erhard 38, 47–8
Mitchell, Reg 53–4, 56
morale 204, 205, 219, 223, 237, 238, 257, 260, 263, 266, 272
More, Kenneth 303
mountaineering 309
Mountbatten, Lord Louis 288, 291, 313
Munich crisis 79, 83, 101
Murnau, F.W. 25
Mussolini, Benito 253

NATO 321, 323
Newall, Sir Cyril 164, 165–6
night fighting 94, 177, 224, 242, 255, 256, 257, 258, 267, 268–9, 287
Niven, David 92, 254, 274, 283, 304, 308
North Weald 76, 198, 207, 210, 225, 226, 265, 302
Northolt 149, 265, 291
Norway, Nazi invasion of 124, 132, 154
nuclear weaponry 323

Observer Corps 2–4, 13, 61–2, 77–9, 80–3, 90, 98, 144, 193, 199, 223–4, 296, 322
officer caste 248, 251
Official Secrets Act 122, 123, 248, 308

Olivier, Laurence 254, 306, 315
Operation Dynamo *see* Dunkirk evacuation
Operation Overlord 290
Operation Sea Lion *see* German invasion, threat of
Orford Ness 64–5
other-worldliness of flying 25, 45, 94, 194, 213, 214, 261, 272, 301
outbreak of war 87–90

Paine, Captain G. 19
Park, AVM Keith 27–8, 36, 75, 99, 126, 136, 139, 140–1, 191, 195–7, 198–9, 202, 207, 209, 219–21, 226, 227, 234, 239, 242–3, 261, 313–15
Pease, Peter 213
Pervitin 181
Phoney War 12, 109, 116
plastic surgery 213
Polish pilots 147–9, 172–3, 253, 315–16
Portal, ACM Sir Charles 87, 255, 259, 260, 291
Portsmouth 178, 189, 208
post-war lives 301, 302–19
Powell, Michael 274, 308
propaganda 42, 43, 103–4, 194, 206
purity of purpose and action 14, 24, 326

radar 62–8, 69, 77, 123, 146, 148, 150, 198, 202, 210, 260, 267, 268
  Mark IV Air Intercept 258
radio communications 226–7
Radio Research Station 62–4
radio silence 198
RAF Club 28

Rathbone, Basil 306
Rawnsley, Jimmy 267
RDF stations 185, 223
    raids on 171–2, 177, 178, 189
Reading, Gwen 300
Received Pronunciation 146, 274
Reynaud, Paul 134
Rhodesia 318
'Rhubarb' missions 266, 271–2,
    288, 304
Richardson, Ralph 254
Richthofen, Baron von 24, 26
Robins, Denise 45, 311
Robinson, Flt Lt Dennis 203–4
Robinson, Lt William Leefe 24
romances 251–2, 278–9, 283–4
Rosewarne, Fg Off Vivien 273–4
Rosyth naval base 111
Rothermere, Lord 27
Rowley, Sqn Ldr Herbert 48–50
Royal Air Force
    creation of 27
    formation of Bomber
        Command and Fighter
        Command 61–2
    post-war 321–2
    recruitment 43–4, 275
    strategic intent 29–30
    Strike Command 323
Royal Air Force Volunteer Reserve
    (RAFVR) 43
Royal Aircraft Establishment 18,
    63, 186
Royal Flying Corps 18–19, 21–4,
    25–8, 35–6, 63, 78, 184
Rudd, Wg Cdr 231, 232, 246,
    270–1
Rudloe Manor 228–33, 245–6, 284
Rusbridger, Alan 323

SALT (Strategic Arms Limitation
    Talks) 323

Scapa Flow 112
September 11, 2001 terrorist
    attacks 324
shadow airfields 196
Shanghai 80
Shaw, George Bernard 199–200
Sheffield 257
shipping convoys 112–13, 152,
    154–5, 157, 174, 176
Short Brothers 26, 187
Sidcots 60
sightseers 116–17, 194–5
silk scarves 23
Sinclair, Sir Archibald 74, 82, 165
Skegness 193
Smith, Ian 317–18
Smuts, Jan 27
Sopwith 26
Spanish Civil War 80, 90, 133
spiritualism 261–2, 307, 308, 309
Spitfire 54–60, 90, 93, 142, 206,
    256, 325
Spitfire funds 199
Stanmore 296, 310
Summers, Capt J. 55
superstition 129–30
Sykes, Maj Frederick 20, 29–30

Tactical Air Forces 290
taking the fight to the enemy 29,
    162–3, 200, 264, 271, 289
Tangmere 91, 114–15, 266–7
Tedder, MRAF Arthur 290
Tempest 293
Theosophy 307–8
Townsend, Gp Capt Peter 44, 45,
    58, 114–16, 243, 262
Travis, Edward 241
Trefusis Forbes, ACC Katherine
    119
Trenchard, Lord 21–2, 29, 30–1,
    32–3, 162–3

Turner, E.S. 297–8
Typhoon 305, 319

Udet, Ernst 49
UFOs 308–9
United States Army Air Corps
    285–6
Uxbridge 75, 220, 221

V-1 flying bombs 292–9, 299
V-2 rockets 298–300, 310
VE Day 312–13
Vickers Supermarine 53–4, 56,
    168
    see also Spitfire

Watnall 247, 278
Watson-Watt, Robert 62–3, 64, 66,
    269
Wells, Edward 253–4
Wells, H.G. 41
Wellum, Geoffrey 44, 58, 59–60,
    90, 127, 129, 155, 193–4,
    271–2, 304–5
Wesley, Mary 278
West Drayton 120–1, 122
Westerman, Percy F. 36
Wilkins, Arnold 62–3

Willoughby de Broke, John 218
Windmill Girls 204–5
women in the services 13,
    118–19
    see also Bentley Park; Women's
    Auxiliary Air Force (WAAF);
    Women's Royal Naval
    Service (WRNS)
women officers 247–8, 251, 276
Women's Auxiliary Air Force
    (WAAF) 5, 7, 96, 118,
    119–24, 205, 217, 247,
    276–9, 311
post-war lives 317
Women's Royal Naval Service
    (WRNS) 144
Wood, Sir Kingsley 74, 110
Woolwich Arsenal 8, 17, 84
Wyndham, Joan 181, 278–9

Y Service 3, 144
Younghusband, Eileen 69–70,
    97–9, 100–1, 121, 124, 146,
    175–6, 231–3, 247–8, 276,
    282–4, 294–5, 299, 311–13,
    316–17

Zeppelin, Count 17, 22–3

Acknowledgements

First of all, many thanks to Wing Commander Erica Ferguson, of the RAF Bentley Priory Battle of Britain Trust, and also to Group Captain T.C. Willbond, for a magnificent introduction to the valuable work of the Trust and for a doubly magnificent introduction to some wonderful veterans. Among those so generous with their time and memories (not to mention excellent lunches) were Patricia Clark, Gladys Eva and Eileen Younghusband. Mrs Younghusband's haunting memoirs *One Woman's War* are available from Amazon, as are Patricia Clark's, entitled *You Never Know* and written under her pen-name Claire Lorrimer.

On top of this, my gratitude to the patient and wise archivists at the RAF library in Hendon. Bentley Priory is now a terrific Battle of Britain museum, with a wide range of startling interactive displays. For information on opening times and how to get there, visit www.bentleypriory.org.

In addition, grateful thanks are also due to raptor-eyed copy editor Steve Gove, insightful and enthusiastically sharp Jennifer Barr at Aurum, Iain MacGregor, whose idea this was, Daniela Rogers for hunting down some excellent images, Jessica Axe for her direction of publicity – and my own dear father Peter, whose recent enthusiasm for flying lessons has proved instructive.